The Mommy Chronicles

Hay House Titles of Related Interest

Books

Baby Sign Language Basics, by Monta Z. Briant
The Bloke's Guide to Pregnancy, by Jon Smith
The Crystal Children, by Doreen Virtue, Ph.D.
The Indigo Children, by Lee Carroll and Jan Tober
Inner Peace for Busy Women, by Joan Z. Borysenko, Ph.D.
Parents' Nutrition Bible, by Earl Mindell, R.Ph., Ph.D.
Seven Secrets to Raising a Happy and Healthy Child, by Joyce Golden Seyburn

CD Programs/Kits

The Best Year of Your Life Kit, by Debbie Ford
Dr. Phil Getting Real, by Dr. Phil McGraw
The Good Night Sleep Kit, by Deepak Chopra, M.D.
Finding Your Passion, by Cheryl Richardson

Card Decks

Car Go Cards, from the Publishers of *Parenting*® Magazine
Rainy-Day Fun Cards, from the Publishers of *Parenting*® Magazine
Sign Language for Babies Cards, from the Publishers of *Parenting*® Magazine
Words of Wisdom for Women Who Do Too Much, by Anne Wilson Schaef

Words of Praise for *The Mommy Chronicles*

"The Mommy Chronicles is a true gift for the mom-to-be or new mom. It takes a brave, honest, and very funny look at the reality of motherhood. A great read for any mom!"
— **Cheryl Richardson,**
the best-selling author of *Stand Up for Your Life*

"Every woman who's considering starting a family should read this book. It's clearly written, funny, and full of a wealth of information about being pregnant and being a parent."
— **Carolle Jean-Murat, M.D., F.A.C.O.G.,**
the author of *Natural Pregnancy A–Z*

"Reading the e-mail correspondence of these very different mothers is a little like eavesdropping on two best gal-pals dishing the dirt when they think no one else is listening. More than anything, this is a story of a friendship that proves to be stronger than differences in pregnancies, postpartum experiences, or child-rearing techniques."
— **Andrea J. Buchanan,**
author of *Mother Shock: Loving Every (Other) Minute of It*

"The Mommy Chronicles, a book of e-mail communications between two pregnant women who then become mothers, can bring comfort to any woman who may feel alone with all the new feelings and events that literally change everyday life."
— **Frank Boehm, M.D.,** the author of *Doctors Cry, Too*

The Mommy Chronicles

Conversations Sharing the Comedy and Drama of Pregnancy and New Motherhood

Sara Ellington and Stephanie Triplett

HAY HOUSE, INC.
Carlsbad, California
London • Sydney • Johannesburg
Vancouver • Hong Kong

Published and distributed in the United States by: Hay House, Inc., P.O. Box 5100, Carlsbad, CA 92018-5100 • *Phone:* (760) 431-7695 or (800) 654-5126 • *Fax:* (760) 431-6948 or (800) 650-5115 • www.hayhouse.com • **Published and distributed in Australia by:** Hay House Australia Pty. Ltd., 18/36 Ralph St., Alexandria NSW 2015 • *Phone:* 612-9669-4299 • *Fax:* 612-9669-4144 • www.hayhouse.com. au • **Published and distributed in the United Kingdom by:** Hay House UK, Ltd. • Unit 62, Canalot Studios • 222 Kensal Rd., London W10 5BN • *Phone:* 44-20-8962-1230 • *Fax:* 44-20-8962-1239 • www.hayhouse.co.uk • **Published and distributed in the Republic of South Africa by:** Hay House SA (Pty), Ltd., P.O. Box 990, Witkoppen 2068 • *Phone/Fax:* 2711-7012233 • orders@psdprom.co.za • **Distributed in Canada by:** Raincoast • 9050 Shaughnessy St., Vancouver, B.C. V6P 6E5 • *Phone:* (604) 323-7100 • *Fax: (604) 323-2600*

Editorial supervision: Jill Kramer • *Design:* Summer McStravick

Library of Congress Cataloging-in-Publication Data

Ellington, Sara.
    The mommy chronicles : e-mail conversations sharing the comedy and drama of pregnancy and
    new motherhood / Sara Ellington & Stephanie Triplett.
        p. cm.
    ISBN 1-4019-0419-X (tradepaper : alk. paper) 1. Motherhood. 2. Pregnancy.
        3. Pregnant women--
    United States--Correspondence. I. Triplett, Stephanie. II. Title.
HQ759.E43 2005
306.874'3--dc22
                        2003025015

ISBN 13: 978-1-4019-0419-7
ISBN 10: 1-4019-0419-X

08 07 06 05   4 3 2 1
1st printing, January 2005

Printed in the United States of America

For Mom,
who continues to show me what it means
to be a great mother, even now that I'm a mother myself.

— **Sara**

For Timothy Carl and Sara Nicole,
you make each and every day full of laughter and love,
and you've made my life entirely beautiful.

— **Stephanie**

Contents

Introduction

We met about six years ago at an advertising agency in Virginia Beach [Stephanie was working as an account executive, and Sara was the writer assigned to work on Stephanie's accounts]. The first time we went to lunch together, we both knew we were going to be great friends—and our husbands hit it off just as well. As couples, we had a lot in common: We'd all been married for about four years and had been getting a lot of pressure from our families about producing some grandchildren.

How clearly we can both remember those relatively carefree, pre-Mommy days: decent salaries, long lunches, dinners at nice restaurants, sleeping late on weekends. . . . As mothers now, it's hard to believe that our lives were *ever* like that. Back then, we felt that having kids meant staying at home on the weekends, watching *Barney,* and changing diapers—and that just didn't sound too enticing at the time. We were having too much fun hanging out on the beach drinking margaritas. These days, we all drink margaritas *while* we watch *Barney.* (Hey, do *you* know any adult who can get through an episode of *Barney* without medicinal help?)

Anyway, here's how the whole Mommy thing started for each of us:

Stephanie: My husband, Tim, and I finally succumbed to the pressure and decided to put birth-control methods on hold and just "see what happened." It didn't take long before there was a big announcement to make.

Sara: Meanwhile, my husband, David, and I had decided to move back to Charlotte, North Carolina, where we lived when we were first married. I found a job there working as a copywriter for an ad agency. Months later, we got a scary wake-up call: David was on a small plane that lost one of its engines in flight. Even though everything worked out fine, it was a pretty terrifying experience. It wasn't long before we decided to get serious about starting our family.

Coincidentally, both of our due dates were just a few weeks apart! We knew that the whole experience was going to be a lot more fun having someone so close to share it with. It turned out to be even better than we expected.

So that's how all this e-mailing began. We kept in touch with each other to monitor the progress of our pregnancies, and we talked out our problems and shared ideas and traded information from all the pregnancy books we were reading. Writing these letters was a great outlet for us to console each other, and of course it made for some terrific male-bashing bitch sessions, too.

About a year into these digital conversations, David began reading our messages. He told us that we should consider turning our e-mails into a book—not only because they made him laugh, but because they were also full of good information. Even so, we aren't exactly sure how we got from his suggestion to the book you're holding in your hands now. We *can* tell you that it involved a lot of crying (both us and the kids), a bunch of conference calls conducted in the garage while screaming children suffered on the opposite side of a locked door, and several family members complaining about a lack of clean underpants. But all that aside, we're very excited to be sharing our stories with you now about our mutual journeys into that mysterious club called "Mom."

Mostly, this book happened because we realized that many of the things we were laughing, crying, and complaining about were universal to all mothers—especially new ones. We wondered why no one had ever told us what motherhood was *really* like. And we were sure that other new moms had to be going through the same thing. That's why our book primarily focuses on our first year of motherhood. Once we left the hospital, it didn't take us long to realize that giving birth wasn't the hard part—after all, there's plenty of information out there to prepare women for pregnancy and labor, and lots of pamphlets and books that tell you how to take care of a little baby and what that baby should be doing every month of its new life . . . but what about the *mother's* new life? Doesn't *that* deserve discussing? We sure think so.

We're just two typical modern-day moms, going through the stuff that mothers deal with every day. Our e-mail conversations simply created a journal of our feelings and experiences; consequently, there's not much we didn't talk about. We were certainly open and honest!

We hope you'll laugh, cry, and relate to us. Most of all, we hope that you'll discover comfort in these pages, along with the assurance that wherever you are in your journey as a mother, you aren't alone.

Chapter 1

Great
Expectations

April 22

From: Stephanie
To: Sara
Subject: Are you sitting down?

Guess what? Yep, I'm pregnant!

I suppose you must think it odd of me to just send an e-mail and blurt out the news in such a manner. But permit me, my dear friend, to explain my plight: As a woman who's been married for four years, every time I call one of my girlfriends and say, "Guess what?" they *always* reply, "You're pregnant!" And for years, I've been a little disgusted by their reply, as if the single most important thing I have to report is that I'm pregnant. I always thought, *Haven't they come to expect more out of me by now than that?*

Or couldn't they at least be a little more creative after the 15th time we've gone through this exchange? You know, something like, "You won the lottery?" or "Your great aunt died and left you her estate worth millions in stocks and annuities?" or "You just returned from your ski trip to Mt. Something or Other (I really should have paid more attention in geography class) in the Swiss Alps, where you survived an avalanche of epic proportions that separated you from your guide and left you to fend for yourself, alone in the wilderness?"

You get the point. Anyway, as you can imagine, it brings me great delight to finally give them the answer they've all been yearning to hear: "Yep, I'm pregnant!"

I know what you're thinking. I've never mentioned that we were "trying" to have a baby. Well, we weren't. That's the first baby-related expression that just cracks me up, by the way (I'm sure there will be more). What exactly do people mean when they say "We're trying"? I used to think that was our generation's polite way of saying, "We're having sex like wild rabbits in heat." And as long as you said it that way—"Yes, we're trying"—it was perfectly acceptable to admit it to anyone: your pastor, your mother-in-law, etc.

Then I realized that for some (and probably most) people, "trying" is actually very complicated. Some poor women are out there tracking their cycles on the calendar, taking their temperatures, and peeing on sticks to determine the best possible moment to conceive a baby. For one couple I know, "trying" became quite a chore. Apparently the best odds of becoming pregnant are by having sex every other day, so when they started trying, the father-to-be was overjoyed. But after a few months of sex on demand, the effort was starting to take its toll on him. I remember him saying, "I would have killed for this when I was 18! But now I'm older, and it's not so easy. Sometimes she's in the bedroom calling me, and I'm like, 'Yeah, yeah, I'll be there. . . . Oh, for cryin' out loud, just start without me!'"

Anyway, it was way too easy for Tim and me. We just sort of decided to stop birth-control tactics and see what happened. And *bang!* Just two months later, I've got a bun in the oven. I'm still in shock, quite frankly. I never thought it would happen so fast. It's so thrilling, yet so scary, too. I have no idea what to expect . . . maybe that's why they call it *expecting.*

Your turn!

April 23

From: Sara
To: Stephanie
Subject: Yes, I'm sitting down . . .

. . . *now!* Oh, congratulations! I wish we were in the same place so that I could give you a hug! I can't believe it! I'm so excited for you and Tim, and I can't wait to give David the news. I'm dying to ask you so many questions: Do you have any idea when your due date is, or will you have to wait until your trip to the ob-gyn? E-mail me back as soon as you can! I want more details!

Now that I've said all the sweet, important stuff, I can't believe that you, the consummate career woman, are with child. How do you feel about all this? And what made you decide to start "trying"?

As for it being my turn, you're a great friend, so anytime you need moral support, I'll be glad to accompany you to the ladies' room, or most anywhere else for that matter. But I have to draw the line when it comes to bringing another human being into the world. I mean, I like you and all, but c'mon!

I'll be glued to my e-mail until I hear back from you. (No pressure.) I'm sure my productivity level for the workday just plummeted. Much love to you and your little "bun."

April 23

From: Stephanie
To: Sara
Subject: Breaking the news

Okay, here's how it all played out. I was actually visiting my grandmother in Pennsylvania when I found out. (Tim was in another state on business.) I told Grandma that I was feeling funny—I was a little queasy all the time, and the only thing that made me feel better was to eat. So I bought a pregnancy test during a trip to the grocery store, and sure enough, it was positive. I was so excited, but a little shocked, too. Naturally, I didn't want to tell Tim over the phone, which meant that I'd have to wait a whole week to give him the news. The next time I was going to see him was Friday night at his mom's house in Charlotte.

I didn't think I could wait that long because it was really hard to keep such a big secret. So I decided I had to tell my friend Laura. She's on her fourth child now, and is the number one perpetrator of the whole "'Guess what?' 'You're pregnant!'" scenario. So I called her and said, "Laura, I have this horrible headache, and it won't go away. Do you think I can take Tylenol?" She told me she didn't know why not. I said, "I mean, do you think it's okay for me to take Tylenol now that *I'm pregnant?*" Then I wish a representative from the *Guinness Book of World Records* had been there, because he would have heard the world's longest scream.

Of course I had to think of some creative way to break the news to Tim. I thought that it would be fun for him to find out exactly the same way I did (but without actually having to pee on the stick). So I decided to wrap the stick up in a little gold box like a present. And I bought a photo frame for Tim's mom that was engraved with the words "Grandkids" at the top. Well, when it came time to hand out the gifts, Tim was busy making a cocktail for his mom, and when I handed him the box, he sat it down on the counter and continued with his work. His mother, however, began opening *her* gift.

I kept saying, "Tim, open your present," and he kept saying, "In a minute." This went on until I was practically screaming, "Open your damn gift, you moron!" (The timing wasn't quite playing out as I'd planned.) Anyway, my mother-in-law got her present open, and she and Tim's sister had already figured out what was going on by the time Tim finally began to tear into his little gold box. The look on his face was hilarious! It was a really fun way to give him the news, and he was very excited.

The funny thing is that I called my doctor, thinking that the big event should be confirmed. I mean, that's what always happens in the movies, right? Well, that's not at all how it works in the real world. The scheduling nurse told me that the tests you can buy over the counter these days are so accurate that they pretty much give you the same thing at the doctor's office, so they didn't want to see me until I was eight weeks along in the pregnancy. I was really shocked. I mean, I have to survive as a pregnant woman for two whole months before getting any direction from a medical professional? What if I do something wrong? I have so many questions. I guess that's why there are so many pregnancy books out there.

So, I'm on my way to Barnes & Noble . . . right after I eat a few more saltines.

April 24

From: Sara
To: Stephanie
Subject: Beautiful gifts

I bet Tim never thought that the best present he'd ever get would be a stick with urine on it. What a great moment. I'm glad you didn't have to hit him over the head with the box to get his attention.

You have to wait that long to go to the doctor? Then again, I guess all you have to do now is eat and throw up. Oh, and lay off the margaritas. Ugh—that's a depressing thought. I guess the sacrifices of motherhood are already beginning!

By the way, have you told your co-workers yet?

April 25

From: Stephanie
To: Sara
Subject: The rabbit died, and everyone knows it

Well, as hard as I've tried to keep my big secret, the cat's out of the bag. I told another woman in my office who'd just returned from maternity leave—since we suddenly had such a huge thing in common (motherhood), I just couldn't help myself. Since I'm only about six weeks along, I'd hoped to keep it quiet just a little longer, because I wasn't sure how the boss would take it. Several women have become pregnant in the last year or so, and all the absences have really put a strain on our small business. Anyway, I felt like someone at the office should know in case I passed out or something. Plus, I just couldn't bear to keep it a secret much longer.

Within a few days of sharing the news, this woman blurted my news out, right in the middle of a production meeting. It's okay with me, though—it was fun to finally get the word out. We women just aren't designed to keep secrets; it's in our DNA. And now I don't have to worry about the "Steph's puttin' on a few pounds" comments, since I swear my belly is starting to pooch out just a little. It's funny, because work suddenly just doesn't seem to carry as much weight as it did before. I can't explain it: I guess it's just the knowledge that there's something big on the horizon. (Hopefully, it won't be my ass.)

May 1

From: Sara
To: Stephanie
Subject: Rabbits are dropping like flies

Hello, my pregnant friend. Remember when you told me that you were pregnant and then you said it was my turn? Well, as it turns out, there's another dead rabbit—and he's here in Charlotte. I guess I was willing to share more than a trip to the bathroom with you after all! Can you believe it? What are the odds?

Here's how it happened. (Well, not actually . . . we all know how it happened. Which, by the way, makes it so weird, even at 30 years old, telling my mom that I'm pregnant. It's like saying, "Hi, Mom! Guess what: I had sex! Aren't you thrilled?!"And she was!) Anyway, remember a few weeks ago when David had that scare going to visit his grandfather? That was an eye-opener—*and* a big kick in the pants to both of us to quit waiting for the "perfect" time to get pregnant. We've been putting it off and putting it off, thinking that we'd have the luxury of making everything happen just the way we wanted, when we wanted. Believe me, waiting on the phone for an airline-customer-service representative to tell you whether the plane your husband is on has crashed or has made it safely to the airport is an emotionally wrenching reminder that your life could crumble in a second. It made me rethink my idea of "the perfect time"—I realized that things are in fact completely and wonderfully perfect right now.

So, when David was finally back home safely, we both agreed that it was time to toss the birth control out the window. And let me tell you, I'm so glad I never risked going without it before, because here I am, pregnant the first month I stopped taking the Pill! I never imagined it would happen that fast. I was so excited about going off the Pill and the fact that there was even a chance it could happen that I went out and got a pregnancy test the first possible day I could do it. You can't imagine my shock: There I was, at home alone on my lunch break, staring at that stick as both lines developed right before my eyes. *Both lines.* (By the way, isn't waiting for that second line the most intense anticipation you've ever experienced?) And even though the second line was faint, it was definitely there.

I was about to explode the rest of the day. I kept thinking that it couldn't possibly be right. I mean, how could I have gotten pregnant that fast? All I wanted to do was to take another test to see if the second one was positive, too. If so, then I'd be sure.

David and I were planning on driving to our new house to check on the construction progress that evening, so on the way home from work, I picked up another test. I snuck into the bathroom to take it before we left—I watched and waited as the first line appeared and then . . . nothing. No second line. *What the hell?* I thought. *Aren't these things supposed to be extremely accurate?* I was totally confused. All I could wonder was, *Well, am I pregnant or not?*

I stuffed the stick into my purse to hide it from David, because I didn't want to tell him until I was sure. Can you imagine: "Honey, I'm pregnant! Yippee!" Then the next day, "Oops, sorry—not pregnant after all." I didn't want that scenario. So we hopped in the car and headed to the new house, me with my pregnancy pee-pee stick safely hidden in my purse.

As soon as I had a chance, I snuck a peek at the test again. I couldn't stand the suspense. And there it was: A second line. It was faint, but it was there. Why it took so long, I couldn't imagine, but that was good enough for me. I finally had to tell David, because I felt like I was about to burst.

We were walking through the house looking at the different rooms, and when we got to the upstairs guest bedroom, I casually asked, "Where do you think we should put the crib?"

He looked at me with this confused expression and said, "We need to have a baby first."

"Well, it looks like we're going to!" I squealed. His mouth dropped open and then he got this big grin on his face and hugged me long and hard. Whenever I walk into the baby's room, I'll think of that moment.

So there you have it. And let me tell you, there's no doubt in my neurotic, skeptical mind that I'm actually, truly, really, for-sure pregnant—especially since I've taken five more tests since the second one I just mentioned. Yes, that makes seven in all. I think the hormones have already affected my brain.

Looks like you've started a trend. I'll be right behind you, pee-ing, vomiting, gaining weight, and having a baby! *Having a baby!*

May 2

From: Stephanie
To: Sara
Subject: I'm supposed to eat what?

I can't believe it! It's going to be so great to share every thrill-ing, painful, weight-gaining moment together! I'm so excited! Can you believe we're actually going to be mothers?

Have you gotten any pregnancy books yet? All the ones I have say that I'm supposed to eat plenty of green, leafy vegeta-bles right now. Don't they know that the only thing we pregnant women can manage to swallow without gagging is soda crack-ers and Diet Pepsi? C'mon, people. Anything green and slimy right now would send me running for the nearest vomit-friendly receptacle.

In other news, it's been quite amusing at the office now that everyone knows I'm with child. The last woman who was preg-nant in this office apparently had a terrible first trimester, and she spent 80 percent of her time puking in the bathroom. The guys in the office found her feverish sprints to the bathroom quite entertaining (for some sick reason). So now they're all look-ing to me to continue the "run and puke" tradition.

Luckily, I haven't had to suffer quite as badly. I do have to confess that, although I feel like I could throw up all the time, I've actually only hurled once, and that was in the privacy of my own home. Nevertheless, *every time* I get up to go to the bath-room (which is about every ten minutes these days), someone in the office asks me if I'm going to go puke. And if I'm in there too long, I swear I think they're all standing outside the door to see if I emerge all sweaty and red-eyed. I think that as soon as they see the doorknob turn, they all scatter and act like they're busy. I must admit, it's pretty funny . . . but if I *was* throwing up, I probably wouldn't find it quite so comical.

The only good thing about feeling nauseated all the time is that it helps to keep me awake. I think I could sleep 24 hours straight and still be tired. No matter how early I go to bed at night, I'm still exhausted all day long. It must take a lot of work to grow a baby, because it's really making me tired. I was thinking about that the other day. Isn't it funny that you really don't have to exert any effort at all toward making the baby grow? Everything else we've done in life that was worthwhile took effort, training, and concentration. Now, all I really have to do is eat healthy and get plenty of rest and I make a baby. Doesn't it seem like I should say, "Okay, in the fourth month, I have to make the eyes, so I'll eat lots of carrots and go to eye-making classes. Then I'll have to grunt and strain and concentrate, and—*ta-da!* I gave the baby eyes." I guess it's just part of the miracle that your body knows exactly what to do and takes over the entire baby-makin' department. I'm basically just a food source and means of transportation. Kinda funny, isn't it?

Gotta run (to the bathroom again).

May 3
From: Sara
To: Stephanie
Subject: Good breeder

I think the grunting and straining comes later . . . you know, in the delivery room.

Supposedly when you feel sick it means that the baby is developing healthily, so I guess that means you're a good breeder. That reminds me: David used to joke about my tiny wrists and tell me that I *wasn't* going to be a good one. And I married him anyway. Go figure. Somehow I doubt wrists have a lot to do with having a baby.

The morning sickness hasn't kicked in for me yet, with the exception of feeling like there's a lot of extra saliva in my mouth. And yes, I am *so* tired. I hit the mattress as soon as I get home around six and usually sleep for at least an hour, then go to bed by nine or ten.

By the way, I know what you mean about people not being able to keep the pregnancy secret. One thing I've learned is this: Don't tell anyone until you're ready to tell *everyone*. See, we thought we'd tell our parents and a few close friends, but it turned out like that old commercial: "And they told two friends, and so on, and so on. . . ." And I have to say that our parents were the most guilty. Oh well—I can't blame them for wanting to share the happy news. Then I decided to tell a few of my closest co-workers in case they saw me running to the bathroom or throwing up during the Monday-morning agency meeting or something. And once you tell some of them, you might as well tell all of them. So the same is true now on our end: The news is definitely out.

By the way, your co-workers really need to get a hobby.

May 10
From: Stephanie
To: Sara
Subject: Modern medicine

Well, I just returned from the big *first doctor's visit.* Stepped on the scale, peed in a cup . . . you know, the usual tortures. But I love my OB—he's also into photography as a hobby, and he takes the most breathtaking pictures of babies in their mother's hands, just after they're born. He showed me these photos of a fetus in the womb, which were taken every month from conception to birth. Wow! It's really amazing how fast the fetus goes from an alien life-form to looking like an actual human baby.

He also told me that he was going to do an ultrasound to see where the egg had attached itself to the wall of my uterus, and to just make sure that everything was in good working order. It's too early to do a normal ultrasound, so he used a probe (I won't go into any further detail), to locate the place where the baby had chosen to take root. At first we were both a little worried, because he couldn't find it. Finally, he located it—on the back side of my uterus. I'm not sure what I was expecting to see; I mean, I knew that the baby wouldn't necessarily be "human" yet, but you can't help but get excited at the chance to get a glimpse of your baby for the first time.

I guess somewhere in the back of my mind I imagined a heavenly choir singing, a ray of sunlight beaming magically through the window and on my tummy, and maybe just *one* recognizable body part that resembled me. But I have to admit: I was a little disappointed at what I saw on the screen. It was . . . a dot. When he printed the image out, the baby was literally the size of the tip of his pen. I never knew you could deflate a pregnant woman. It was pretty anticlimatic. But he did give me my due date: December 9. That's pretty exciting to find out . . . except for the fact that every other mom I know has told me that it means nothing—the only person who decides the due date is the baby. But there's some weird security in having a date to cling to.

It's fun to know that I have another visit in a month, and that there will be lots of changes between now and then. And I'm also required to take these huge prenatal vitamins, which are like trying to swallow one of the knobs on the stove. So I must ask the powers that be, "Why would you make such a large, hard-to-swallow pill for pregnant women, knowing that we're already swallow-challenged? Are two smaller pills too much to ask?" What's wrong with the world?

May 26
From: Sara
To: Stephanie
Subject: Why do they call it morning sickness . . .

. . . when it lasts *all day?* Okay, morning sickness has now definitely set in, and I have no idea why they call it that, except for the fact that it begins first thing in the morning. They should call it "feeling like you're about to throw up all day" sickness. The name "morning sickness" sounds like you get a little queasy in the morning and then go through the rest of the day just fine. Well, I'm here to tell you that it's an ugly mistruth. I feel like I've always got about a gallon of saliva in my mouth, and the only way to stand it is to keep something in my stomach at all times.

It's much worse when I feel hungry—must be nature's way of making me eat.

A probe? That doesn't sound so good. I just had my first visit to the OB, too. No probe, though—my doctor got out this little wheel/chart thing and said that I conceived on April 11. You should have seen David when I told him that. He starts saying to himself, "April 11 . . . April 11 . . . I know! We were . . . " (I'll spare you the details.) Apparently this was the most important information to be learned from my first prenatal visit.

You know, by my calculations, I should be about six weeks pregnant, but I'm actually *eight* weeks. Since they count from your last period, it's like you're already two weeks pregnant when you conceive. I know I had a really dense look on my face when Dr. Beurskens was explaining this to me. The best response I could manage was, "Huh?" And due to their way of counting, you're actually pregnant for ten months, not nine. Why do they always say nine months then?

My doctor said that everything looks right on track, and she gave me a due date of January 4. Next time, at the 12-week visit, we get to hear the heartbeat. Then I have the ultrasound at 18 weeks. It's all so incredibly exciting! Maybe that's why I feel like I'm going to throw up all the time.

May 31

From: Stephanie
To: Sara
Subject: Worries

That cracks me up about David figuring out when you conceived. He was probably trying to figure out what he did right, you know, for the next time. And I agree with you: Why *do* they call it nine months when it's definitely ten? Was there once a time in our history when humans were only pregnant for nine months? Does it take longer for babies to bake now? Does it have something to do with alignment of the sun and the planets? And why hasn't anyone corrected that before now? It's a vast mystery to me.

Anyway, on to today's current news. It looks like Tim's company is going to move us to Atlanta! He just got promoted to

National Sales Trainer for AutoTrader.com, which is perfect for him! He's so hilarious and loves to perform—they're going to love him.

But I'm completely freaking out! How am I going to pack our entire house, leave a home where we've lived for 12 years, find a new job, and totally pick up and move . . . all while gestating? I don't know what I'm going to do or how I'm going to survive this. It seems much bigger than I can handle right now.

Don't get me wrong—I've always wanted to live in Atlanta, since there seems to be so much opportunity there. When I first graduated from college, I turned down a job there so that I could move to Virginia Beach and be closer to Tim. I guess part of me always wondered where that would have taken me, but now it's the last thing I want.

How am I ever going to find a job? No one's going to hire me knowing that I'm going to go on maternity leave in six months! What am I supposed to do, lie during the interview? I'm not showing yet (at least not with clothes on), so it will be easy to conceal my little bun. But I'd feel terrible sitting in a job interview and not telling. What should I do? I'm worried about quitting my job at the ad agency, too. And I can't imagine leaving all our friends here in Virginia! Ugh—all this on top of pregnancy hormones? I think I'm going to self-implode at any minute.

June 1
From: Sara
To: Stephanie
Subject: Multiple life changes

How many life changes can one person be expected to handle at once?

Don't worry: People have babies and go back to work all the time. And legally, they can't discriminate against you because you're pregnant, right? I'm sure everything will work out fine. Just try to have patience. You don't have to figure it all out right this minute. Things will fall into place—just take it one step at a time. Or should I say, one *life change* at a time.

At least you and Tim will be a few hours closer to us now! I expect you to drop by whenever you're in town visiting Tim's mom!

Can you believe that we're both moving during our pregnancies? At least mine is just across town—yours is a whole different ball game. But the good news is that we'll both be settled by the time the babies arrive.

Gotta run. Hang in there!

June 3
From: Stephanie
To: Sara
Subject: New job in "The Big City"

Amidst all the details of moving and quitting my job, I remembered a contact of mine from my days in the cable world. He was a VP in the Atlanta office for the Family Channel, and he'd offered me a job about six months ago—of course six months ago, I had no interest in moving to Atlanta. Nevertheless, I decided to pick up the phone and find out if he was happy with his most recent hire; if not, maybe he'd consider me. But when I dialed his direct line, I got quite a shock. The new VP who'd apparently taken this guy's place was Bo LaMotte—an old friend and co-worker of mine. Bo and I had worked together selling cable-TV advertising for a few years in Virginia Beach, and then he left to go work for MTV in New York. I almost fell out of my chair when I heard his voice!

I said, "Bo, Tim and I are moving to Atlanta!" He responded, "That's great! Do you need a job?" I said, "Yes! But I'm four months pregnant." He replied, "That's okay, just promise me you'll come back after maternity leave." And there it was—just like that! A great job back in the cable-TV industry, with a wonderful, understanding boss, and I didn't have to lie about it! It was a tremendous load off my shoulders. I'm so relieved.

The downside is that now our move is going to happen faster than expected. Tim doesn't have to be in Atlanta until the fall, but my new job starts in just three weeks. I'll have a temporary corporate apartment for a couple months, and by that time my husband and the rest of my worldly belongings will arrive in Atlanta. So it looks like I'll have to go it alone in the big city for a few weeks. At least Tim's company is handling our move, so I won't have to pack a thing—the moving company will do it all. I'll just have to unpack. Now all we have to do is find a house and sell ours. Sounds so easy, doesn't it?

June 8

From: Sara
To: Stephanie
Subject: Our baby's new home

I'm so glad you found a job—and with your old friend to boot! That will make moving and starting a new job easier. You have so much on your plate that you deserved to have your job hunt be this easy. I can't believe you have to tackle all this right now, plus find a new OB! After all this, childbirth is going to seem like a breeze.

We finally moved into *our* new house this weekend. We didn't have electricity until Sunday and it got pretty hot, but we made it okay. And, being pregnant, I didn't have to carry much! Of course, as you know, it's all the unpacking that's really the pain. But I don't care—I'm so excited to be in!

The house really turned out great. After living in that tiny condo (900 square feet), the new place feels huge! It really is our dream home.

It's great to be able to wake up and look at the lake in the morning. I was unpacking more stuff last night and I thought, *This is where we'll bring our baby home. And this is the house our kids are going to come home to from school or after spending a night with a friend. Right here, they're going to learn how to swim and fish and catch lightning bugs.* It seems surreal. I feel so ready to "nest" and be a Mommy.

June 10

From: Stephanie
To: Sara
Subject: Whose body is this, anyway?

I'm so excited for you about your new house! What perfect timing: Not only did you get out of carrying all the heavy stuff, but with all those nesting hormones kicking in, you'll be unpacked in no time. What a dream come true.

As for my pregnancy update, not only has my bladder basically taken control of my entire schedule, but the books are scaring the hell out of me! Have you read that certain body parts are going to change color—and stay that way? I didn't sign up for that! I don't recall seeing any brown nipples in the Victoria's Secret catalog or *Sports Illustrated* Swimsuit Edition. I'm sorry, but I refuse to believe it. I firmly believe that whatever is pink now will remain that way, baby or no baby. I can live with stretch marks and even wider hips, but brown nipples? Ooh, that's disgusting.

And what *is* with all the peeing? I'm *so* freakin' tired of going to the bathroom! And why does your body make you have to pee several times in the night? Just when you're more tired than you've ever been in your whole life? Why? Why? *Why?* I've never bought so much toilet paper. And on top of it all, you're supposed to drink lots and lots of water for the baby? Give me a break.

June 12

From: Sara
To: Stephanie
Subject: Too much information

I was at Babies "R" Us the other day (by the way, can you believe that place? I was totally overwhelmed), and they gave me a little brochure that showed all the stages of fetal development right up to and including the baby being born. I'm talking fully detailed, four-color, in-your-face photography. Looking at the photos of the fetus was fine, just a little freaky. It was that last one of the baby coming out that got my attention: There was nothing natural looking at all about that. I think I would have rather not seen that picture. I'm sure the nightmares will start anytime now.

I, too, have read about the nipple thing. I guess this is just one of the many things that are happening to us that are sadly out of our control. Maybe it's just the beginning of the end, and it explains why you see so many women who become mothers (especially stay-at-home moms) donning sweatpants and old T-shirts and skipping makeup most of the time. It's probably the result of a long list of pregnancy-related cosmetic changes that began with brown nipples—finally, they just give up the fight altogether and surrender to the sweatpants.

Although I'm planning on staying at home once I have the baby, I don't want to give up the good fight for fashion and personal hygiene. So please, if you ever see me out in public with my hair in a scrunchie, wearing leggings and a sweatshirt, or God forbid, a Christmas sweater, you have my permission to do an intervention.

June 18

From: Stephanie
To: Sara
Subject: Christmas-sweater intervention and new job

You mean Christmas sweaters are bad? Okay, I'll give you the Christmas sweater, but I'm not, under any circumstances, giving up my scrunchie collection. (Yes, I said *collection*.)

Well, here I am, four months pregnant and starting my new job! There are only about seven of us in the office, as we're based in California, yet this is a very career-minded group. They're going to die when they find out that Bo hired a pregnant woman! i'm going to hide it as long as my belly will allow, so they're probably just going to think that I really eat a lot.

I'm so glad that I told my new boss up front. That way, when we do break the news, he can tell my co-workers that he knew I was pregnant when he hired me, and it won't look like I pulled one over on him. His credibility is important to me because there was never a moment of discrimination over my pregnancy (which is the way it should be). And it felt so good to be considered on my merits and not have anything taken away because I'm going to become a mother. Unfortunately, I don't think all bosses are like that, so I know I'm really fortunate.

Right now I've got it all: the career, the family, and the appetite of a 400-pound sumo wrestler.

Have you felt the baby move yet? It's hard to concentrate on it since there are so many other changes happening to our poor bodies right now between the indigestion, the stretching, and the bloating. But I definitely noticed a feeling in my belly that I'm sure is the baby moving around. The best way I can describe it to you is to imagine a goldfish swimming into the side of its bowl. It's like a little bump surrounded by water. It's so weird and so amazing all at once.

Gotta run for now!

June 23

From: Sara
To: Stephanie
Subject: The sound of a washing machine

Wow! We got to hear the baby's heartbeat today, and it was so incredible! It sounds like a little washing machine in there—a wonderful, reassuring sound. It was a little scary at first, though, because it took Dr. Beurskens a while to find the heartbeat. It was like the little baby was hiding out in there. But we finally found it, and after breathing a collective sigh of relief, the doctor, David, and I just listened with delight. I think I could have stayed there and listened to that sound all day.

I don't think we're going to find out the sex of the baby ahead of time because we want that moment in the delivery room. I've always dreamed of hearing the doctor say "It's a girl!" or "It's a boy!" right at that joyful moment. I just hope that we can hold out during the ultrasound. I know *I* can—David's the one I'm worried about. He's dying to know.

I really have a girl feeling, and I even have a girl name picked out already. Maybe that's a sign . . . who knows? But it's fun to wonder. Another woman who works near me in our office is pregnant now, too. She's just a month or so behind me and isn't finding out the sex either. All the guys are betting on who's having what—there's even talk of starting an office pool. I swear, men can find a way to bet on *anything*.

June 25

From: Stephanie
To: Sara
Subject: Making a baby

I know, the whole heartbeat thing is truly amazing. Did you ever think about the fact that you're walking around with not one, but *two* hearts in your body right now? Weird, huh? When I heard my baby's heartbeat for the first time, all I could think of is that it's so incredible to know that its heart is already beating on its own—that all that stuff is taking place inside my body, even when I'm not thinking about it. The whole time I'm working or driving or cleaning toilets, my body is busy making a baby. And now it has a heart?! Wow!

The heart rate was slow for us, which indicates a boy (or so the old wives' tale goes). I hope that's right, since there hasn't been a boy born on my side of the family in more than 70 years. I'm sick of gymnastics, ballet, cheerleading, and dresses. I want to take my son to baseball practice and buy him little trains and dump trucks. I can't wait to find out, but I really want that big moment in the delivery room. I don't think we're going to find out beforehand either.

July 6
From: Sara
To: Stephanie
Subject: Rookie of the year

Hey, woman! We had our monthly agency meeting today, and I got our "Rookie of the Year" award, which is given to the new person who has excelled in their first year. (Of course it's not like it's a huge agency: There were probably only four new people hired this year, but I'll take it!) I can't believe I've been with Corder Philips Wilson almost a year now. It's gone by so fast.

Anyway, they printed up a certificate for me and everything. (That's one of the benefits of working in an ad agency—you can do all that fun design stuff conveniently in-house.) The certificate says "CPW recognizes Sara for her ability to balance building a home, starting a family, and writing damn good copy." Isn't that funny? I felt like Sally Field: "You like me! You really like me!" It really made me feel good about my work. I was glad to know that they're happy with my writing. I'd kind of felt insecure about it because I've spent most of my time at CPW either distracted by building the house or being pregnant. On the other hand, it makes me feel guilty to know that I'm not coming back. Of course *they* don't know that yet. I'm hoping I can work out an arrangement to work from home for them after the baby is born. Keep your fingers crossed. For now, mum's the word (no pun intended).

July 6
From: Stephanie
To: Sara
Subject: Congratulations!

"Mum's the word"? You should be ashamed of yourself. Not about the award—about your sense of humor. (Just kidding).

Congratulations, girlfriend! There's nothing I like to hear more than a mother (or, in this case, mother-to-be) excelling at her job. That's awesome.

Plenty of people like you, by the way—you're just too hard on yourself. What's not to like? You're gorgeous, talented, and have exquisite taste; plus, David says that when you're out on the lake, you "look good wet." Not many people do, you know, so that's a real compliment.

Keep up the good work on the job, and they'll work something out with you. Don't worry.

July 20
From: Stephanie *[now five months pregnant]*
To: Sara
Subject: Incredible ultrasound!

Today was the ultrasound! We saw our little baby's face, hands, and feet; and we saw it move and even smile and suck its thumb.

Tim and I haven't been able to come to an agreement about whether or not to find out the baby's sex. I don't want to know because I feel like it's going to be a huge reward to look forward to. I believe that the anticipation is going to help me get through all the pain, pushing, and struggling. Tim, on the other hand, wants to know *really* badly. He says that he wants to be able to prepare himself. Frankly, I don't understand what he has to prepare for: It's all blankets and bottles in the beginning—he doesn't have to worry about buying footballs or Barbie dolls for a couple of years.

I also want us to find out together—I mean, it should be something that we share. I'm afraid that if he finds out, he'll tell his family or friends, and I think *I* deserve to know the sex of my baby before anyone else. We just can't settle the debate. I *don't* want to know, just as strongly as he *does*. So we're really at an impasse. Even as we drove to the doctor's office, we still hadn't settled the dilemma.

Of course I was about to burst—I had to drink so much water, and the baby was crowding my bladder anyway. I was so uncomfortable! I thought I was going to wet my pants by the time I finally got my turn on the ultrasound table. (You'll be happy to know that they do give you the chance to pee and get more comfortable beforehand.)

The whole thing was incredible! It made everything seem so real, and we really realized how close the time for Baby to join us is (about 130 days to be exact). We have the cutest printout of the bottom of the baby's foot, and it looks just like Tim's foot. It was so amazing to see the baby move, blink, and hiccup. I finally got to see what's been kicking me for the past few months.

When it was time to find out the baby's sex, the nurse asked us if we wanted to know. We just stared at each other and explained to the nurse that we couldn't come to a decision. So she wrote it down on a piece of paper and put it in a sealed envelope, which she gave to me. That way, I could decide whether we wanted to know or not.

But when we got to the car, Tim said that he didn't really need to know anymore. He'd thought that finding out the sex would make it more real for him, but once he saw the baby, it was real enough. So I hid the envelope, and that was the end of it.

August 7

From: Sara *[now four and a half months along]*
To: Stephanie
Subject: The first time I saw your face . . .

I'm feeling so much right now, I can't even begin to describe it. We had the first (and most likely only) ultrasound today. I know I may be biased, and those images are pretty murky, but I'm telling you that this little baby inside me is a cutie pie. It has the cutest little nose I've ever seen. The baby sucked its thumb, played with its feet, and then promptly went to sleep, so our wonderful little first peek at our baby ended entirely too quickly. I wanted to beg the ultrasound technician to do it again, but I contained myself.

We held strong on not finding out. Even though the technician carefully avoided showing us any of the "private" areas (not that I could have distinguished anything). David is convinced we're having a girl. I have a pretty strong feeling that way, too, but who knows? I think it would be great to have a little girl, but either way I'll be happy.

I'm such an emotional basket case lately. A couple weeks ago we adopted a second dog, another golden retriever we named Luke. He's six months old and the sweetest little thing. He hadn't been treated well by his previous owner, so he's very happy to have found a good home. I was so excited to get him and give Sam a buddy—keep in mind that I initiated the whole thing. But two days after we brought Luke home, I'm bawling my eyes out wondering if Sam (our first child, just of the canine variety) still knows that we love him or if he thinks we've abandoned him, or if anything will ever be the same now that we've gone from a one-dog family to a two-dog family.

Somehow I don't think it's the change in the number of *dogs* in our house I'm really worried about, but it took me a day or two to figure that out. Poor David: He just listens and brings me more tissues. I hope I'm simply a victim of hormones; otherwise, my child is going to need an awful lot of therapy. And so am I.

My other big problem is tomato sauce. I can't get enough of it. I mean I *really* can't get enough of it: marinara sauce, Bolognese sauce, even salsa—I don't care. As long as it's full of pureed tomatoes, I must have it, and in large quantities. I have an addiction that I can only imagine compares to that of the crackhead. I'm the joke of the office because I'm constantly bringing in large Styrofoam takeout containers loaded down with pasta and sauce at lunchtime.

"Baby wants spaghetti again today?" somebody's always asking, as I sprint out the door every day promptly at noon. I even found a restaurant close to the office that has great spaghetti and serves big helpings. I'm sure I'm their customer of the month, but recognition is the last thing I want. In fact, I may have to start wearing sunglasses and a hat when I go in there. And it's so embarrassing at the office that I never go eat down in the lunchroom—instead, I huddle over my massive portion at my desk, hoping that no one will notice . . . and I eat it all. And it feels worth every bit of humiliation.

It seems that this poor baby is destined to be born to a weepy, spaghetti-addicted, 250-pound Christmas-sweater-wearing freak.

September 9

From: Stephanie
To: Sara
Subject: Happy anniversary . . . let's eat!

Today is our fifth wedding anniversary. And what does every pregnant woman want for her anniversary? To go out to eat—what else?! Yum!

My pregnancy book says that now that the baby is at the six-month point, it's about nine inches long and weighs at least 1¾ pounds. (It sure feels a lot heavier than that!) The book also says that I need an extra 300 calories per day. This is *not* a problem for me. I found out that I feel my best when I have a little food in my stomach, so I've learned to snack almost constantly. I have an entire file-cabinet drawer filled with snacks: pretzels, cookies, crackers, granola bars, Twizzlers, peanuts, you name it. It looks like the Keebler elves have taken up residence in my desk. And I don't think my co-workers mind at all: Every afternoon the buffet opens, and these are people who have no guilt about taking food from a pregnant woman.

I'm traveling a lot for work lately. Since my territory covers four states (Tennessee, Texas, Arkansas, and Louisiana), I'm trying to see all my clients before I'm too pregnant to fly. I'm so happy to be working in the cable-TV industry again. I really love my job. My boss and co-workers are so much fun that it's really going to make returning to work after the baby comes a lot easier. Anyway, I know I wasn't meant to be a stay-at-home mom because I'm one of those weird people who likes to work. And besides, if I stayed at home all day, I wouldn't have any excuse for not cleaning my house.

September 14

From: Sara
To: Stephanie
Subject: My glamorous life in advertising

I don't know how you do it with all the flying. I just found out I have to go to Albany, New York, to watch a demonstration of a product that blows open doors for firefighters, the military, and the police. It's new and innovative because it opens the door without hurting anyone on either side of the door (from blowing debris). So they've got me—their pregnant, hormonal, spaghetti-eating copywriter—flying up to watch this big gunlike prototype bust open some steel doors (which is every girl's idea of fun!). Even though I'm just a teensy bit removed from the profile of their target audience, this is supposed to help me write better ads. I'm sure they're thrilled to have me on their creative team!

It's a trip on the client's private plane, a day out of the office . . . I should be excited, but I'd rather just stay in front of my computer all day. I hate to fly anyway, but being pregnant has just made it worse. I wish I was further along so that I could say I was too late in my pregnancy to fly, but no such luck. I never get to go anywhere except occasionally to a client's office or a photo shoot—now I get to go somewhere and it's to some old armory to watch doors being blown open. I'll try to contain my excitement.

I know what you mean about work: I really like it, too, but somehow I don't think it's going to be that hard to leave my job. It's great to get paid to write, but I'm really not writing what I want. I've always looked at copywriting as a means to an end— a way to hone my skills and still get a paycheck—and felt that there was something bigger out there for me. I'm just not sure how or when I'll get to it.

I've always wanted to stay at home with my kids, but I haven't broken the news to my boss yet. He hasn't asked either, God bless him. None of the partners have. We have so many women who work in the agency that I guess they've learned to handle the whole pregnancy thing gracefully (and ethically). There are actually two other women pregnant in the office right now, and with the number of married thirtysomething women employed here, there are bound to be more with child soon.

Anyway, I'm going to tell my boss soon because I want to give him time to replace me. It's not like there are tons of copywriters out there, so it may take a while. I hope I can do some freelance from home for them, though—I'd love to continue working with some of my current clients.

I wish I could stash what *I* crave in my desk drawers . . . but it'd be a bit difficult to keep spaghetti and chips and salsa in there. This is so typical of me: I don't crave snacks, I crave *meals*. Three hundred extra calories a day? I'd bet I'm taking in an extra 1,300. And I'm enjoying every minute of it. (Damn!)

September 14
From: Stephanie
To: Sara
Subject: The spaghetti drawer

What do you mean? Sure you can stash spaghetti in your drawer. Ever heard of Chef Boyardee?

I think the blow-the-doors-open-without-flying-debris thingy sounds pretty cool, but you can keep the whole private-jet experience. To me (and my own personal flying phobia), the words *private jet* mean "small plane with fewer lives to lose, therefore less caution is required for maintenance."

In any case, good luck with it and try to enjoy it!

September 15
From: Sara
To: Stephanie
Subject: Reassurance

Thanks for the words of comfort. Could you possibly say something a little scarier about private planes? Sure, I was thinking it, but did you have to *say* it?

October 8
From: Stephanie
To: Sara
Subject: Pillow talk

Can you believe we're almost at the end of our second trimester already? This is week 28, and my trusty pregnancy book says that by the end of today, I'll have been pregnant for a full seven months. It also says that the baby will gain more than one pound this month. If it gets any bigger, it's going to hurt me.

I can't believe how much it kicks. Sometimes I have to laugh because the kicks are so hard and fast and grouped together that I swear the baby is having a temper tantrum. It happens a lot when I'm sitting at the computer in the afternoon. It seems like when I'm sitting still, that's when Junior gets aggravated. And sleeping is impossible these days. Poor Tim is going to have to go to the chiropractor because I've managed to adopt every pillow we own: one for my head; one for my arm; one for between my knees; and, as an added bonus, sometimes I like one against my back. Thank God we have a king-size bed, or I'd be spending nights with my pillows, while Tim sleeps in one of the guest rooms.

They're starting to put all the Christmas decorations out in the stores, and I'm getting so excited. The baby will be here before Christmas, and it's just surreal to think that I'm going to have a baby between now and then. Aren't you getting excited?

I think I have to go to Babies "R" Us again today. I love that store! I want everything they carry! It cracks me up because when I was single and renting an apartment, I went into a Home Depot with one of my home-owning friends. And I remember thinking, *What in the hell is so interesting about this store? What is all this crap?* Then when Tim and I bought a house, I couldn't wait to go to Home Depot! It's the same way with baby stores now. I used to think, *Who could ever use all this ridiculous stuff, like toilet-seat safety hooks, outlet covers, and cup holders for a stroller?* Now when I know I have to go to Babies "R" Us, I'm so excited, I could pee my pants (of course I do that every time I sneeze anyway).

It's just funny how life reveals things to us in stages. And speaking of stages (nice segue, huh?), Tim's doing great at his new job. He's come up with all this crazy stuff for the training program. He found a production company who re-created the set from the *Late Show with David Letterman,* and Tim does a whole training program while impersonating Dave. He also impersonates Regis Philbin and does a *Who Wants to Be a Millionaire?* program—and, to my dismay, he also does a program based on the show *The Weakest Link,* where he impersonates the host (you know, that red-haired lady who insults everyone). He even wears a black dress and a wig!

I don't know what happened to him: This is the same guy who was self-conscious just walking to the salad bar at a crowded restaurant when we were dating—now he's performing in a Fortune 500 company in front of hundreds of people. But it's an amazing program that he's put together, and the employees are loving it. This move to Atlanta turned out to be a really good thing for both of our careers. Plus, I'm beginning to realize that despite my early Yankee roots, I really belong in the South. I'm really feeling very much like I belong here. I'm a country girl at heart: I love NASCAR racing and fried chicken, and I love to bake pies. I have five, yes, I said *five* deviled-egg plates (a sure sign that you're a Southern girl), and we did leave our Christmas lights up until March last year. So there you have it. I've got it all, except the accent—that just didn't quite stick.

Gotta run for now—talk to y'all later.

October 10

From: Sara
To: Stephanie
Subject: The missing link and deviled eggs

Maybe Tim should change the name of his show from *The Weakest Link* to *The Missing Link.* Sorry, I couldn't resist. He wears a wig? Has he thought about what that's going to be like when it's career day at his kid's school a few years from now?

Okay, my *mother* doesn't even have five deviled-egg plates, and she's the quintessential Southern woman. When, pray tell, would one possibly need five deviled-egg plates? I'm assuming that these were wedding-shower gifts from elderly women at your mom's church. Those Southern church ladies sure love to give a girl a deviled-egg plate.

It really is wild feeling the baby move. Although the other day at work the baby must have gotten its leg or arm or something hung up under my rib. Even though I was extremely uncomfortable and short of breath for about 30 minutes and could only sit in one position to not be in severe pain, somehow I just knew that's what it was. I could actually feel that little limb stuck under my rib.

Hey, remember that trip to Albany I was telling you about? Well, I went and yes, I survived. But I have to tell you what our client did while we were up there. We were all about to eat lunch, and he was asking me how I was feeling and so on, when he reached over and touched my belly! I was shocked. Of course I didn't say anything to him, but c'mon! I thought that was a bit inappropriate. He's a client, and he didn't ask. Why is it that people think that just because you're pregnant they can touch you there? Why would they want to? It really creeped me out.

Yes, we're getting closer to the big day! David and I can't settle on a boy's name. Our girl's name is Anna, a name I've liked for a long time. It's classic, and it sounds good for a little girl or a grown woman. But we're not sure about the middle name yet—I like Grace, but David doesn't. We may go with Marie, since that's the middle name of both David's mother and grandmother, and it goes well with Anna. It would be nice to have a family connection with the name, too.

Boys' names are harder, though, since there are fewer to choose from. We both like Sean, so that may be an option. I have such a strong girl feeling that it probably won't matter anyway. I really feel that this baby is a girl. If it's a boy, that's great, too, but I'd like to have a daughter at some point.

Okay, gotta go write some burly-man ad copy about breaking down doors now. Yep, I'm still working on this project. Ugh.

Chapter 2

The Final Countdown

November 10

From: Stephanie
To: Sara
Subject: The pregnant and handicapped

Here's one to look forward to, since you're following so closely in my very pregnant footsteps: For the past two days, I've felt a lot of pressure at the bottom of my belly. When I get up from sitting or get out of the car, I have to stand there for a few minutes before I can walk. The baby has dropped a little, so it's now basically resting right on my pubic bone—*very* uncomfortable. The midwife said that I'd probably feel this way until the baby drops the rest of the way when it's closer to the time of birth. Great.

You know that "waddling" that I vowed never to do? Well, any hopes I had of maintaining a poised walk have gone out the window, along with my sexy size-three underwear (okay, size five). Waddling has now become my major means of transportation.

I've become one of "those" women—the ones in the mall who look like they can hardly put one swollen, water-retaining leg in front of the other. Those poor women we looked at before we were pregnant and thought, *For cryin' out loud, get her a wheelchair already. I've seen handicapped people move faster than that.*

Which brings me to another point: If I ever get into politics, I'm going to lobby for pregnant women to be allowed to park in handicapped-parking spots. There are too many of those things anyway—I mean, have you ever seen a parking lot where every one of these spots was full? When the lawmakers developed the formula for the number of spots, were they planning on all the handicapped people showing up to shop on the same day? What a waste for us hot, heavy, bloated women who are walking for two. Anyway, I digress (as usual).

I had a doctor's appointment today, and the baby's heartbeat was really fast (indicating a girl). I want a boy so badly that, although I hate to admit it, I couldn't help but feel a little disappointed. I know it won't matter once the baby's here, but I just want to think footballs and G.I. Joes, not dolls and weddings. Isn't it ironic how this is the biggest life-changing event ever, yet we don't get to choose what we're having? It just goes to show that God really does have a sense of humor.

I suppose that Tim and I could just go ahead and find out the baby's sex. But since it's our first, I just want to have that "big moment" in the delivery room. I think that waiting to find out when the baby's born will give me something to look forward to—sort of a goal to get me through all the pain and pushing. I can't wait to find out!

My friend Laura was here visiting last weekend. She has four children, so when it comes to pregnancy and childbirth, I just run right out and do everything she tells me, no questions asked. Anyway, she gave me some good suggestions on what to pack for the hospital (besides all the stuff you'll learn in childbirth classes), and since she's racked up some significant frequent-flyer miles in the maternity ward, I figure she knows what she's talking about. Thought you might be interested:

1. Bring some comfortable sweatshirt/hang-out type clothing. If you're in the hospital for a whole day before giving birth, you'll want to walk to the nursery or the cafeteria, and you might not want to be stuck in your jammies and a robe the entire time.

2. Snacks are *extremely* important. If you give birth in the middle of the night, you don't get to eat until the cafeteria opens, but you'll be *starving* after the physical exertion of labor. Plus, there's a very good chance that David will need them, too.

3. Bring lots of socks and underwear. You'll ruin most of them because of the blood and fluid and stuff after the baby's born, so bring ones you don't mind leaving behind. She also recommended button-front pajamas, which have "easy access" for breast-feeding purposes.

4. Bring a couple of outfits for the baby and some diapers so that Junior doesn't have to wear hospital-issued onesies, which are made of some sort of fabric derived from sandpaper. By the way, Laura also said to bring *two* of your favorite going-home outfits just in case the little angel decides to "christen" one on the way to the car. It makes for bad "coming home from the hospital" photos.

I think I'm entering that nesting stage. I started Christmas decorating today, and my suitcase for the hospital is almost completely packed. (It was so much fun packing for the baby—it all seems real now!)

Okay, done sharing. Have a great weekend. As I reminded Tim, you and David are spending your last few weeks *alone* together, so make the most of it!

November 11
From: Sara
To: Stephanie
Subject: I can't concentrate . . .

. . . on work! All I want to do is practice breathing techniques, buy baby clothes, and read childbirth books. I don't have time to write a new ad campaign—I have too much baby stuff to do! This is making me crazy.

Can you believe you're only a *month* away? Are you excited? Nervous? Apprehensive?

You mentioned there was a book you were reading on pain-management techniques—is it called *Birthing from Within*? I saw it the other day and thought it was the one you mentioned. We did breathing exercises in childbirth class last night (now you know where all this is coming from . . .) and the instructor suggested that we practice at home, with me holding an ice cube in my hand for a minute at a time to simulate the aggravation of a contraction. (However, she also said that the ice cube would be nothing compared to an actual contraction. . . . I wonder if they say that stuff just to psych you out.) Did you and Tim do anything like that?

In some ways, I feel very apprehensive about labor, and other times I feel like *bring it on!* I want to see what my pain tolerance, endurance, and mental strength really are. I've never had a broken bone or anything, so I really don't know how I'll deal with pain of this magnitude. I hope I don't disappoint myself!

Are you planning on getting an epidural, or are you going to try to do it without one? (I'm full of questions today, aren't I?) I agree with you about not finding out about the baby's sex. I think it's going to make for a really great moment in the delivery room, even though it nearly killed David not to find out when I had my ultrasound. I think that if I'd wavered, he would have jumped at the chance to find out. But we resisted the temptation—and not knowing has actually been a lot of fun.

Write back when you can. I know you have plenty of other stuff to do. Pregnant women should get maternity leave *before* birth, too.

November 15
From: Stephanie *[six more weeks to go]*
To: Sara
Subject: Just breathe

I'm laughing so hard from reading your last message . . . you sound like the typical woman about to have a baby! Remember, all the books said that it would be hard to think about anything else toward the end.

Yes, I'm reading *Birthing from Within*, and I *highly* recommend it. (In fact, I almost bought it for you, but you once made the statement that you had too many books already.) The author is an art therapist, and she has her subjects draw pictures to relate their feelings and fears about labor and birth. The last half of the book is awesome: It teaches you how to analyze pain and find ways to deal with it. In fact, the ice-cube exercise is in that book, too.

Tim and I did breathing exercises in childbirth class, but I didn't care much for them. I plan on using the ones I learned from *Birthing from Within*, along with the ones I use when I'm lifting weights, when I'm in pain and struggling and concentrating. That's the closest thing I can compare it to.

I feel the same way you do about labor: Sometimes I'm nervous, but other times I just want to prove to everyone that I can do it. I'm convinced that it's 90 percent mental. When I watch that show on TLC, *A Baby Story,* there are women who get through it and hardly make a peep, like there's nothing to it. And then there are women who freak out and give up before they're even halfway through. Can it *really* be that different for everyone?

Yes, I'm going with an epidural—what are you, nuts? My friend Laura (the one with four kids) had her first two naturally, but then she decided to have an epidural with her third. She called me afterward to say, "Stephanie, *I am an idiot!* I can't believe I put my body through all that pain. I'd never go without an epidural again!"

I'm not really convinced that "natural" childbirth has that many advantages, anyway: You still have to make it to four or five centimeters dilated before they'll even administer the epidural, which is why I'm hoping all those pain-management techniques will help. Besides, I just think it will be a much more "natural" and enjoyable moment for me if I'm not fighting the pain. I watched my sister through her entire labor, and it wasn't pretty. But then again, her baby was premature, and she hadn't prepared by reading or taking any classes. Preparing and educating yourself gives you the ammunition to fight the pain, because you understand what's happening to your body. However, when I tell my sister about the techniques for managing pain in the book, she just laughs at me.

I think you and I have the mental toughness to be fine. I've been told that fear makes the pain worse because you're more out of control. The more you know, the less you'll fear. And being able to relax (as much as possible) is key for moving labor along faster. We're a lot like animals, because if our "birth place" is causing fear and apprehension, then labor slows down (like an animal that can hold off the birth process until the environment is safer).

Do I think I'll "lose it" toward the end? Yes. But it's temporary, and knowing that will help. Do I think I'll cry and make weird sounds? Yes. But who cares? One of the books I'm reading was very empowering because it teaches that it's entirely *up to you*. No one can help you—not the doctors or the nurses or anyone. And since you realize that it *is* up to you, you don't have to succumb to everything they tell you to do. If it's not what you want, then don't do it. It's *your* child and *your* labor. That helped me a lot because I usually take the "Yes, ma'am, I don't want to be a burden" approach that our mothers taught us.

Anyway, I'm having one of my pregnancy headaches today, so I'm hating life. Even my vision isn't quite right. But I'm working at home, so that helps. I also think that the "pregnancy insanity" is why I've been working on so many projects. If I didn't have the luxury of working at home two days a week, I think I'd go crazy. I can get so much done around the house in between phone calls and e-mails. I'm thankful that I have work, though—otherwise, I'd sit around the house all day (eventually I'd run out of baby stuff to do) and drive myself crazy just *waiting*.

Well, time to go feed the baby. It starts kicking the crap out of me when it's hungry. Try to concentrate and be patient—when you *are* in labor, you probably won't want to be! As for me, I'm just trying to soak up these final weeks of being pregnant. I'm really going to miss it! Not feeling the baby moving inside is going to be like losing an arm.

By the way, have you decided who you're going to allow in the labor/delivery room with you?

November 16

From: Sara
To: Stephanie
Subject: Tough girl in leather pants

I think you're right about the mental-toughness thing. I feel pretty sure that I'll handle the pain all right. It's just weird when you don't really know what to expect. (My mother says that it's like bad gas pains.) I've dealt with migraine headaches all my life, so I do know something about dealing with pain. I just don't want to do anything that will ruin the experience of giving birth. I have a good friend who's a nurse, and she talks about deliveries she's witnessed where it's a beautiful experience—the mother and father are calm and focused, the lights are dim, and soft music plays in the background. Then there have been others she's seen where the mother's screaming, "Get this f#$%*ing thing out of me!" I really hope I don't get so whacked out that I say something like that—what a way to bring a child into the world! Yet I might not be the other extreme either (somehow I think the soft music might annoy me).

I guess I'll go for the epidural, too, but I'm trying to approach it all with an open mind. My plan is to just see how my labor progresses and how I'm handling the pain and make the decision then. My sister didn't have an epidural with either of her kids, since she says that back then they didn't hand them out as freely as they do now. She said the pain is rough, but nothing you can't stand. However, I think they say that if you get Pitocin it makes it worse than if you go into labor naturally.

As for the delivery room, I'll let people come in and out during the labor, but once it's time to push, then it's just going to be David and me. I want that to be our moment (plus, I don't really want everyone seeing me in my full glory, if you know what I'm saying).

You're right: It *is* going to be weird not to be pregnant anymore, but I'm really starting to want to be skinny again. (Not that I really was that way before I got pregnant, but it just seems like it by comparison now.) I even had a dream the other night that I was wearing leather pants, which might be a sign that I'm ready to have this baby.

Of course, I doubt that I'll be able to afford leather pants considering the way David is spending money lately. I think he's on some kind of last hurrah before the baby comes. I guess he thinks that there won't be any money left for *his* toys after the baby's born, so he's trying to get them all now. He's working on me to get a hot tub and a Ping-Pong table . . . you know, really useful things that we need to spend money on right now. I think he must have pregnancy insanity, too. And God forbid I spend money on a crib or dresser for the nursery—how frivolous! He doesn't understand that, for a woman, this is even more important than planning a wedding. This is something I've looked forward to all my life, and he's nickel-and-diming me on everything. But, oh, we *must* have the top-of-the-line Ping-Pong table. I'm glad he has his priorities in order.

Here's my big news for the day: I told my boss that I won't be coming back after the baby, and he was great about it. (I don't think he was all that surprised.) He said, "I hate that you aren't coming back, but I completely understand and respect you for it." That was about the best thing he could have said to me. Everyone—my co-workers and all three partners—has been awesome to me, and I'll miss the interaction with everyone. I've really made some good friends here. Anyway, my last day will be December 18. I feel kind of sad about it now that the cat's out of the bag—it hadn't seemed like I was really leaving before.

November 21

From: Stephanie
To: Sara
Subject: Male nesting

First, a question I've been pondering: Why is it that at the drugstore, the smokers can get their cigarettes just inside the front door, but the sick people have to walk all the way to the back of the store—which is where the pharmacy is—to get their prescriptions filled, infecting all the healthy shoppers who are only there for toilet paper and a new lipstick? And why am I suddenly so bothered by this stuff?

That's great news about your boss—I'm really glad he was so gracious about it. That's the way it should be; after all, pregnancy is just part of life. I don't know why we feel so much pressure and stress about telling our superiors. It's like when you were a little kid and knew you were about to get in trouble for doing something really, really bad. It's so easy to lose perspective—I mean, creating a family is a thousand times more important than any job anyway. But I'm so glad that it went well.

This baby must be coming soon, because I am *so* uncomfortable! I can't sleep at all, and I'm extremely irritable. Everything is a struggle—for the first time in my pregnancy, it's really become a burden. And Tim is clueless. Last night I was trying to get out of the car with my big coat and purse, a shopping bag, and a bottle of water (after walking around a race track all day, by the way), and he says, "Can you hurry up? It's cold, y'know."

I wanted to smack him. I told him that I felt like that kid in the movie *A Christmas Story* . . . you know, the Red Ryder BB gun and all that. Remember the little boy whose mother has wrapped him up so tightly, in so many layers of snowsuit, that he falls and can't get up because he can't bend his arms, and he just lies there struggling and yelling, "Help! Help me!"? That's what getting out of a car is like these days.

I figure it's been a while since you and I had a good man-hating session, so here you go. Tim is going through some kind of a male nesting period right now. He's been bitching about how much money I've been spending recently (baby supplies, Christmas decorations, family gifts, food, etc.). I've been trying so hard to get *everything* done before the end of this month. But suddenly, he decided that we needed a TV in the living room (for when everyone is here around Christmas).

So, just like that—after *one day* of deliberations—we went out last night and bought a 27-inch TV and a stand. (Do you know how long it took me to sell him on the idea of mattresses for the guest rooms?) We get the TV home and suddenly he's one big ball of motivation. Hanging mini-blinds, assembling the TV stand . . . I had to make him stop to come to bed at midnight last night!

I'm starting to regret going to our childbirth classes so early. Tim had much more consideration and empathy for me during and immediately following those classes, and that's now worn off. And *now* is when I need it the most!

I think he's stressing lately, too, but can't really put his finger on the cause of it. He played video games (his favorite escape) until almost 2 A.M. on Friday night, and then slept too late on

Saturday to accomplish anything. Then he played video games again Saturday afternoon and then again until the wee hours of the morning! Then, of course, he's tired and wants to take a nap, or wants me to drive home from our day at the track. I'm a total bitch because *I'm* tired from not being able to sleep from the baby kicking me and having an upset stomach. (Naturally, I had previously pointed out that he should go to bed instead of wasting time playing video games.)

Meanwhile, the house didn't get vacuumed or cleaned, and nothing was accomplished. And worst of all, I didn't get to spend any time with him because he was concentrating on his games. I was really looking forward to us being together because he had trainees in town all last week and didn't come home until 10 P.M. or later every night. I was really hoping that we'd be able to cherish these last few weeks "alone" together, but we're both obviously so stressed out, irritable, and busy that I can forget any third-trimester romance. This is going to be nothing short of pure survival.

It's funny how some of the things that attracted you when you were dating are the very things you hate about your husband after you're married. I used to love Tim's lifestyle—he was always ready to play and have fun and be silly—but now I need him to be responsible and accomplish some grown-up things, and all he wants to do is be a big kid. In his mind, we have plenty of time to finish getting the guest rooms ready and stock up on frozen food for the Christmas/new-baby guests. So, as usual, I've decided to take matters into my own hands. If he doesn't help me, I'm hiring a maid! (Exactly how long have I been threatening to do that?!)

We're going to Fayetteville to be with my family this weekend, so I'm looking forward to all the doting (and having a fresh audience to complain to). And I predict that in his usual manner, Tim will find some reason to make us leave late, thereby reducing the number of hours he has to spend with the Baptists. My family doesn't drink at all, because although I've never found the Bible to condemn drinking, apparently Baptists go to hell for drinking (at least in my family). At Tim's family's house, it's a big party from the time we walk in the door until the time we leave. But hey, it's not going to kill him to go a couple of days without a beer. Anyway, this is why I have a theory that he somehow manages to find ways to procrastinate.

I can pack for him (which he never does the night before—it's always on the way out the door in a chaotic mess), I can do everything in my power to get him organized, but *something* always happens at work, or there are last-minute errands he needs to run. There's always a stupid reason to delay our departure, and it's usually something that could have been avoided with a tiny bit of planning. Of course this ritual drives me insane because I want to get home before it gets too late (my family also goes to bed early). So I know that tomorrow, no matter how much I prepare myself mentally to be patient, he's going to piss me off, and good. That, coupled with the pregnancy hormones, is not going to make for a pleasant five-hour road trip. I wonder if I can hook a video game up to the cigarette lighter in the car to lure him in there. Hey, desperate times call for desperate measures.

Anyway, thanks for letting me vent. Chat back when you can! Motto of the day: "Men are ineffective."

November 22

From: Sara
To: Stephanie
Subject: Trying to tighten that belt

It's funny you mentioned *A Christmas Story*. We had a client meeting this morning and it was freezing, so I was all bundled up. I had to get in the back of a van to go the client's office. I could hardly hoist my leg up high enough to climb in the van because my belly was getting in the way. I had my lovely black peacoat on that, thankfully, can also be worn with a loose belt, which has become shorter and shorter in recent months. I'm surprised it didn't come untied as I was hefting myself into the minivan. And my boss comments, "You look like the kid from *A Christmas Story!*" (Yeah, bite me.)

It's definitely getting harder to move around—I feel like a turtle on my back getting out of bed some mornings. And I don't know what would be worse: being pregnant in the blazing heat of summer or being pregnant now, when we have to wear all these layers of clothes that make us even bulkier. Before long I'm going to have to push the driver's seat in my car back so far that my feet may not touch the pedals.

Speaking of winter coats and pregnancy, I never thought about that issue until now. Like I said, thank God my coat has that belt so that it can expand with me, but otherwise I guess I would have ended up buying a whole new coat just for a couple months of pregnancy—'cause these buttons sure wouldn't meet the holes right now. Hell, the two sides of the coat are barely meeting as it is, and it's all I can do to tie the belt. It makes for a really fashionable look, as you can imagine. But by God, I'm warm! I did purchase a lighter-weight coat that has been fine most days, especially since my body is a furnace right now. But that was only about $40—I'd hate to shell out $100 or more for a maternity winter coat. (Do they even make such a thing? I've never noticed.)

And I can relate to the "male nesting." David and I were having a discussion at 11 last night about having Roman shades made for the dining room, and it was *his* idea. I was in such a state of shock I could hardly speak. This is the man who still wears the same shoes he owned in high school. But I'm not complaining, since this time it's about something *I* want and not a Ping-Pong table.

I feel the same way about these last few weeks of alone time: It's not happening! Nextel has a big promotion going on now so David's clients have been buying phones left and right. It's great timing in terms of his paycheck, but he's been up every night until 2 A.M. entering orders. The corporate-account executives have to enter all their orders themselves, and it's quite a process—especially when you have to do it after meeting with clients all day. So if he's not entering orders, we're going to a childbirth or an infant-CPR class, or taking the dog to obedience class (my goal is to have a well-behaved dog by the time the baby arrives). Plus, we've been on the go every weekend lately, *and* we're going to Virginia for Thanksgiving *this* weekend—which, thank goodness, will be our last trip home before the baby. (Riding in the car for four hours isn't really my idea of fun anymore.) I'm hoping that David and I will get some time in December, but then there's Christmas to get ready for. It's crazy . . . what were we thinking having babies during the holiday season?

I think David has gone into hyper-responsibility mode—at least financially. We are *so* okay, we have money in the bank, and we're investing; yet you'd think we were on the brink of poverty to hear him talk. He can't stop worrying about it. I think maybe he's panicking about losing my income, but it's not like we haven't done things to prepare for this.

Tim playing all those video games is probably some subconscious attempt to hold on to his freedom before he becomes a dad (just like David's Ping-Pong table). I really have a feeling that once these babies are here, we'll have nothing to worry about.

Yes, men *are* ineffective, so by all means, hire a maid! Hell, you're about to have a baby, and you're hosting Christmas at your house—I'd say that more than qualifies you for some help. I'm going to do that, too. I get indigestion so bad bending over now that I just can't do everything I used to. You don't have to be Superwoman, Steph. Get some help at home, and be good to yourself.

I hope you haven't left for your parents' house yet so that you can enjoy my bitching! Have a great Thanksgiving with the Baptists, and a safe trip! Tell Tim it will be good for him to dry out for a weekend. It cleanses the system.

November 27

From: Stephanie
To: Sara
Subject: Nesting and scrubbing

Worrying about finances must be a fatherhood thing, because Tim is *exactly* the same way right now! It doesn't matter how much money we have in the bank—he doesn't want me to spend *any*. All he talks about is mutual funds, IRAs, savings accounts, and raises for next year. It must be guys' way of preparing somehow.

We started working on our Christmas village last night (we assemble a fabulous one under our tree), so Tim's all into house-mode this week. Thank God—it's great to have him back! Of course, he has another training class in town all next week again, so he'll pretty much be AWOL. I'm so lovey-dovey toward him lately; I just want to cuddle all the time, and I keep telling him how crazy I am about him. He laughs at me and says, "It must be the hormones."

It looks like his whole family is coming to visit the day after Christmas (sister, brother-in-law, and baby from Denver; brother from New York; Mom and Dad), and I'm really looking forward to having them all visit. I just hope that the baby is on time or even a little early so that I can be a little more "gathered" by the time they all get here. Just in case, I've supplied Tim with coordinating Christmas plates and napkins, along with all the frozen appetizers and lasagna to keep everyone well fed; he's also in charge of stocking up on the booze to keep everyone happy. I figure if it's too much for me, my bedroom door has a lock on it.

As for the domestic help, I probably should line up somebody, but I'm in full nesting mode right now, so I'm kind of looking forward to scrubbing toilets every night. And besides, nobody can do it as well as I can, right? Let me tell you, girlfriend, I can clean a toilet like nobody's business. When Tim was selling cleaning chemicals to hospitals, he brought home a video that they used to train the maids on how to sterilize a bathroom between patients. I was forced to watch the entire presentation at least four times, and some of it stayed with me. You can rest assured that when your derrière touches my toilet seats, the only thing you have to worry about is chemical burns.

So how was the CPR class? Was it worthwhile? Ours got canceled, and I'm trying to decide if I should reschedule or just get my money back. It's four hours long, and I've had it with the classes. What do you think?

Isn't it weird to think that there's a complete baby inside of us right now? It's not a little alien-looking thing anymore—there's a whole little person in there, with working parts. It's completely Sci Fi Channel if you really think about it. Wouldn't it seem more civilized if we laid eggs or something?

It sure would be a lot easier to push an egg out! Then we could spend the next several months at home, sitting on our eggs, watching all the soaps and ordering Chinese food. Plus, our husbands could help us sit on them, too, so it wouldn't be all up to us. Oh well, we'd probably still get fat with all that sitting and eating, and we'd still get "pregnancy butt." There's just no way around it.

Oh, by the way: My pregnancy journal says that the force of a contraction when in labor is equal to 55 pounds of pressure. That's how hard it is to squeeze the baby out. Oh yeah, that's not going to hurt at all. Ugh.

November 27

From: Sara
To: Stephanie
Subject: Stumbling through pregnancy

I can't believe that you're going to have that many people at your house at Christmas! Breast-feeding is going to work wonders for you—you can just excuse yourself to be alone anytime you want! How are you feeling? Are you going to the doctor once a week yet?

You know that thing about getting clumsier when you're pregnant? Well, I just took a big spill in the middle of the office. I was walking down the hall reading a memo (my first mistake—walking and reading at the same time), when I tripped over a big cardboard box that someone had left there. It was pretty funny because it was one of those falls where you think you're going to pull it out and not go down, so I stumbled and stumbled for about 30 seconds before I actually fell. Our office is in an old refurbished warehouse with hardwood floors and it's very open, so the sounds of my fumbling and stumbling reverberated through the building, sending everyone running out of their cubicles to see if I was okay. Fortunately, since it was such a slow fall, it sounded way worse than it was. I was just sitting there in the middle of some flattened cardboard laughing by the time my co-workers came on the scene.

Of course the CPR class was worthwhile, you idiot—it could save your baby's life! Get back to that hospital and take it. However, I can't believe they make you pay for it; that was the one class our hospital offered for free. Seriously, the class was good. I recommend it just because if (God forbid) you're ever in the situation, you'll definitely want to know what to do. Plus, they give you literature that tells you what to do in almost any scenario. It made me feel more at ease having that information—at the same time, it also made me more paranoid, learning about all the things that can happen to a little baby.

I can't believe that there's a human being inside each one of us right now either. Eggs might be more civilized, but I wouldn't want to sit on a nest all day. At least being pregnant we can still walk around and do stuff like clean toilets. (You watched the video *four times?* If that's not love, I don't know what is.)

It's funny—I used to think that newborns were so tiny, but now that one's about to come out of a very small part of me, they look freakin' huge.

November 28

From: Stephanie
To: Sara
Subject: Just stay out of my way—I'm cranky

Yes, I'm going to the doctor every week now (yippee). As if the yearly poking and prodding wasn't bad enough, now it's every Wednesday. I still feel pretty good, but it's getting a little harder every day—the baby just grows so fast, my muscles can't keep up with the workload. The baby feels huge now. And it hasn't slowed down at all—it actually hurts me sometimes when it moves. I'm just a big punching bag.

I walk very slowly these days, and I let everyone else maneuver around me. Just stay out of my way: I'm heavy and cranky, and the hormones are a deadly time bomb, waiting for any excuse to explode into a fit of hormonally charged pregnancy rage (or tears, depending on the stimuli).

I hope you're okay from your fall. That must have been at least a little scary. They say that when the baby drops, your center of balance will change again, so be careful. On that note, I bought some new (stretchy) shoes that fit my poor, swollen feet. They look like corrective shoes, but they're comfy and have good support. Fashion can kiss my ass right now. I just want to be able to walk around without falling down.

I have to tell you our latest issue. Even though I asked him about it before my mom bought her plane ticket, yesterday Tim decided that he wants us to be alone in the delivery room. Great. I so wanted my mom there for the labor, and I feel that it's really unfair to ask her to be there through all that and then leave for the big moment. It would mean so much to her.

I asked him, "If you were having a big surgery, wouldn't you want your mother there?" Of course he said no. (Yeah, right.) He asked me to put myself in his shoes, and I responded that I'd want him to do whatever he needed to do to get him through it. He also said that he thought it should be a private moment for us (with five other doctors and nurses in the room), and I can understand that.

The problem is that now I have to break the news to my mom. I know she'll cooperate without complaining, but I also know that it will hurt her a little, too. Tim appreciated my giving in, and he doesn't want to hurt my mom either. I'm still going to ask her to come for the labor, since I think it will be good for Tim to have a backup. It's not that I don't trust him—I just think that he'll need a break, or he'll need some time to put in his Bubba teeth and entertain the nurses' station (I know him well).

What a dilemma . . . probably the first of many. But I know that putting Tim and me first is the right decision.

November 28
From: Sara
To: Stephanie
Subject: Stretch pants

I know what you mean about fashion: All I want is a comfortable pair of stretch pants (and I *never* thought I'd hear myself say those words!). At least I *do* reserve the stretch pants for home, but that could change. I feel really big now, too. I went to the doctor last week, and I've gained 27 pounds—so much for keeping to the 25-pound mark. And, of course, the kind doctor reminded me that I still have the Christmas feeding frenzy to get through. Next visit I get the beta strep test, which I learned involves a vaginal and rectal culture. Oh, goodie!

You're sure right about the baby feeling big and kicking harder. My baby's whole body flinched the other night while I was sleeping, and it woke me up. It was wild! Sometimes the movements are so strong they catch me off guard.

I finally bought *Birthing from Within*. Boy, those first few chapters are a little out there, especially where she talks about making a plaster cast of your pregnant belly and letting the father wear it! Now come on: Can you see David and Tim wearing casts of our bellies and boobs?

Based on what I've read in that book and other places, I'm starting to think I'd really like to try to have the baby with no epidural. Of course I may get to two centimeters and feel completely different. Have you done the ice-cube exercise?

I think you did the right thing by putting Tim first on the delivery-room issue. As much as you want your mother in there, you do have to take him into consideration first. And she probably understands more than you realize. This weekend, for example, my mom made a point of telling me that when she had her first baby she couldn't wait for her mother to leave. She told me not to hesitate to tell her to hit the road. I was surprised, but remember, they've been through this before.

Besides, your mom will have plenty of time to enjoy her grandchild—and you and Tim should have some special memories that are yours alone. I don't think you'll regret it. David and I have already talked, and after a certain point in the labor, I want it to be just the two of us. I know that for me personally, it will be more comfortable that way. I think this is going to be our most amazing moment since we got married, and I want it to be just ours. You know, this is probably the first of many times to come where we'll have to put our "new families" first.

November 28

From: Stephanie
To: Sara
Subject: Extra-big-girl cotton nightie

You in stretch pants? The only reason I believe you is because I'm usually in my $5 extra-big-girl cotton nightie from Wal-Mart from the time I get home till the time I get up in the morning. One of the best things about living in a new town is that nobody knows us, which means no surprise guests.

Don't worry about the Strep B test. It's no big deal. Just a quick swoosh or two with a Q-tip—no cold metal tools required. I wasn't looking forward to it either, but I was pleasantly surprised. It's being checked for dilating that hurts.

As for the ice-cube exercise, I can't say that I've actually done it. However, I'll bet that I'd be immune to it. My hands and wrists are so swollen that I've had to resort to walking around for hours with ice on them to prevent my wedding rings from having to be surgically removed. My wrists and hands are so painful, and they look like little carrots because of the water retention and swelling. I woke up in the night and thought I was going to have to go for x-rays this morning because my wrist hurt so badly. I can't even make a fist. Is this what poor Tim feels like after a good night of downing Bloody Marys? If so, I'd quit drinking. (As for Tim making a cast of my belly . . . tell David to get with it—ours is on the mantel!)

We've been working on Christmas decorations. I've gone to painstaking lengths and great detail, not to mention multiple trips to the craft store, to make the house perfectly beautiful: swags over the archways in the living and dining rooms; all-gold table accessories; and of course, coordinating everything with the tree. Last night, Tim drags in the old artificial Christmas tree that was a hand-me-down from his parents. In all my visions of Christmas with our families and our new baby, we were never sitting around an old Charlie Brown Christmas tree that even most homeless squirrels would refuse. He said that it was too much effort and took too much time to go buy a real tree and tie it on the car and drag it in the house—he had too much to do.

Then it happened: He made a fatal error . . . I'm almost embarrassed to tell you the next six words that came out of his mouth: "What do *you* have to do?" Of course the words, *Um, you mean like give birth?* came to mind. But for one fleeting moment, the hormone levels were low enough that I was able to control my mouth. Instead, I took his hand and led him to the kitchen. On the door of the fridge, I've been keeping a little dry-erase board with all the "To Do" items that are left. I've done this partly for my own sanity, and partly so that he could see what was still left to do before the baby and the holidays. And, instead of erasing what I've accomplished, I just cross it out so that I can feel like I'm making progress. I didn't say a word, just left him there reading the list. (As if it was the first time he'd ever seen it after all those beer trips.) Of course, he's more worried about what total the list will add up to monetarily, but the list itself is a very good thing.

So I solved my own tree dilemma by driving my big pregnant belly to Home Depot. (Hey, where else do you get a tree in a big city?) I picked out a nice seven-footer, the kind Home Depot guy strapped it to the roof of my Infiniti, and I drove home and directed Tim to drag it into the living room. Of course I had to listen to him bitch about all the needles and the mess—but it's so beautiful and smells so good that it's totally worth all his complaining. It's definitely the finishing touch to my hormone-induced nesting rampage.

Thanks for the reassurance on the whole Mom-in-the-birthing-room thing. I think I'll be happy that Tim and I have that moment, too. I left when my sister was ready to push. She asked me to stay, but even though I didn't know anything about birthin' no babies back then, something told me that I wanted to save that moment for myself. So I know it will pay off.

I'm fairly useless at work these days, waiting for the baby. Just getting ready in the morning and making that one-hour drive every day is getting almost impossible. One of my books said that during the last couple weeks of pregnancy, the baby could kick hard enough to knock a book off your lap. So we've got that to look forward to.

Chapter 3

The British Are Coming
(Stephanie's Birth Experience)

November 30
From: Stephanie *[ten days before delivery]*
To: Sara
Subject: Emotional roller coaster

Pregnancy is one big emotional roller coaster!

Yesterday at my doctor's appointment, I'd made *no* progress at all: The baby hasn't dropped as low as it should by now, and I had no thinning, no dilation . . . nuttin'! My midwife even did a quick ultrasound to make sure that the baby was in the right head-down position, and all is well (more about the baby's ears later).

Anyway, what a disappointment! I was so sure that we were getting really close—I mean the baby just feels so *heavy*. Then last night, out of the blue, I lost my mucus plug. (Isn't it funny that once you get pregnant, it's okay to use words like *mucus* and *dilation* and talk about the general condition of your female parts?) I called the nurse this morning to see if that's truly what it was, and she confirmed it, adding that I have hours, days, or up to two weeks before the baby comes. There is absolutely *nothing* definite about labor, and I wish someone would just give me a freakin' hint!

I know I need to just relax and let it happen, but that's *so* hard to do because I'm so keyed up about everything. I have just a couple more things that I want to do (including getting the two guest rooms cleaned). I think that after I finish that, it will be easier to sit back and wait it out.

So, back to the ultrasound. . . . I can read x-rays better than most people (at least in my own mind) because when I worked at the veterinary hospital, the doctor there was also a great teacher. He used to take us into the darkroom and point things out to us, so I do see things in ultrasounds that many people can't—it's sort of a way to train your eyes to look at the positive and negative space and shapes, and so forth.

Anyway, having said that, based on yesterday's ultrasound, our child is all Tim: It has his ears, the side of his face, his jaw, his forehead, his nose, etc. Tim says he doesn't see it, but I swear I can. And I have to admit that as much as I adore my husband and think he's got it going on in the looks department, it just pisses me off that after carrying this child for nine months in *my* body and then going through the pain of birth, it could very possibly have not gotten even one of my genes!

Of course the one trait we didn't want to pass on to our children is Tim's rather large ears, which have been a source of constant teasing and torment his entire life. So last night, he's walking around the house holding his head in his hands, going "Poor baby, poor baby." And every time it would kick me hard, he'd say, "That's not a kick—an ear just got stuck."

So here I am in pregnancy limbo. Basically, the nurse told me to watch for my water to break and/or to pay attention to my Braxton Hicks contractions, and if they get into a pattern, I should call. I'm afraid that if it doesn't happen by the end of next week, I may be an emotional and psychological wasteland . . . which will make me really fun to be with at the Christmas parties we have next week. Anyway, I'll keep you posted!

November 30

From: Sara
To: Stephanie
Subject: Yikes!

I can't believe it. God, I feel like this is happening to me, too! (Well, not literally. . . . It's just that we've talked so much throughout all this.) It's so amazing that this is about to happen for you! I can't even explain what I'm feeling, but I'm sure you know.

Well, if your poor big-eared baby is a girl, it will at least have one of your parts. Do you still have your girl feeling? (And were you using your x-ray-vision skills to check out that part of the body on the ultrasound?)

We took our breast-feeding class last night, and the teacher claims that you can bring on labor by stimulating your nipples. (Speaking of which, words like *nipples, milk flow, mucus plug, uterus,* and *Kegel exercises* are all part of my normal vocabulary now, too.) So go home and have major foreplay, and maybe that will get things going!

How many weeks are you now, 37? (This is all so confusing, since 37 to 42 weeks is full term—that's not a due date; it's a due *month!*) Are you considered early or right on time? And have you felt any Braxton Hicks contractions yet? Sometimes I feel a tightening, but it doesn't last for 45 seconds like the books say.

Since I began writing this e-mail, I've slipped into a major panic. I mean, if all this is happening to you now, then I know I'm not far behind. I still don't have my dresser for the baby's room, my house decorated, my Christmas shopping done . . . dear God!

If the messages from you stop, I'm going to start calling and checking on you. Put us on your phone list for when you go to the hospital. I'll only have about 500 more questions for you then. I'm so excited, I can't stand it! Boy, do I wish you lived in Charlotte now!

November 30

From: Stephanie
To: Sara
Subject: Due month

You're cracking me up! I can tell by the way you're writing that you're in a panic. So many questions. . . .

I'm 37 weeks. But I've always said that this baby was going to come early because my first doctor gave me a due date of December 9, but then the doctor here in Georgia changed it to December 19. There is definitely no exact science to this.

The bad news in all this is that it could be another week to ten days before anything happens (which would still make me early, so my theory was correct). I've talked to my girlfriends, and some of them told me that once they lost their mucus plug (gosh, I wish there was another term for that, it just sounds so gross), they went into labor within 24 hours, but then others said that it took another week or two. It's so frustrating! There aren't any definitive answers, just when I need them the most.

I'm back to the boy feeling again. The heart rate was only 140; however, the midwife said that the fetal heart rate slows a little as the baby grows. As for Braxton Hicks, I've had those daily since about six months; and last night they were more severe, more intense, and lasted longer than ever before. But "the girlfriends" say that true labor pains feel more like bad menstrual cramps that start in your back and lower abdomen. I've had some crampiness, but not enough to put the suitcase in the car.

The baby is extremely active—I think it wants to get out! And I wish that it would find the exit soon before it hurts me. As for the foreplay, I need a few more days; I mean, I still have some gifts to wrap! Besides, the thought of sex right now . . . oh, don't think so. And after all this talk about mucus plugs, I'm sure that the only reason Tim would even think about touching me would be out of sheer mercy alone. I'm not exactly a dream date these days.

No, you aren't far behind at all, girlfriend. But don't panic; there's still time. I think that our bodies give us enough warning signs and pre-labor symptoms that you'll know when you're close. Besides, it's like I keep telling myself, *The baby doesn't care if the tree is decorated or the beds are clean.* As long as the milk is flowing and it has a place to rest its head, it'll be perfectly happy. *We're* the ones that make ourselves crazy with all these visions of perfection in our heads. (And, on that note, I'm nesting like crazy today!)

If I lived in Charlotte right now, trust me, you'd be bored. Amazing what excitement one little chunk of mucus can cause, huh? In fact, Tim's mom has called me three times today to see if there's any progress. I think she's as excited as I am (almost).

Right now I'm just trying to get all my nesting crap done so that I can wait it out in a relaxed state.

Of course you're on the labor call list. I'll be sure to keep you posted and look forward to giving you every gory detail!

November 30

From: Sara
To: Stephanie
Subject: Your little chunk of mucus . . .

. . . caused quite a stir with me, too. I was so excited that I wanted to run through the office yelling, "My friend lost her mucus plug! My friend lost her mucus plug!" (The British are coming! The British are coming!) I reconsidered when I realized that no one else would appreciate the news as much as I did.

You must be in a state of constant anticipation. I bet you're analyzing every little twinge or pain (I would be). I'm so excited. Thanks for keeping me in the loop.

Take care.

Godspeed.

And may the force be with you.

November 30

From: Stephanie
To: Sara
Subject: The British are coming

"The British are coming"? Oh, that's going to send me into labor laughing. Maybe you were wise to keep the little mucus thing between us, though. Somehow I don't think that your co-workers will appreciate it the same way: "Yeah, whatever. It's the weird pregnant chick again. She's either falling or yelling about bodily fluids all the time. And do you think it would be too much to ask for her to find a pair of pants that fit?"

Talk to you tomorrow!

December 1

From: Sara
To: Stephanie
Subject: Houston . . .

. . . do we have engagement? Just checking in for a status report.

December 1

From: Stephanie
To: Sara
Subject: Still nuttin' . . .

. . . but I *am* feeling kind of squeamish and very, very tired. This baby better come soon because I'm "nesting" us out of house and home. The more time I have on my hands, the more stuff I keep buying to decorate, etc. I have a project in every room, and I just made yet another trip to Michaels. I'm in a tacky, over-the-top, decorating frenzy. It looks like the Christmas section of Wal-Mart exploded in our living room. As Jim Carrey would say, "Somebody stop me!"

I'm trying to keep busy so that I can stop obsessing about *when* the baby will arrive. But I promise to call if any "developments" occur.

December 1

From: Sara
To: Stephanie
Subject: Me again

Okay, I'll try to make it through the weekend without calling you 50 times. Just take your cell phone with you to the craft store.

December 6
From: Stephanie *[four days before delivery]*
To: Sara
Subject: Trial run

Here's your latest update: We spent a little time in the hospital last night. After having cramps all day, everyone kept telling me to call the doctor, so I finally did. I was having some pretty serious Braxton Hicks contractions throughout the day, so I figured it wouldn't hurt to call.

My advice is to choose your words *very carefully* when talking to your obstetrician on the phone. She asked me if the baby was moving normally, and I innocently said, "Well, come to think of it, it hasn't moved as much as usual."

Next thing I knew, I was going to the office for them to monitor the fetal movement and heart rate. Luckily, I had my bag packed just in case. Tim picked me up, and we spent about an hour or so at the doctor's office. The baby's heart rate had one funny dip (extremely low rate), so my doctor decided to admit me to the hospital to monitor the baby's heartbeat overnight. If it looked risky, they were going to induce labor this morning; if it was in severe distress, a C-section. But mostly they just wanted to be extra careful, so we had a good dry run.

Anyway, I spent about four hours with an IV and a fetal monitor. Around 10:30 P.M., the doctor came to look at the printout and said that everything looked fine and I could go home. Thank God! The women's-center wing of the hospital was so full that they had me in a triage room, which is normally just a temporary room they use until they figure out where to put you permanently. So the bed was literally 30 inches wide, there was no chair for Tim, and *no* Jacuzzi tub (the horror of it all)! I would never have been able to sleep there.

The reason for the weird heart rate is partly because I was dehydrated, and possibly due to the baby moving so much that it sometimes pinches or puts weight on the umbilical cord, causing a dip in its heart rate. I was nesting so hard yesterday that I didn't take the time to eat enough or drink enough water. A little dehydration can knock your electrolytes for a loop, which can turn out to be a bad thing for Baby. Amazing how important a little H_2O is!

So what wisdom did I learn on my little practice run that I can pass on? Having an IV in your hand is a bad plan—my hands are so swollen that it was really sore—so try to get them to put it in your arm. Plus, you won't feel so handicapped. Also, bring a washcloth or two to the hospital; curiously enough, they didn't have any. I guess if you want to wash at a hospital, you get a nurse and a sponge. And bring your own pillow—the ones in the hospital are like little devices of torture. I don't care how silly I look walking through the hospital lobby, I'm not going again without my favorite pillow(s).

I think you're right about labor not being as bad as everyone reports. . . . My contractions on the monitor were really high, and the nurse said, "Wow! Are you feeling those?" And it just felt like some tightening—nothing painful. I could hardly tell I was having them. I know they'll get much worse when they're the real thing, but her reaction definitely gave me a little confidence.

The encouraging thing is that the doctor checked my cervix at the office, and I was a fingertip dilated. She checked again at the hospital and said that I was one centimeter dilated—and she thought that she'd see me again within 24 hours! But today I'm still not having any true contractions. We're just sitting around waiting. It's pure torture. I'm so ready to go—I'm not afraid, I just want to get on with it! It's time.

My office Christmas party is tonight, and while it's going to be an effort for me to get dressed and waddle there, our vice president is coming in from L.A., and I'd like to meet him. Plus, my boss has worked really hard to put this dinner together, and a couple people can't make it, which makes morale look bad in front of the VP, so I *really* want to go. If I'm not having active contractions, I may just go and put my suitcase in the car. Hey, nothing like a meal from one of Atlanta's best restaurants to give you the strength to push, right?

So, I'll call if things progress today like the doctor predicted. Who knows?

I have to go drink water and clean something now. How are *you* doing?

December 7

From: Sara
To: Stephanie
Subject: Pillows and electrolytes

Wow! That must have been pretty scary for you—I'm so glad the baby's all right. But overall it sounds like things are moving in the right direction. I'm sure that the doctors take the "better safe than sorry" attitude when it comes to pregnancy. And at least you got a chance to see what it was like to check in to the hospital and see what they have and don't have. That's good to know about the pillow—I'm putting together a list of items to take right now. After all, I'd rather have too much that I don't need than be without something I do.

I didn't know they gave IVs in your hand; I thought you got them in your arm. (Come to think of it, I've never even had an IV.) And I had no idea that water had such an impact! It's scary to think that it could affect the baby's heartbeat. No one ever told me about the electrolytes thing . . . anyway, keep chugging.

How was the Christmas party last night? More important, what's your status this morning?

December 7

From: Stephanie
To: Sara
Subject: Big fat stinkin' nothing!

Yes, we did go to my company Christmas party last night—I mean, why pass up a fabulous meal, not to mention good company, right? At least it took my mind off the big event for a few hours. Of course, I had nothing appropriate to wear that my big round belly would fit into. My boss's sweet wife let me borrow a beautiful black-velvet pregnancy suit (she's got great taste). She'll never know how good it made me feel to get dressed up at the peak of feeling so big, heavy, and stressed. It was such a great night—even though everyone was really surprised that I was actually there.

I wish that doctor had never told me "24 hours." What do they know anyway? It's very frustrating, and it's been making me crabby. So today I've decided to just try to get it off my mind. I'm going to go walk around the mall and run some errands instead of sitting around waiting. I'm not even cramping today. It's really weird.

Thanks to the way I was feeling the other day, I was *so sure* that this was the beginning. I was having all the symptoms and everything. Maybe this is nature's way of making you really want it. Tim's anxious, too. Every morning before he leaves he says something like, "Keep incubating, will ya?" I've given up the one-hour drive to the office—I brought all my files home on Monday, and I can do just as much here. I simply can't handle an hour drive in the car twice a day right now. It's too uncomfortable and unsettling to face Atlanta traffic when my belly barely fits behind the wheel. (Not to mention how uncomfortable it is to sit in one position for that long.)

Anyway, I'm off to the mall for my lunch break. Maybe the walking will help, who knows? Hope all this will prepare you to be patient when you see the first signs. They could mean days or weeks—just remember that.

December 8
From: Sara
To: Stephanie
Subject: I'll understand . . .

. . . if you decide to stop checking your e-mail and answering your phone. I'm probably making this worse by continuing to check your status every day, but I can't stand it! So are you feeling anything? You've got to understand that whenever I don't hear from you I automatically think you've gone to the hospital!

We went to David's company party last night, and I started feeling major Braxton Hicks contractions, which lasted for longer than any before. (It's wild when you start to feel anything happening!) Anyway, it was a really fun night. All his female co-workers kept telling me how great I looked and asking me all sorts of questions, so much so that by the end of the night I didn't even know what to say anymore. Some of them touched my belly, and I didn't even mind. Maybe I've gotten over the whole touching thing . . . I guess going to the doctor every two weeks to be poked and prodded helps you kind of lose your modesty.

My friends have said the nicest things to me, and David has, too. I realize now how much that means to me, and how good it makes me feel about myself. One thing I promise myself is that I'm going to shower my child with compliments and praise. It's easy to forget that everyone needs to hear those things, whether we think they do or not. So, on that note, I don't know if I ever told you this, but you look awesome pregnant. I really mean that. And you're going to be a great mom.

One more thing: Remember my "Rookie of the Year" award at work? Well, we had our monthly agency meeting yesterday, and I got another award. This one was the "Earth Mother" award, which recognized me for my "ability to hide basketballs under her shirt while eating her weight in spaghetti daily. (We'll miss you.)" My boss is a nut. I guess I wasn't concealing that whole spaghetti obsession from anyone.

Let me know what's happening today if you get a chance. I want to hear about everything you're experiencing!

December 8
From: Stephanie
To: Sara
Subject: Poise

No, I don't mind you checking—in fact, I look forward to it!

I'm glad the party was so much fun. It really is nice to be on the receiving end of all the attention and good wishes. And the knowing smiles of other mothers have been fun for me, too. It's like a secret society—wouldn't you just *love* to know what they're thinking when they knowingly look at you and smile?

I'm going to ask the doctor today why I've "stalled out." I was so sure that it was the beginning of the end, and so was she! I'm sure nothing's wrong, but I can't help but be a little concerned. (Tim says that one of the baby's ears probably got hung up on something.) In an effort to keep my sanity, I've begun to wonder why it is that I'm trying to rush all the pain and agony anyway. For years, I've heard pregnant women talk about how ready they were—they couldn't wait to "get this thing out" of them. I don't feel that way at all. I mean, I can't wait for the baby to get here, but I'm not miserable. I'm a little uncomfortable, but so what? Five hours into my labor, I'm sure I'll be saying, "Why did I want this to hurry and get here?"

The worst part is the fact that I've lost what little grace I had left. My "waddle" has turned into nothing short of a limp, as I try to haul the weight of this belly around. I walked out of our Christmas party the other night using as much poise as possible: shoulders back, chin up, heels clicking at a fast, steady pace. As soon as we got to the parking deck, I was like, "Okay, Tim, slow down. I have to go back to the pregnant walk": shoulders slumped over, back arched too much to make up for the weight on the front of me, hanging on to my poor husband's arm, shuffling along like an elderly person in a nursing home. What's happened to me?

Longer Braxton Hicks contractions are a good sign. When those turn painful, and start lower in your abdomen (or back), you're in business! Have you noticed how wobbly your joints are? You know there's actually a hormone that makes our bones soften so we can expand to give birth, and it wreaks havoc on your joints because they get very loose. That's partly why we're so clumsy. Is this what it feels like to be old?

One thing I've wanted to share with you is that although I realize that they're trying to compliment me, I've actually hated it when people have said, "You're due when? No way, you're so small." I don't want to hear how small I am! Compared to the body I know, I feel like a freaking barn! Who wants to be told how small they are when they're concentrating every day on the baby growing inside them? But I thank you so much for your sweet words. Even with all the aches and the clumsiness, isn't it amazing to be able to create a life inside your body? A body whose only redeeming value nine months ago was for transporting our brains and occasionally donning something to keep our husbands happy? What an amazing and awesome privilege. I've never felt so thankful about being a woman. I love it!

Well, better go get some work done. We've decided to put up a second tree in the den—what the hell, I've got the time, and it will keep my mind occupied. I'll let you know what the doc says.

December 8
From: Sara
To: Stephanie
Subject: Joys of womanhood

I've never wanted to be a man (except occasionally on camping trips when I had to pee in the woods). Being a woman isn't easy, but the shoes and pocketbooks alone make it worth it to me. I can't imagine not being able to carry a purse—that's one of the great joys in my life. (It's one of my shallower qualities, but I am not ashamed!) Plus, we can wear any color we want without feeling that our "manhood" is being threatened. My husband can't even bring himself to wear a vest, for crying out loud. Women don't have all those silly hang-ups. (On that note, wouldn't it be neat if we both had girls?)

If the tables were turned and David was the one carrying this baby, I think I'd feel very jealous. I'd want to know what it was like, and I'd feel like I was missing out on something. But he doesn't feel that way at all—he's *glad* he's not the one pregnant. It just goes to show why God gave women this responsibility. Obviously, He picked the right people for the job. Plus, can you imagine all the complaining, moaning, and groaning we'd have to hear if *they* were pregnant? Being spared that is definitely worth a month or two of swollen ankles.

Patience, however, isn't my virtue: I'm already anxious, and I could have a month more to go! I don't know how you're standing it. It must be hard not to be in control, just to wait. I'd be running around putting up multiple Christmas trees, too. Just remember, you're going to have to take all those trees *down* as well. And when that time comes, you'll have a little baby around keeping you busy on top of it.

All I need is something else to make me clumsy. *Poise* is a word that's never been used to describe me. I'm the girl who fell down while ice skating, knocked a big horn of a knot on my head, and proceeded to get up five minutes later . . . only to fall again and cause another big knot to pop up on the other side. I looked like a little eight-year-old blonde-haired devil. Let's hope my child doesn't inherit that gene of mine (or my freakishly long middle toes).

Let me know what the good, yet perpetually wrong, doctor has to say. Not that it matters. . . .

December 8

From: Stephanie [two days before delivery]
To: Sara
Subject: Doctors: What the hell do they know?

Well, the midwife seems to think that I have at least another week to wait. I'm still only one centimeter dilated—no changes.

When I asked her why the doctor seemed so sure the other night, her theory was one I'd already thought of: The first doctor who checked me isn't as generous with her measurements as the second doctor (who is known for being a little more generous with her measurements). So when Doctor #2 thought I went from a fingertip to one centimeter in three hours, she thought I was in labor. Which just concludes my belief that medicine is anything but a science—it's all opinions and educated guesses.

I really like my midwife, though: She was making fun of the other doctors and told me to quit whining since I'm not even due till the 19th! I suppose she's got a point. She also said that if there was still no progress next week, she'd schedule me to be induced the week of Christmas, since she doesn't let any of her patients go past 41 weeks. I really don't want that to happen, for many reasons. I just read an article that said when you're induced, your labor is much more painful and much longer because your body isn't ready. And second, Tim's family is going to be here on the 26th, and I really don't want a full house. I was hoping to have the baby at home for at least a few days before I had to entertain a house full of guests.

So, needless to say, I'm really hoping that the baby decides to join us well before Christmas (not to mention all the cute "My first Christmas" outfits hanging in the closet!). There's still plenty of time.

Meanwhile, can you say "nipple stimulation"?

December 9

From: Sara
To: Stephanie
Subject: You still there?

Are you there today? I haven't heard from you—could this be it? Write back if you're there.

December 9

From: Sara
To: Stephanie
Subject: Hey!

Are you having a baby today? I can't stand it—I'm calling you right now!

December 15

From: Stephanie
To: Sara
Subject: There are moments you wait for all your life

Well, I'm home from the hospital, and back on e-mail, just in time to give you all the gory details before it's your turn. Only the details don't seem quite so gory now—once you're holding your little baby in your arms, the pain and medical details seem quite small and trivial. But here's how it played out.

Remember how the midwife told me during my appointment on Friday that I probably had a week or two to go? *Two weeks*— I couldn't stand it! So I decided that I needed a project to keep my mind off the looming occasion, so on Friday night, Tim and I began working on a last-ditch nesting/decorating effort to put another Christmas tree up in the den. We stayed up late working on it, and then we finally gave up and went to bed, figuring that we'd finish it in the morning.

At about six o'clock on Saturday morning, the baby was kicking so hard that it woke me up. I lay there feeling the intense kicks and actually whispered, "Baby, calm down or you're going to break my water." And just a few seconds later, I literally heard a "pop" and then felt the trickle of warm water. I jumped up and ran to the bathroom, still in disbelief that the big moment was about to begin. I woke Tim and told him that I thought my water had broken. He sleepily said, "Really?" and hugged me.

Then the excitement began to set in. I called the doctor to let her know, and asked her if I had time to take a shower—I figured that this might be the last one I got till who knows when. It's funny, because it's nothing like what you see on TV. We weren't in a big hurry: We both took our time getting ready, and I even applied some makeup and tried to look presentable. It was so exciting, weird, and immensely overwhelming to realize that our little baby would be with us the next time we returned home. Two of us were leaving, but *three* of us would be coming back.

The drive to the hospital was a little uncomfortable. I was having some mild contractions, and the speed bumps in the hospital parking lot felt more like we were driving off cliffs. But I got through that, and Tim helped me inside. We registered at the front desk, and I was taken up to the triage room. They put a test strip in my underwear to confirm that I was leaking amniotic fluid, and then I was admitted. My midwife wasn't on duty, so as every pregnant woman fears, the people I'd come to know and trust wouldn't be delivering my baby. This very petite woman with long black hair walked into my room (I swear, she looked like she was about 16 years old), and very sweetly introduced herself as Dr. Soundararajan (Dr. S), the person who would be delivering my baby! I didn't know what to think. (It wouldn't take long to find out that she was the best doctor anyone could ever hope for.)

My contractions had all but stopped by now, so it was time to walk the walk—around and around the maternity-ward hallways. It was like some kind of weird Mommy-to-be Olympics. There were other women doing the same thing: One hand was pushing the IV stand, the other hand was trying to hold together the robe (or hospital-issued gown with the big opening in the back), husbands in tow. And we walked and walked and walked . . . and then we walked some more. By the way, add running shoes and a workout towel to your list of what to bring with you to the hospital.

Despite my marathon, our little baby just wasn't ready to join us—my contractions weren't strong or regular at all. Pitocin was added to my IV bag to speed things up, but it didn't help. Finally, I began to have a few more contractions mid-afternoon. By this time, both my mom and Tim's mom were there, and everyone was in my room waiting for Baby and me to do *something*. I was doing everything I'd read you were supposed to do to get things moving. However, once you're strapped up to an IV and fetal monitor, it's almost impossible to do anything besides just lie there.

One of the things I love most about Dr. S is that she has very small hands, and I was amazed at how she moved them around my pregnant belly to feel the position of the baby. She told me that she felt like the baby's head was turned slightly, and this may be what was slowing things down. So she explained that she wanted to reach up and straighten the baby's head, and I was going to hate her because it was going to hurt. The labor nurse suggested that they go ahead and give me the epidural. Of course I questioned that, since all the books and classes teach that the epidural slows everything down. The nurse adamantly told me that if my doctor was going to turn the baby, it was going to hurt a lot, and there was no sense putting myself through that if I was going to eventually receive the drugs anyway. I figured she knew more about it than I did, so they gave me the epidural. Now, the good and the bad news is that I received this wonderful blessing even before I felt what hard contractions feel like. So I'm afraid I have no advice for you on what it's like or how bad it hurts—but I can tell you that if you decide not to have an epidural, you're nuts.

The epidural itself was a little strange. I sat on the side of the bed with my arms over Tim's shoulders, and it was his job to hold me completely still while the doctor inserted the needle into my spine. This sounds much worse than it is—the anesthesiologist numbs the skin before he sticks you, and it just sort of burns a little. The weird part is that it felt like a bolt of lightning shot through my right leg. My leg jerked forward and I kicked Tim in the knee (you know he deserved it). But it's really nothing to be afraid of—it's not like you can feel the needle in your back. They tape it into place, and you can lie back comfortably, or as comfortably as you can in a rock-hard hospital bed.

Anyway, the doctor was able to move the baby's head into a better position, but still, I wasn't progressing well at all. Then we started to get worried because the baby's heart rate started having little dips, which are the beginning signs of distress. So, on top of the four tubes of IV and medications that were already trailing from my hand, I was given a mask to help get oxygen through my bloodstream and to the baby. I looked and felt like a chemistry experiment, with all the tubes and fluids hooked up to my hand.

All this helped the baby's heart rate, and Dr. S decided that it was time to make some decisions. She had to leave me and go to another hospital to perform an emergency C-section, so she instructed the nurses to give me a fresh bag of Pitocin. She explained that we were going to give it another hour, and if I showed no progress, I'd need to have a C-section for the baby to be born. I agreed. More than 14 hours had passed by now, and I was growing frustrated and tired from all the waiting. I was completely numb from the epidural, so I couldn't tell if my contractions were getting any stronger. I'd read about what was involved in a C-section, so I was prepared for it. I was trying to remain open-minded, even though I knew that it would be a more difficult recovery, and it certainly wasn't my first choice for bringing my baby into the world.

While my doctor was gone, the Pitocin and my body began to work. We could see the contractions on the monitor growing stronger and longer; by the time Dr. S returned, I'd dilated all ten centimeters and all systems were go. When she checked me, she happily cheered, "Congratulations—you're ten centimeters!" I was so happy and relieved that I couldn't have been more ready to push! It was like I'd just had a pep rally right there in my hospital room.

At this point, things started happening fast: Dressers were converted into tables full of metal instruments and baby-fixing equipment; people started changing clothes, putting on masks, moving furniture, and getting ready. The hustle and bustle was exciting.

In contrast, I—the one who was supposed to do all the work—was completely useless. I was so numb and paralyzed from having had the epidural for so long that I couldn't even lift my legs off the table, which was a little disturbing. They made me sort of roll up in a little ball, and then Tim held one heavy, useless leg while the nurse held the other, and it was finally time to push. I gave one push, and Dr. S. stopped me. "Okay," she said to the room. "Hold on, she's going to be a good pusher."

Tim, who was holding my dead 20-pound leg, said, "I knew you were going to be a good pusher."

I think it was then that the doctor realized that there was meconium in the amniotic fluid (meaning that the baby had pooped on the way out). As you probably know, this can be a life-threatening thing during birth if the baby aspirates any of the meconium into its lungs. So, in addition to the doctor and nurses, a respiratory-therapy team was called into my room as well.

So much for the private moment Tim and I were dreaming of . . . I think there were a total of eight people in the room, all standing opposite the bed (on the "home-plate side," if you know what I mean), staring at me. But it didn't matter: I had bigger things on my mind. Once the team was in place, the doctor told me to start pushing again. One of the nurses was trying to help me by counting to ten during each push. But she was frustrating me because I couldn't hold my breath and push as long as her ten-count was lasting. She had one hand on the back of my neck and was pushing my head forward, which was making me very uncomfortable.

After a couple of pushes, the doctor said that she could see the baby's head. I got so excited—to think the head was there already! One of the delivery nurses said, "Oh, you don't have a mirror!" I told her I wasn't sure I wanted to see, but she insisted that it was really awesome to watch. When they put the mirror where I could see my progress, I was a little disappointed. The doctor showed me the "head" she was talking about: It was about a two-inch patch—you couldn't even tell it was a head. This really motivated me to work harder, so that's when I decided to take matters into my own hands.

I told the nurse to let go of my neck, and then I asked my doctor, "Do I have to wait for a contraction to push? Or can I just start pushing?"

Dr. S. looked pleased, and said, "No, you can push as much as you want."

So I started pushing *my* way. No ten-count, no Lamaze breathing—just like I'd imagined, I used the same kind of pushing and breathing that I use when I lift weights. It must have worked, because the baby was born in just 20 minutes, with probably less than six or seven pushes. (I sure am thankful for the book that taught me to take charge if I needed to.)

It was a little scary at first, though, because the baby wasn't making any sounds. Dr. S. had explained that as soon as the baby's face was out, she was going to stick her fingers in its mouth to keep it from breathing until they could ensure that it wouldn't aspirate any of the meconium. Even knowing all this, it was scary not to hear our baby cry. We were concentrating so much on it breathing that I barely heard the doctor say, "It's a girl!" I think I sort of sighed in relief, but I do remember saying something like, "Really? I was so sure it was a boy."

And then the betrayal happened: As soon as the baby was out, everyone who had been taking care of me and cheering me on rushed to the other side of the room with the baby. I was completely alone, except for my faithful doctor, who remained to do the cleanup. Tim was also standing, very concerned, over the bassinet, while the respiratory team worked on our baby girl. Finally, I could hear her first cries. She wasn't responding as well as they would have liked, so she was given a shot in her thigh that got her first responses kick-started.

An entire hour went by before I was allowed to hold her—I couldn't even see her from across the room! It was nothing like I'd imagined at all. In fact, the nurse was about to administer some other kind of shot when I stopped her and said that it would have to wait: I needed to hold my baby (another out-of-character, take-charge moment). So I did.

Sara, there is no moment in life more awe-inspiring than the first time you hold your newborn baby. As I looked in those big, dark eyes, it was so hard to believe that *this* is what had been inside my body all that time. It was, by far, the greatest moment of my life. Nothing could equal that feeling—complete, overwhelming joy and amazement. From the first moment I saw her, I was absolutely, totally, and deeply in love with her.

When she did cry, it was funny: It sounded like she was saying, "A-lah, A-lah." Even the nurses laughed, and Tim said that maybe she was Muslim. Finally, she was doing well, and the nurses wrapped her all up and put her in a little glass bassinet and took us to our room so that we could all rest together. I was exhausted, mentally and physically. It seemed so strange to look across the room and see that little baby and know that she'd been inside my body just moments before. And yet, there she was—lying there breathing air and sleeping—right there in our world.

And then she began to cry . . . and I didn't know how to make her stop. I tried everything I knew to comfort her, but it wasn't working. A nurse came in to help and told me to try putting the baby in bed and cuddle with her, that often the warmth from the mother's body would help comfort a new baby. It worked like a charm. And it was the best thing I could have done, because it made me feel so close to her. She went from being that "little stranger" sleeping across the room to my precious little baby, snuggling with me, needing me and the warmth of my body. It was my first connection with her, and from that moment on, I knew what to do. The reason it felt so strange to see her on the far side of the room is because it *was* strange. I needed her next to me—and she needed that, too. I cuddled her and thought about how she'll never be as close to me again as she was when she was inside me, just a few hours ago. As happy as I am that she's here, there's something sad about losing the privilege of having her inside my body and all to myself.

In retrospect, I have to say that although I was so programmed to have this birth be entirely up to me, it was anything *but* natural. The science of medicine kicked in from the moment I checked in to the hospital. Nothing really went like I'd planned or imagined. So the best thing you can do is to check in to that maternity ward with an open mind. The only real goal should be to get the baby out safely. Also, I have to say that the epidural is definitely the way to go. Ironically enough, having an epidural made my birth experience much more natural and enjoyable—instead of concentrating on the pain, I could focus on watching my perfect little baby enter the world.

The next morning at the hospital, they brought forms for us to fill out for her birth certificate. I was holding her, so Tim began to fill out the paperwork. When I glanced over at him, he was crying. When I asked him why, he said that it was because it was the first time he'd written her name. His little daughter was really here. He was a dad, and we were a family.

I can't wait for you and David to experience this. You can't imagine how immediately eye-opening and life-changing it is. You've never known the depth of love you could achieve until you've seen your baby. And the things you notice, which you've never paid attention to before, make you feel like such a fool. There's just so much around you that you miss when you haven't known life with a child and haven't felt the pressure to protect her from the world.

I love watching those sweet smiles in her sleep. The way she wrinkles up her forehead and stretches when she's trying so hard to wake up—it's such an effort for a tiny baby. I can't stop kissing her perfect face. The joy and meaning that comes with being a mother is more than I could have ever dreamed. Tim and I fell in love with her the first second we saw her. I can't predict what the future holds for this tiny new person, but right now she's mine, and I just want to hold her and kiss her sweet little face. She is pure joy. My cup runneth over. Her birth announcement will read:

There are moments you wait for all your life . . .
We announce, with great joy, the birth of our daughter
Sara Nicole Triplett
Sunday, the Tenth of December
1:53 AM
6.6 pounds
19 inches

There's the Culprit
(Sara's Birth Experience)

December 18
From: Sara *(13 days before delivery)*
To: Stephanie
Subject: First day home

The photos of Baby Sara are just adorable. She's absolutely beautiful! I'm so glad that everything turned out well for both of you. Reading your e-mail makes me all the more excited for my little one to arrive. I can't wait to see what he or she will look like—I'm so filled with anticipation.

My last day of work was Friday. It wasn't as hard to leave as I thought, especially since I'll most likely still be doing some work for the company on a freelance basis. I guess that since I have something so exciting coming up, leaving isn't so sad. I'll miss my co-workers, though—many of them have become good friends.

The challenge of being at home will be in not doing too much, especially since I'm in full nesting mode. At least at work I was basically sitting all day, but here I want to do a million things—Christmas is almost here, and family will be coming soon. Like you, we're going to have a full house: Even my sister with the two kids is coming—that's big, since they're used to having Christmas in their own home.

I'm having someone come clean my house tomorrow. That wasn't a luxury at this point—it was a necessity. I'm just not that mobile right now; plus, my blood pressure has been creeping up. Lately I've been seeing some little spots in front of my eyes sometimes when I stand up too quickly. I didn't think anything of it, but apparently it's a sign that my blood pressure is getting high and a reminder to relax. I'd never mentioned it to the nurse until she asked me about it the other day.

It's funny, I feel like I've mentioned so many little feelings that I thought could be symptoms of something to the nurses and doctors, but they weren't anything. Now the one thing I don't mention *is* something. Maybe I was getting complacent about telling them things, which is a good lesson: You should mention everything you feel because you never know! Anyway, the doctor told me to sit down, put my feet up, and take it easy (which is the hardest thing for a woman to do). Add Christmas and company coming, and that makes it about impossible! But I have to put things in perspective: The important thing is the baby.

I have my company Christmas party tomorrow night. It will be fun to go one last time . . . except, of course, for having to haul my big self into a black velvet maternity dress (why, oh why, didn't I opt for a pantsuit?). The party is in this beautiful old country club, and the food is just to die for—hopefully, I won't go into labor before the crème brûlée. I still think I have a little way to go, and my mom thinks that everyone being here at Christmas is going to be what sends me into labor. I'll keep you posted.

Meanwhile, Merry First Christmas to little Sara! Send me a picture of her in one of those cute outfits you talked about!

December 20
From: Stephanie
To: Sara
Subject: Sara #2

I'm so sorry I haven't written—I've had a house full of relatives and a new baby that I just can't put down. I still can't believe she's really here. While my family was here visiting, I had portraits made of all of us with Sara #2. We're sitting in front of the Christmas tree with this tiny brand-new baby, and the pictures are just beautiful. There's something so special about seeing a great-grandmother holding somebody so new.

Okay, I know you're dying to know about the baby's name. As much as I'd love to tell you that we named her after you, that's not exactly the case. You see, Tim and I had a terrible time agreeing on names. Every time I'd say, "I like this name," he'd say something like, "No, there was an ugly girl in my high school with that name," or "No, I dated a girl with that name." When we finally came across the name Sara, we liked it a lot because it's one of those classic, never-go-out-of-style names. And the only person that came to mind was you.

Tim said, "Hmm . . . Sara Ellington—I like her." I said, "Yeah, me, too. I even like the way she spells it, without the 'H.'" So that's how it happened. I guess in a way, she sort of *was* named after you. (Then again, if Tim had dated a girl named Sara, it never would have played out.) But let me just say, I can only hope that she'll grow up to be as great as you.

Everything is going fine. I'm actually amazed at how quickly my body recovered. I felt pretty normal in just a few days' time. Little Sara cries a lot, though—we finally broke down and gave her a pacifier, and that helped tremendously.

She's so *tiny*. Her clothes seemed to swallow her, and it made me feel so bad for her because she looked so uncomfortable. I had all these adorable little outfits all washed and hanging neatly in her closet impatiently awaiting her arrival. And none of them fit her. Who knew she was only going to weigh six pounds? Thankfully, my mom and dad rushed right out to the nearest baby store to buy as many preemie outfits in *pink* as possible. The preemie size fit her much better, and I was so thankful that she looked more comfortable once her little clothes weren't drowning her. When our next baby comes, I'm going to have a couple of preemie-sized outfits ready and waiting. The "Newborn" size should really be labeled "Six weeks +." I'm convinced that if anything came out of our bodies the size of "newborn" clothing we'd need more than an epidural to get them out!

Gotta run for now—there's a hungry baby calling me! Chat back when you can. I know you must be counting the minutes now, but just try to be patient. . . .

December 28
From: Sara
To: Stephanie
Subject: The pressure's on!

Hi, Mama! I'm writing this in the hopes that you may have one brief moment to check your e-mail today.

Here's the latest: I went to the doctor today, and my blood pressure was like 150-something over 100, which is too high. So I'm basically supposed to take it easy tonight, go back to the doctor again tomorrow, and they may send me straight to the hospital if my blood pressure is still up. This could be it! Although I'm a little worried about the blood-pressure thing, I'm so excited (which probably isn't helping to lower my blood pressure)! We're so close now. David is going with me tomorrow, and we'll be ready to roll if the doctor admits me. I'll let you know!

By the way, I forgot to tell you that at my company Christmas dinner everyone chipped in and gave me a card and a gift certificate to Babies "R" Us. I was so touched. They presented it to me at dinner—I completely was not expecting it, but it made me feel so good. My boss and I talked, and it looks like they *will* be able to use me for some freelance projects from home after the baby is born. I'm really happy about that.

What you said about little Sara is so sweet. I consider it quite a compliment that I share a name with such a special girl.

December 29
From: Stephanie
To: Sara
Subject: Anything yet?

Hey! Are you havin' a baby or what? What the hell are you waiting for? Sorry, I had to ask. Do you feel like you're getting any closer? Any signs? I'm so excited for you. There's nothing better in the whole wide world than holding that little angel in your arms for the first time. They look right back at you with their slimy little eyes (the doctor puts antibiotic ointment in their eyes immediately after birth to protect them from any germs that may have gotten in during birth), and it's just pure love.

Bringing them home is the best, too . . . to think that this perfect, new little someone is going to be with you for the rest of your life. And it's perfect because you love them so much, all that matters anyway is just that you'll be together, always. I know I'm sappier than usual—it's still the hormones. But it really is the best thing ever. So call and keep me posted, okay? If you forget to call me on the way to the hospital, I may be forced to rename Sara (and since we couldn't think of any other names, I'm hoping I won't have to do that).

As for me, the breast-feeding thing is a little tricky. I'd been trying very hard to follow the *Babywise* book and stick to a feeding schedule, but Sara lost weight her first week home, so we had to take her to the pediatrician. When I told her that I was following that book, she told me to go home and throw it away. She said, "This is a newborn baby, and she needs to eat whenever she's hungry, not on your schedule!"

I felt so bad—to think that the reason she's been crying so much is probably because she's hungry. The doctor also told me to supplement my breast-feeding with some formula to help get Sara's little tummy full until my milk becomes more plentiful. It's really hard to tell if the baby is getting anything or not when you're breast-feeding. I haven't gotten that engorged feeling yet, so I'm thinking that my milk supply is taking a while to kick in. But I'm going to be patient and keep trying. It's an amazing thing to be able to feed your baby with your body, and I really want to succeed at it.

I don't know when I've had so little sleep. I just doze off and on all day whenever Sara does, and I think that's the key to survival with a new baby. And speaking of napping, she just fell asleep. The problem is that *Oprah*'s on—so do I take a nap or do I watch TV? Sleep or intelligent adult conversation . . . it's a tough call.

Keep me posted!!

December 29
From: Sara *(two days before delivery)*
To: Stephanie
Subject: Not yet

Well, I'm writing you from home, not the hospital, since my blood pressure was a little better today. I was almost—no, I *was*—

disappointed. I thought I might be heading in for the Big Show. David did go with me, and the doctor sent us home with instructions. I'm going to give them to you verbatim: "Go home and have sex, and lots of it. You need to have this baby."

Can you believe that?! As we were walking out of the office, David looked at me with a grin and said, "You heard the man."

I felt like saying, "Can't you just give me some Pitocin instead?" David's pretty happy about this, though—and how can I argue with him? It's doctor's orders! I wonder if a female physician would have told me the same thing? Hmm . . . guess it's worth a try. I'll let you know if it works.

December 29
From: Stephanie
To: Sara
Subject: It's all they think about

Are you kidding me? A female doctor would have said, "Honey, get yourself a great spa pedicure, then go straight home to put your feet up; order a good pay-per-view movie; eat a pint of Ben and Jerry's; and then take a nice, long nap."

I swear, sex is all they think about, even at times like this. But on the other hand, you should be glad that David still *wants* to have sex with you at this stage in pregnancy. I don't think Tim wanted to *look* at me at that point, let alone have sex. Anyway, let me know if it works.

January 4
From: Sara
To: Stephanie
Subject: The little culprit is here!

Here are the first pictures of our little one. It's been a hectic couple of days, as I'm sure you know!

My birth experience was everything I could have hoped for. The nurses (who do the vast majority of the work), my doctor, David . . . everyone was so supportive. My sister had told me a month or so ago that the pain was manageable, and it was—of course I did have some help from the good ol' epidural.

Anyway, here's the play-by-play. My water broke at about one o'clock in the morning on December 31. (Let's just say that we followed our doctor's advice, and yes, it worked!) I called the physician on call, Dr. Pixley, and he told me to come to the hospital. We didn't panic or rush, since I wasn't having any contractions. We were just so excited—it was like, "This is it! The moment has arrived!" (It was a very similar feeling to the weekend of our wedding, but with even more excitement.)

I showered and fixed my hair, and we got to the emergency room at about 3 A.M. David videotaped me getting out of the car, asking me questions like a reporter the whole time: "So, how do you feel? Are you nervous? What's your call, boy or girl?" (He's such a geek.)

They checked me in to one of the birthing suites, and Dr. Pixley came to look in on me. He decided not to start me on Pitocin until the morning, and David and I were both instructed to get some sleep. They hooked me up to all the monitors and turned down the lights. It wasn't the most comfortable or restful sleep, but I did sleep. And poor David, in the recliner, did as well.

The next morning at about eight, Dr. Pixley came in and said that they were going to start me on Pitocin to get things going. The nurses were short staffed due to the holidays, so my Pitocin didn't get started until about 11 A.M. Every nurse that came into my room was sweet, petite, and cute . . . until it was time for my enema. Then Big Bertha, with the voice of a truck driver who's smoked Marlboro Reds for 30 years, comes in out of the blue and announces that she's here to administer it. She doesn't ask, but *tells* David to leave the room. (I was thankful later.) I can sum up my enema experience by simply asking you to recall the bathroom scene in the movie *Dumb and Dumber* . . . times ten. Every time I thought it was over I'd shuffle back to my bed, only to turn right around, IV pole in hand, and shuffle right back to the bathroom, praying that I'd make it in time. (You don't set any speed records shuffling with an IV pole.) Big Bertha knew what she was doing getting David out of there: Seeing that would have been much worse than witnessing childbirth.

Okay, now that we have that ugly scene out of the way, let's move on. The next few hours were basically filled with pretty strong, but very manageable, contractions at about four- to five-minute intervals. David had football on the TV, which was fine with me because it reminded me of watching games with my dad when I was growing up, so it was comforting. David also helped me through the contractions—one of the nurses showed him some great ways to apply pressure to my back (I had mostly back labor), and that was a lifesaver.

Dr. Pixley gave us an ETA of right around midnight—in fact, it could have been the first baby of the New Year, which didn't sound so wonderful to me right then. Midnight was a *long* way off.

The nurses kept coming in and turning up my dosage of Pitocin, which really started to get on my nerves after a while. I asked for a little medicine to help me cope with the increasing pain. (I wanted to see how that worked before I started thinking epidural.) The nurse got the okay from the doctor to administer some Nubain through my IV. Ah, Nubain . . . what a nice relief that was. It gave me a little burst of energy, and I started singing to myself, "Nubain is great/ Oh yeah, uh huh/ I love Nubain." I was even considering naming the baby Nubain for a moment. Then, just as quickly as it came in to my system, it seemed to leave. The nurse said it was still there, but it sure didn't feel like it. Now I just felt sleepy and still in as much pain. I started to chant through my teeth, "Nu-bain sucks, Nu-bain sucks."

By this point I was having to sit up and lean forward as much as possible to get through the contractions, which seemed to be gaining more in speed than in strength. By leaning forward, and with David pushing on the pressure points, I was able to get through the contractions pretty well. (However, my sitting up and leaning forward created a problem for the nurses, who couldn't get a good reading from the belt strapped around my belly because I was moving around so much.) The problem now was that the three- or four-minute break I'd been getting was gone. The pain never totally subsided; it just decreased for a bit (and not for long), and then it came back strong again. It was really starting to wear me down. I'd gotten to six centimeters by this point, so I figured that it was now or never for the epidural.

I looked at the nurse and said "I'd like to have my epidural now." I was actually quite cordial throughout the whole thing, believe it or not. I'm sure David was as surprised as anyone.

I remember thinking a few months back that the whole idea of an epidural might freak me out enough not to have one. You know, the whole "big needle in the spine" thing. Well, let me tell you, that anesthesiologist could have said, "Ma'am, I'm going to have to administer this through your eyeball," and I would have answered, "Do what you have to do, just give it to me. Now!"

The epidural didn't totally take the pain away for me like I've heard it does for some people (maybe I was too far into it by that point)—but it made a huge difference, and my labor was much more manageable. I could lie back a bit finally, which helped the team read all the monitors on the baby and me more accurately.

My blood pressure was a concern, but it held out okay. The nurse checked me again and said, somewhat surprised, "You're about ready to push." She said she could feel the baby's head.

Wow! Dr. Pixley was right on: He'd told me he thought that when my cervix started dilating, everything would go pretty quickly. He said it just had that feel to him.

I was fortunate enough that my regular ob-gyn, Dr. Beurskens, whom I've been seeing for ten years, was now on call. What a stroke of luck and a blessing! I was so happy that she'd be delivering my baby. The only problem was that she'd left the hospital to go home for some rest, thinking that I'd be in labor a while longer. She'd instructed the staff to call her when it was time, and they were trying to reach her; but in the meantime, they told me that I was going to start pushing. My wonderful nurse, Laura, who saw me through, assured me that the head nurse was there and was perfectly qualified to deliver my baby if my doctor didn't make it in time. I totally trusted Laura by this point, so when she said that she'd let the head nurse deliver one of her own babies, I said "Okay, let's go."

Fortunately, I didn't push long before Dr. Beurskens walked in. The nurses had finally reached her on her cell phone, and she was already in her car. When she arrived, she said, "I just had a feeling that I'd better get in the car and come back over." She went to get scrubbed up, and I pushed some more. It was hard work—plus, the epidural was working so well that I couldn't feel any of that "magical pressure" they told us about in childbirth classes. You know, the one that's supposed to make us want to push so bad? I felt nothing. They actually turned my epidural down so that I could feel a little.

But thank goodness for that epidural, because it enabled me to stay somewhat still while pushing so that the nurses and my doctor could keep a close eye on the baby's heart monitor. The baby's heartbeat was fluctuating, causing my doctor some concern. They gave me some oxygen, which worried David more than me. I was so consumed with trying to push that I couldn't think about or comprehend anything else, which was probably a good thing at the time. (No time for panic.)

I'll never forget Dr. Beurskens's words when the baby's head came out: "There's the culprit." In my drug-and-pain-induced state, I didn't think a thing of it. I just thought she was making a joke, like, "There's the little one who's been causing you all this pain—there's the little stinker!" Looking back, of course, that makes no sense, but hey, I'd been in labor all day!

What she was talking about—"the culprit"—was the umbilical cord, which was wrapped around the baby's neck, causing the heart rate to fluctuate. David told me later how deftly and quickly Dr. Beurskens slipped the cord off and over the baby's head. Maybe the head nurse would have been just as responsive to the situation, but I sure was glad my doctor was there to handle it.

After one more push . . . there she was, our baby girl. Time of birth was 8:40 P.M., and I'd only started pushing at 8:00! Dr. Beurskens joked, "You might have your next one in only a couple of pushes."

They put the baby right on my chest, and David and I counted her fingers and toes and were just awestruck at how perfect she was. Her head wasn't pointy, her skin was clear—I could not believe (and still can't) that she was inside me. What a little miracle. Make that the *biggest* miracle of all. And what an overwhelming relief to know that your child has made her way into the world unharmed and perfect. Our little New Year's Eve baby.

They wrapped her up, and all David and I could do was just stare at her. I have never felt joy like that in my life. I was bursting with energy and felt like I could have run a marathon (if only I could have moved my legs). Meanwhile, David was the proudest father I can imagine. He kept saying how perfect she was, and the excitement didn't go out of his voice for hours. One of the nurses commented that she wished all fathers were like him. I'll never forget that.

We were beside ourselves with joy and thanked everyone in the room profusely. And that was the overwhelming feeling of that moment in our life—gratitude. We've been blessed with a perfect baby. What greater gift can there be?

David went out to the waiting area and announced the good news to my mom, my sister, and his parents, who were all on the edge of their seats. (A little bit later they came in to greet their new granddaughter and niece.) Then we called all our friends, many of whom were celebrating at the same New Year's Eve party, to announce the good news. Over the phone we heard our friend Mick yell to the crowd that Anna Marie had been born.

By the time they put me in a regular room, my younger sister and her fiancé had gotten to the hospital from Virginia, and I was starving. David went down to the hospital grill (which, thankfully, is open 24 hours) and got me a grilled-cheese sandwich and some French fries. It was the best thing I ever tasted in my life. Then the four of us and little Anna watched Dick Clark drop the ball in Times Square: It was the start of a new year . . . and a new life.

We welcome to this world
Anna Marie Behnke*
December 31
8:40 P.M.
Six pounds, ten ounces
19 1/4 inches

[**Editor's note:** "Ellington" is Sara's maiden name, which she's using for this book; however, "Behnke" is her married name.]

Chapter 5

Postpartum:
Here Come the Hormones

January 4

From: Stephanie
To: Sara
Subject: Big sentimental mess

Hi, fellow Mommy! Thanks so much for the photos—what a wonderful surprise! Anna is so beautiful! Have you ever seen anything so perfect?

I'm a big sentimental mess: I was holding Sara while I was looking at Anna's photos and telling her how much fun she was going to have with her friend at the lake every summer, and I just started to sob. But they're tears of joy.

It's the *best*: She kept me up until 3 A.M. again, I haven't had a chance to eat anything today, I have two loads of laundry waiting for me, and I've changed at least six disgusting green diapers since midnight last night . . . and I'm madly in love with her. Go figure.

Anytime you want to send more photos, don't hesitate! I'm also looking forward to talking to you—but take your time. The phone is your enemy. I understand.

January 6

From: Stephanie
To: Sara
Subject: Are your ankles back yet?

Hope all is going well with you and little Anna. How's the breast-feeding going? Do you have your ankles back yet? You'll be amazed at how small they look when you see them back to normal. It will make you feel very skinny . . . until you see your butt—ha! (Speaking entirely for myself, of course.)

My parents gave us a digital camera for Christmas, so I'm going to be *really* annoying with the photos. Have you stopped to think about how bad it's going to suck for little Anna, having to celebrate her birthday on New Year's Eve? Tim and I have often talked about eventually moving to Charlotte (Atlanta doesn't feel permanent for us), so we'll just have to have one big party for Sara and Anna in the middle of December.

Gotta go for now. Take care, and enjoy every minute!

January 7

From: Sara
To: Stephanie
Subject: What a week!

Well, I'm finally feeling somewhat back to normal and have a minute to write.

What a week! Thank you so much for the adorable preemie outfits—what a great idea! I never would have thought of buying preemie sizes, but you're right: The 0–3 months' size is way too big for a newborn, unless they're one of those huge 11-pounders or something. It's nice to have some things that actually fit Anna right now, and she looks adorable in them, too! Thank you also for the bath soaps and the book. You've given me hope that at some point this adjustment must get easier because you were obviously able to leave the house for a little while to go shop for gifts!

I can't believe how much Sara's changed already. Her eyes look so big! Are they blue? And that Santa suit is great—where'd you find it?

Everything is really going well here. I'm doing fine with the breast-feeding, and that awful engorgement stage is over (ouch!). I stopped at the grocery store on Friday after taking Anna to the doctor for her one-week checkup, and I was just praying that I wouldn't see anyone I know since I was standing in the checkout line with nothing but a huge box of hospital-grade maxipads and a head of cabbage. Nice. I'm feeling better now, though. (As for the cabbage, I read that if you put leaves of it in your bra, it helps to relieve the pain of engorgement. And believe it or not, it does work! Plus, we had coleslaw for dinner . . . just kidding.)

Anna seems to have her days and nights confused: She sleeps much better during the day, and then at night she wants to get up almost every one and a half to two hours. This morning she did sleep for three solid hours, so David and I took advantage and slept late, too.

We've been giving her a little formula along with the breast milk to keep her full longer, but I'm finding this whole breast-feeding thing to be kind of confusing. One pediatrician told me not to worry about supplementing with formula; another said it's okay, but only after I've nursed her first—in other words, I can't skip any feeding or it will mess up my supply. And since I'm not one to just expose myself anywhere, I'm wondering how I'll ever leave the house for more than 15 minutes. I was able to pump some milk, however—it took about a half hour to get an ounce, but it felt like such an accomplishment. I could finally see that something was actually in there! Then I thought, *Why am I celebrating? Half an hour for <u>one ounce</u>? How do people do this?*

How are you adjusting? Have you had any postpartum blues? I was fine until yesterday when my mom left—I've missed her ever since. I really wish now that she lived close enough to stop by every day. Having a daughter of my own makes me think a lot more about what kind of daughter *I* am. It's kind of overwhelming to become a parent yourself: You realize how time and life march forward, whether you want them to or not. I'm already having nightmares about the day Anna leaves for college. Can you believe that? Hopefully some of this is hormones talking. I feel like this wave of emotion has come over me, and I hope I won't be a sappy mess the rest of my life. Being a mom sure does make you look at things a lot differently, doesn't it?

Also, I guess that since there's so much anticipation surrounding going into labor, when it's over it's kind of a letdown, especially when all the visitors leave. David was off work and here all week; he goes back tomorrow. I'm going to miss him being here during the day, but it will be fun to bond with my little girl, too.

My whole birth experience was just awesome. I wouldn't change a thing: David was great, as were the doctors and nurses. I'm so glad that I was able to experience a vaginal birth. It was just amazing. It's funny how we focus so much on the labor and delivery, yet to me, getting through this adjustment period at home afterward is so much harder than that. I sure wish you and I lived closer now so that we could share even more of this time together.

January 8
From: Stephanie
To: Sara
Subject: Baby talk

Thanks for the photo! I see that Anna likes a pacifier, too. Tim and I laugh at how much they look and sound just like Maggie Simpson with the pacifier.

Aren't we so lucky to have made such beautiful, perfect babies? Damn, we're good. I hope they can grow up together—although they'll probably hate each other because we want them to be friends so badly. Either that, or they'll both be in constant trouble together. They'll be gorgeous, and David and Tim will be fighting off all their boyfriends.

Anna has your eyes—do you see it? As I suspected, Sara didn't get anything of mine except my hair, smile, and, you know, the girl parts. Everything else is Tim's—her toes and hands and little legs look exactly like his. It's so amazing. We can't tell yet what color her eyes are going to be, but I'm hoping she gets Tim's eyes as well. He's one of those disgusting people who will be 100 years old and never have to wear glasses.

I'm so glad the outfits fit. It made me feel so bad for little Sara when everything swallowed her—especially since she looked so tiny and pathetic anyway. When my parents brought me all those cute, pink, preemie-sized clothes, they fit her perfectly and she looked so much more comfortable. So when I heard that Anna's weight was close to Sara's, I knew that you needed something pink from the preemie rack just to get you through the first month or so.

We had a doctor's appointment today, and everything's going well: She's grown one and a half inches and weighs eight and a half pounds already! I was very excited about that. You have to understand that I've endured years of my sister teasing me that my children were going to starve to death because my chest is so small. It was good to prove the taunting wrong!

Take heart, little mother: It *does* get better, and fast. Taking Sara out in the real world today went pretty well. She likes the car ride (it soothes her to sleep), and I think that she also likes the excitement of getting out of the house. She was as good as gold at the pediatrician's office—didn't cry at all, except for the shot in the thigh (ouch!). What is it with doctors and babies? It's like they sit around saying, "Let's see . . . we'll find the most tender, sensitive place on the body and stick it with a big needle." At the two-month visit, Sara will get four injections at once—eek! I'm not looking forward to that one. Poor little baby.

Anyway, you *will* get out of the house, just be patient. It's not that difficult; it's just a pain to have to carry the car seat around everywhere. I'm going to try to tackle the grocery store tomorrow. And I figure if she cries, she cries—everybody will just have to get over it. She certainly isn't the first child to cry in public; it's not like they're going to announce, "Crier in aisle four!"

It's interesting how hard it is to identify with all these stages of life until they happen to you. I wish that there was a way to teach our children how each stage feels so that they're more considerate of others along the way. We stopped at the camera store on the way home, and the young girl behind the counter made me stand there with that 50-pound infant carrier/car seat and wait and wait. I thought about how she'd hurry a little more to help me out if she knew what it entailed to be a mother.

As for the Santa suit, Tim's sister had given it to me when I first got pregnant. Of course it was huge, so (are you sure you're ready for this?) *I actually sewed!* These maternal hormones must be powerful things, because I don't even know how to sew. But I figured out how to change it from pants with little boots on the feet into a little skirt. I even altered it to make it smaller. And

I added the fur trim (which, I'm happy to report, was accomplished with a hot-glue gun).

You know, I think we have to look at motherhood like it's a career. I just know I want to be really great at it—better than I've been at any job or activity I've ever been involved in. I always worked so hard to do well at my job and always based my worth on my career. Now I couldn't care less about what people think, and whatever they *do* think about me certainly has nothing to do with what I do for a living. I just want to be a great mom. And I love that I've overcome that whole "being defined by my job" thing (not to mention the "going to the grocery store without makeup" hang-up).

My point is that you shouldn't worry about not going back to work because in just a few months you'll have time to do things for yourself again. Try to remember that everything with babies, good or bad, is just a stage—and no stage is permanent (it just feels that way sometimes).

If it makes you feel any better, my worries about *not* staying home involve having to leave my little angel with a stranger—someone who isn't going to dote on her, hold her every time she cries, and kiss her at least 500 times—for eight hours a day! I honestly don't know how I'm going to get through that. I'm actually hoping that we get laid off. I can't imagine what it's going to be like to only spend three or four hours with her each night. It breaks my heart like nothing ever has. I'm crying right now just thinking about it. (Could it be the hormones, or have I really become that maternal?)

I have to tell you that Tim got *big* husband points at Christmas. He gave me a gorgeous ring with Sara's birthstone in the center, surrounded by little diamonds (and little diamonds down the band, too). Plus, he got me a silver locket for her photo and a silver bracelet with a charm that has her name engraved on it. Wow! I love the idea of taking a little "Sara souvenir" with me everywhere I go.

The ring is my favorite (feel free to make suggestions to David), although Tim said it was a funny story how he stumbled upon the engraved-bracelet idea. During his usual last-minute Christmas-shopping dash, he decided to have a quick drink at a bar in the mall. (Hey, I'm not complaining—after all, nothing like a little "liquid holiday cheer" to loosen up the old purse strings.) Anyway, he struck up a conversation with the person next to him, who happened to own a jewelry store. This guy told him about the bracelet idea and invited him back to his store where he gave him, as Tim calls it, "the beer-buddy discount."

I'll let you know how the grocery-store outing works out. Take care and enjoy every fleeting moment! And give little Anna a kiss for me!

January 10
From: Sara
To: Stephanie
Subject: I've got the blues, baby (or vice versa)

I hate to say it, but I'm *not* enjoying every fleeting moment right now. David went back to work the other day, and I've been a mess ever since. I stood at the window watching him leave at 6:30 A.M. in the pouring rain and just cried my eyes out. All I could think was, *The world is going on without me. My support team* [Mom and David] *has left, and I'm all alone.* I guess these are the baby blues they talk about. Whatever it is, it's not fun, and I hope I'm over it soon.

Sorry to cut it short, but I don't feel much like writing now. I wish I felt better—it really stinks to have so much to be thankful for and feel so awful.

January 16
From: Sara
To: Stephanie
Subject: Postpartum

I'm still not feeling any better. Everyone says to give it time, but in the meantime, this is awful (I've never been good at waiting anyway). It's just so hard to understand how I could be so euphoric two weeks ago and now feel like I'm in the depths of woe. I feel I have no control, even though I wake up every morning and take a little mental reading to see if I'm going to feel any better that day. For some strange reason I feel better in the evening than I do in the morning—maybe because David's here, and everything is more manageable. I don't know. There's so much I just don't understand about what I'm going through. I want to take action, to do something to make myself feel better, so I've been doing some research on the Internet.

It's really hard to talk about this. I hear you reveling in every moment, and you have no idea how much I wish I could feel like you do. People are sending me gifts for the baby, but I can't even bring myself to open them. And what if this doesn't get better? I'm really afraid that I'm going to be a horrible mother, and that was the one thing I always knew (or thought I knew) that I'd be great at. What in the world has happened to me?

January 18
From: Stephanie
To: Sara
Subject: You're not alone

I'm so sorry that you're feeling bad. Please feel free to call me anytime you get bored or sad.

I certainly know at least some of what you're feeling. For example, the other day I was pulling my hair out, too. Lately, Sara isn't awake unless she's crying. And I can't seem to console her—she's just plain cranky. I hate letting her just lie there and cry, so I keep picking her up. By the time Tim got home, I was in tears because I wasn't able to accomplish a single thing all day long. I was trying so hard to have dinner ready, and I had clothes in the dryer that were wrinkling, yet I couldn't get away from the baby long enough to do a single chore because she just kept screaming. I get so upset with myself because I want to be good at this mom stuff, but I get so frustrated with her—and angry—and I hate having those feelings. But I'm hoping that it's all just part of learning to be a parent.

Anyway, my point is that you certainly aren't alone. You *have* to go talk to your doctor about what you're going through—I'm certain you'll feel so much better and happier with a little medicinal assistance. Please don't feel weird about that. Obviously postpartum depression [PPD] is very common, or they wouldn't have a cure for it.

One thing that helps me is to think about just how short this period is going to be. In a couple of months, our girls will be completely different, focusing and ready to play with us. I hope that the doctor can help you because you should be able to enjoy this time—it goes by so fast. I hope you realize that these feelings you're experiencing aren't you; they're just courtesy of hormones taking over your body.

In a badly needed effort to get out of the house, Tim and I decided to venture out to a movie, baby in tow. Movies are a great getaway for new moms and babies: The theater was dark and cool, and Sara slept right through the entire film. At one point, she got a little restless, but I just kept rocking the car seat the whole time. Plus, it was so loud that I don't think anyone would have heard her cry anyway. Plus, it was so dark that if she had made a peep, I could have easily nursed her back to sleep.

And we realized yet another revelation: You can't believe how much more you understand things in movies that you never would have even noticed before you became a parent. I told Tim that I needed to go rent and rewatch every movie I've ever seen, since there's so much I missed before I became a member of the parent club. It's like the difference between watching a 3-D movie without glasses and then with them: Knowing the love of a child gives everything more depth.

Today I met Tim and his boss for a lunch meeting. I'd come up with some concepts for a few of their training meetings, and the boss asked if I could meet them and do some more "concept-ing." Sara slept through the whole two-and-a-half-hour meeting, and it was nice to get a chance to use my brain again for some-thing other than feeding schedules or to determine how many scoops of formula it takes to make a four-ounce bottle.

Before I know it, it'll be time to go back to work. My mom's going to come and keep Sara for my first week back to make it easier on me . . . which is when I may be calling you to cry on your shoulder. God, I'm dreading that week. I just can't even think about handing my baby over every morning to someone else and only spending time with her in the evenings and on weekends. It actually makes my stomach hurt to think about it. I honestly don't know how I'm going to survive it. I'm afraid I'm going to be a horrible employee: Work is so far down on my list of priorities now—and the fact that the company was just sold and our futures are in a state of limbo doesn't help my attitude.

I've been down this corporate-acquisition road before, and it's never pretty. I just got my yearly review, and it was awesome. I'm going to hang on to it because it might be the last good one I get until my kids are in college. Oh, well. . . .

Send me a photo of little Anna when you get a chance. I bet she's changed already.

January 19

From: Sara
To: Stephanie
Subject: Mama called the doctor

Thanks for your message. No offense, my friend, but you don't know what I'm feeling, and I'm glad. It's way beyond just a moment or two of being frustrated or overwhelmed—it's a constant dark feeling that never seems to go away. That's why I think that this is more than just the "baby blues."

David and I ended up going to see one of the doctors in my ob-gyn group. The nurse had called in a prescription for me, but I wanted to talk to a doctor before I just started popping pills. Dr. Beurskens was on vacation, and I was really disappointed because I wanted to talk to a fellow mother about this—I thought a woman might be able to understand better than a man. But since I didn't want to wait, I went to see Dr. Gourley. And believe me, he understood. He was awesome! He said that the main culprit here is sleep deprivation, which reduces the levels of serotonin in the brain, causing depression. He told us to try letting David get up with her through the entire night so that I could get a solid night's sleep. Apparently, two or three hours at a time don't do the trick for the old brain. So that night we did just that, and it did help some. He also recommended that I exercise, but of course the weather has been positively awful ever since. If that doesn't work, he gave me a prescription, so there's that option.

Dr. Gourley also made me feel very empowered on the breast-feeding point. You see, I've really wanted to quit, but I've wrestled with this huge amount of guilt because of all the classes I took and books I read about how much better it is for the baby than formula. But more than anything, I just don't like it—it makes me feel trapped. I'd even secretly hoped that I wasn't producing enough milk so that I'd have a physiological reason to quit; physically, it's working fine . . . but mentally, it's awful.

Dr. Gourley said that his wife breast-fed for "about 15 seconds," and she just knew it wasn't for her. "Look, I'm a doctor," he said, "and all my kids were bottle-fed—and they're *fine*." He even picked up the picture of the three of them on his desk (they're all teenagers now) and showed it to me.

That was the best thing he could have said to me. It was like I needed permission to stop, and I was getting it from no less an authority than a doctor. So I think that I've decided to stop breast-feeding: I'm not enjoying it, and I think it's contributing to my PPD. I have this need to just get my body completely back to normal. But I still have guilt about it, I have to admit. I feel like I was so brainwashed in those classes that I can't help but think that I'm a horrible mother for stopping.

Anyway, the whole conversation was so helpful, and it really gave me a boost. He genuinely got what I was going through, which surprised me (guess that teaches me not to be sexist!). Best of all, he gave me hope. At one point in the conversation I said something like "if it gets better" in reference to my current mental state, and he stopped me in my tracks and said, "No, it *will* get better." I left his office feeling like, *Okay, I can make it now. I know there has to be a light at the end of the tunnel.* I doubt that Dr. Gourley will ever know how much he helped me.

I went back to my old office today to have lunch with everyone. When I told my boss that I was going stir-crazy, he said, "Just let me know and I'll hold your job." Maybe I can work some type of flexible situation out. Who knows? At least it's an option. It felt good just to be there today, and to be missed by everyone (they also gave me some freelance work).

How's Sara sleeping? Anna takes lots of naps during the day but only sleeps for about three hours at a time at night if we're lucky. Last night she was up from 2 to 6 A.M. I was ready to scream. I feel terrible that I'm so frustrated, but I want sleep *so* much! I can't wait until she's sleeping through the night. That seems like heaven right now.

January 20
From: Stephanie
To: Sara
Subject: First morning sickness and now this

I'm so glad that the doctor helped. Hey, pop the pills if you're not feeling great—don't hold back.

That's very interesting information about sleep deprivation. I've been wondering why it is that even though Sara sleeps from two until nine most mornings, I'm still feeling so tired that I have that sick feeling in my stomach when I wake up. And even though it seems like she sleeps for a long time, it's not constant because I'm waking up to feed her every two or three hours. Maybe I need to ask Tim to take care of her on Friday nights so that I can sleep, except my milk-engorged baby-food makers would explode without her eating during the night, so I can't win. We need each other, I guess.

Of course I have to tell you that my breasts are absolutely beautiful when they're full of milk. I have the cleavage I've always coveted (without the surgery). The irony in this is that they're also too sore to touch, so poor Tim must relish them from a safe distance. Life can be so cruel.

You're so lucky about your job. I'd give anything to have a flexible schedule or the opportunity to work at home—in fact, that's exactly the situation I'm going to try to find once the company acquisition is complete. Tim's mom was talking about me going back to work this morning, and I had to leave the room because I started to cry again. I don't know how I'm going to get through it; I just can't imagine being away from my baby for eight hours a day. No matter how difficult she can be, it's still heart wrenching. It makes me want to throw up (first morning sickness, and now this!).

Give yourself a break on the whole breast-feeding thing, will you? I hate that your modesty is making it harder for you. I, on the other hand, have been known to whip them out in parking lots, malls, and even on a tour bus once. Hey, you don't mess with Sara's meals. But I agree that the Nipple Nazis put way too much pressure on us new moms. Doing what's right for you *is* the right thing. Anna will be fine. Besides, with you two for parents, she's got worse things to worry about, like all those future therapy sessions. Ha!

January 21

From: Stephanie
To: Sara
Subject: If little Sara is in the swing and her lips are purple, is that bad?

Just kidding. Okay, I'm having some serious burnout already. Tim has been so busy with his national sales meeting that I haven't had any time alone—even a shower is a race between crying spells. I was really frustrated and having a bad day yesterday. Sara wouldn't stop crying, the house was a mess, I'd spilled soda all over myself, and just then the doorbell rang. It was the exterminator. I told him to make himself at home—I was a little busy. He obviously saw my frustration and sensed that I was in a mood. At one point I was running up the stairs to get yet another diaper and I ran directly into him and almost knocked him down.

He looked at me and said something along the lines of, "You know, you should cherish every moment, because it goes by really fast—"

I interrupted him and said, sharply, "I know, I know, we're just having a bad day."

And it really, really pissed me off. That's not what I needed to hear at that moment, especially from a *man*. He obviously knew that he'd rubbed me the wrong way, because he did the rest of the house and left without saying a word. I, on the other hand, was in the next room fuming and plotting his murder. When I heard the front door close, I thought, *That's right, bug-man, better get out while you still can.*

Some of our friends got together a few nights ago at a bar/restaurant, so Tim and I brought Sara with us. I can't believe I'm now one of those mothers I used to criticize for bringing a baby to a bar! But it was great, because no one knew that we were coming. Everyone wanted to hold her, and it was probably a little soon to be passing her around—but on the other hand, our plan was to take her with us from the very beginning so that she'd get used to our lifestyle. I think that the more she's around people now, the more accepting she'll be of them later.

Sara's having these weird crying spells from 10:30 P.M. to 1:30 A.M. every night like clockwork, and I'm getting a little worried. Even though the doctor said that it was perfectly normal for a baby to have a "fussy time," her little hands shake and quiver, and her legs kick like crazy. She's so tired, but it's as if she can't stop moving. I read that babies' nervous systems are still developing and they sometimes have these spells up to three months of age. I just feel so sorry for her.

She's starting to smile now. Not exactly on command, but close. And she laughs sometimes, too. What could possibly be funny to her? Who knows? Anyway, gotta go for now.

January 21
From: Sara
To: Stephanie
Subject: Hanging in there

I know what you mean about criticizing other mothers—I did the same thing. But we've already taken Anna to restaurants, on a boat, to the grocery store . . . you name it. I *have* to. Getting out is the best medicine for me. I'm still having a hard time. It gets better at night, and it's better if I go out somewhere.

I can't stop feeling trapped—it's like the walls are closing in on me. My mom keeps telling me that it will pass, and I sure hope it does, or I'm going to be the worst mother ever. This is the hardest thing I've ever had to get through.

Gotta go. Anna's saying, "Feed me!"

January 23
From: Sara
To: Stephanie
Subject: What happened to my life?

Well, I haven't started popping pills yet. I made the mistake of looking up the medication on the Internet and started reading about the side effects. Now they tell you every possible thing that could happen (I'm sure even Tylenol has side effects), and it freaked me out. And I have to admit that I have some reservations about taking antidepressants. I know I shouldn't, but I think that part of me will feel like a failure or something if I take them; but at the same time, I don't want to deprive Anna of anything either.

Anyway, I'm feeling better. Yesterday was especially good, so I'm still giving it some time, but not much longer—I'm ready to start feeling like my old self again. I don't know how people deal with this for very long.

I'm sorry you have to go back to work—I know that must be killing you right now. Doesn't all this make you appreciate your mother more? You never really know all the choices and sacrifices that are involved until you become a mother yourself. And it's just not the same for men: If I decide to go back to work, no one will look at David and think, *He should be staying at home with the baby.* I can imagine how you feel. When I think about going back full-time, the thought of putting Anna in day care really bothers me, too. I think that having someone come to your house would be less stressful.

Have you found someone to look after Sara? At least your mom will be there the first week—that will really help. And just remember that you don't have to do anything you don't want to. I know you made a commitment to your boss, but if it's just killing you to put your child in day care, you're not going to do anyone any good by continuing to work.

As far as my flexible work situation goes, I'm not sure what that would be. Why don't more companies have in-house day care? That would be such a great solution. I wish I could take Anna to the office with me, but somehow I don't think that will fly. I'm trying to let everything settle down before I jump into anything. It seems that you and I both have to deal with two big adjustments at once: motherhood and leaving work or going back to it. I feel torn right down the middle.

Today David and I set up our will. That was depressing. I hate thinking about that stuff, but we had to do it, especially since we're parents now. We had to decide who would be Anna's guardian in the event something happened to both of us. I have to tell you that this was *not* a good time for me to be thinking about this stuff. Lately my head has been filled with thoughts of impending doom and everyone around me dying. It's very strange and unnerving. I've hardly told anyone that—
it sounds so creepy—but apparently, these are the hallmarks of depression. It's like some black cloud takes over your brain, making it hard to even do the most basic daily tasks because

that cloud creeps in no matter what. I've always loved decorating, taking care of my house, cooking, and reading, and I don't feel like doing any of those things right now. I feel like I've been robbed of the simple pleasures I used to enjoy. I hope I can get back to myself somehow.

Oh, another tidbit on the sleep thing: The Chinese torture their prisoners of war by waking them up every few hours and never letting them get solid sleep. And researchers have been able to cause depression in lab rats by depriving them of sleep. Who knew? You'd think that in all those childbirth classes, someone *might* have mentioned that part of this whole process! I was prepared for labor and childbirth, but I wasn't prepared for this. And don't you ever wonder what our lives are going to become? Will there come a point when all we can do is go play putt-putt and eat at Chuckie Cheese?

January 23
From: Stephanie
To: Sara
Re: Child-survival classes

I agree with you on sleep deprivation not being mentioned in childbirth classes. I think pregnant couples should be required to take "child-survival classes." I mean, the stuff you learn in childbirth class is fine; but let's face it, unless you're going to have a natural delivery (no drugs), the doctors and nurses pretty much take over. Whether you take a class or not, that baby is coming out one way or another.

It's once you get them home that the real challenge begins. And most of us were so busy worrying about giving birth that we overlooked the fact that once we got our babies out of our bodies, we had to help them sustain life (not to mention our own) once we left the hospital. None of the reading I did to prepare has been a true testament to what happens to your life—the schedules, the sleep deprivation, the workload, the emotions, the healing process of your own body, how demanding a new little human can be. It's altogether devastating, and at the same time, magnificent in every way.

Sara sleeps from 1:00 until about 10:30 every morning, and I've been feeling guilty for not getting up earlier to get some things done before she wakes up, but I'm so tired that I just need to sleep. So your information about needing to sleep more than three hours at a time to feel rested has helped me a lot.

I'm glad that you're feeling better. Don't hesitate to take the pills—it's really no big deal. The drug companies have to list all those ridiculous side effects to cover their butts. You need to feel better to be a better mom for Anna. That's more important than your hang-ups about taking medications. That's just your ego talking (sorry, but this is tough love). It's not like you to be feeling these things; it's not your fault, and you haven't done anything wrong. So stop making excuses and just take the pills!

I'm going to give the going-back-to-work thing a chance and see how it goes, how Sara makes out, and how I feel. I don't think Tim realizes just how much it upsets me, though. I usually hide it from him because I don't want him to think that I cry too much. And I know he's not as concerned as I am because he hasn't spent as much time with her and doesn't have the same bond. I know that if I decide to quit, he's not going to make it easy on me. He's gotten really used to my salary and isn't willing to change our lifestyle.

I'm having second thoughts about an in-home caregiver. Nannies make around $15 per hour! Eek! And I keep having these nightmares that I come home from work and the nanny and Sara are both gone. My next-door neighbor loves her baby's day-care center: They limit the number of infants to six, and she can't say enough good things about it. So Tim and I are going to go interview them on Friday morning, which isn't exactly a pleasant chore. It's kind of like scheduling a root canal. It makes my stomach hurt when I think about how much time I have left, but there's really no good solution aside from quitting my job. The other thing I like about a day-care situation is this: Who knows *what* they can do to your little baby alone in your house—at least at a day care there are witnesses. (Maybe I'm watching too much *Dateline NBC*.)

As for the Chuck E. Cheese comment, I've been looking for an excuse to go there for years—I love the place! I only wish they made one of those plastic-ball pits in parent-size.

February 1

From: Sara
To: Stephanie
Subject: Taking medication

Well, I finally decided to start taking the medication. I ended up going with a newer one, which I just feel better about for some reason. Maybe it's the advertising, but it seems like this is the latest and greatest in antidepression medication, so I figured why not go with the best. I think I feel a little lift already. Maybe it's the placebo effect, but I'll take anything I can get at this point. It's not much, but it's something and it gives me encouragement. The fine print says to give it at least two weeks to get in your system, then you have to increase your dosage every week until you're up to what your doctor prescribed. So it's a gradual process filled with more waiting! But if it makes me feel better, then it's worth it.

I think I was starting to stress out so much about whether to take the pills or not that it's a relief to at least have the decision made. I'll keep you posted on what happens. . . . I haven't told many people about this. I still feel a little bit like a failure, although I do know that this was out of my control. I gave it a month, and I tried everything to feel better—and not much changed. I don't know how someone could go very long like this without getting some relief, and I sure hope it helps me.

By the way, you're obviously much more qualified to be a parent than I am—I didn't even know how to *spell* Chuck E. Cheese.

February 5

From: Stephanie
To: Sara
Subject: Better living through chemicals

Would you stop it? You're not a failure—you're the victim of your own hormones. They're brutal, and they affect us all differently. Thank God you got smart and started taking something. Sometimes I think every mother should leave the hospital with two things: (1) their baby; and (2) a prescription with refills to last until the child is age four.

Hang in there, and call if you want to talk.

February 15

From: Sara
To: Stephanie
Subject: The worst is over (I hope)

After two weeks of medication, I'm definitely feeling better. Not totally back to normal yet, but definitely better, and more like my old self. And at least I'm not crying every day—that's an improvement!

This whole thing fascinates me: What does this pill do to my brain to make me feel human again? It's such new territory that I don't think the doctors even really know. But it proves to me that there's certainly a physical/chemical aspect to this whole postpartum thing.

David and I went out to dinner last night for Valentine's Day, with little Anna in tow. She was very good, and we had a nice meal. She had on a cute little outfit with little red hearts all over it, which she got from my sister-in-law. She got a lot of compliments.

Going out to dinner is nothing unusual for us—I swear, eating out has saved my sanity. I was going so stir-crazy that once I realized it was pretty easy to take Anna with us to a restaurant (she pretty much just sleeps in her car-seat carrier), I've greeted David with the words, "Want to go out to eat?" almost every night when he walks in the door.

I also think I may have had a touch of seasonal depression as well. It certainly didn't help matters that the day David went back to work (when Anna was a week old), it started raining and didn't stop for two weeks. I've never looked so forward to spring and warm weather. I'm dying to see leaves on the trees, since everything looks so barren now.

I'm so glad I decided to take this medication—in fact, I wish I'd started sooner because I'm really starting to enjoy Anna now. It amazes me that in all the childbirth and breast-feeding classes I took that *no one* mentioned postpartum depression. It's a dirty little secret that no one talks about. That's just terrible, because so many women have to deal with PPD, and if they're like me, they have no idea who to talk to, or they're afraid to mention it to their girlfriends. You don't want anyone to think that you're a bad mother, even though it's entirely not about that. And since no one talks about it, you think you're a freak until you start reading that at least *10 percent* of women go through this. Where are they? They're staying silent for the most part. And they aren't teaching any classes at the hospital, that's for sure.

When I was pregnant, David and I went to this class called "Taking Care of Baby," which basically taught us how to change a diaper, swaddle the baby in a blanket, and give it a bath (like I couldn't have figured that out on my own). Instead of that waste of time, there should be a class called "Taking Care of Mama." As a pregnant woman, you're about to go through this huge life change—probably the most transformative period of your life— and no one feels the need to give you the slightest clue about it. The mother is left out of the whole equation. You check out of the hospital with your little instruction sheet on how to take care of your body and a prescription for ibuprofen. As for the massive emotional, mental, social, and financial turn that your life has just taken . . . well, you're on your own there, sister.

That's what gets to me about these Nipple Nazis. The mother factor is never considered in breast-feeding. It's all about how good it is for the baby. Well, what if it's *not* good for the mother? Shouldn't that be considered as well? I feel like going to the hospital and crashing one of those classes and telling those mothers-to-be what it's *really* like.

Okay, I'm getting off my soapbox now. Good luck with the child-care search!

Chapter 6

We've Decided to Let the Baby Stay
(But We'd Like to Get Rid of Our Husbands)

March 5
From: Stephanie
To: Sara
Subject: OP syndrome

After viewing at least 22 photo e-mails from you over the last three days, I'm wondering if Anna's wishing you never got that digital camera. Sara, who also suffers from OP ("overly photographed") syndrome, has literally learned to cry whenever we bring out the camera. There are so many ways to torture them, aren't there? I feel like it's a little revenge for all the nights of sleep deprivation.

I made such a "Moronic Mom Mistake" last week. I had to go to San Antonio for a trade show (it was just an overnight trip), so Tim took off work to stay with Sara. We decided to try to give her a bottle the night before I left, even though this was the first time we'd done so since she was three weeks old. We didn't think twice about it: After all, she took a bottle nightly for the first three weeks of her life (until the breast-milk quantity got regulated). *Big* mistake. She'd forgotten how to drink from a bottle and totally refused to eat. I purchased five different kinds of nipples and bottles, and we tried everything we could think of to get her to cooperate.

I'd worked and worked to pump a month's supply of breast milk, and she wouldn't touch it. She was screaming because she was hungry and frustrated; Tim was frustrated; and I, still suffering from overactive hormones, was nothing short of traumatized. There was no way I was going to get on that plane until I was sure that my child wasn't going to starve to death (or dehydrate). I was trying to figure out how I was going to tell my boss that I couldn't attend the trade show because I was afraid my child would wither up and die, without sounding like some kind of maternal freak. It was one big, fat, ugly crisis.

Finally, Tim said, "Every time the milk touches her tongue, she starts to cry." Hmm, a clue . . . I took the lid off, and the milk was sour. So I went to the freezer to thaw another bag of milk—it too, was sour, and so was the next bag. The brochure the hospital had given me said that breast milk could sit out for several hours before freezing it. So, for convenience's sake, I'd let a bottle sit out for several hours and keep pumping milk into it over the course of the day until I had at least four ounces. Obviously, I let it sit out too long, because I had to throw out *an entire month's worth of milk!* That stuff is pure liquid gold!

I was devastated. All those trips to the kitchen in the middle of the night to put milk in the freezer! All those painstaking details, making sure to write the date on every bag, double-bagging everything to keep it fresh, not to mention the sore nipples from the damn breast pump. Tim and I held a vigil over the trash can as I discarded the entire supply—again, as hormonal tears streamed down my face. Now I have to pump like crazy to have enough stored for when Sara starts day care . . . *next week!* She finally did drink from the bottle when we gave her formula; thank God you can interchange that stuff with breast milk! It was crazy—I think I lost four pounds that night (which is actually okay).

Now that Tim has her acclimated to the bottle, he's giving her one once every evening just to keep her used to it. He really likes feeding her, and it's been great bonding for them both. In fact, my time away did wonders for their relationship—he was so much more attentive to her when I got back. It was an amazing difference: He was interested before, but now he's really into her. So I'm really glad that I had to make the trip.

We have to take her on a plane next month, and I'm not looking forward to it. Tim's grandmother is having a 90th birthday party/family-reunion thing in Massachusetts. Although this month's *Parents* magazine had a whole article on how to fly with your baby, I'm still dreading it. I'm mostly worried about her safety, as well as how her little ears will react to the pressure. But we also have a wedding in New York in June and a vacation in Virginia Beach planned in July, so I guess she'll be a world traveler before she knows it! Poor little baby. It's such a big world when you have busy parents.

Right now, Sara's in her swing watching *Oprah* (I'm serious).

March 7
From: Sara
To: Stephanie
Subject: Liquid gold

Having pumped for an hour to squeeze out only one blessed ounce of that liquid gold, I feel your pain, my sister. It must have taken you hours upon hours to compile that stash—I can't believe every single bag was bad. Thank God for the people who invented formula, right? By the way, my mom told me that the "formula" she fed my older sister was a concoction consisting of evaporated milk and Karo syrup. If she grew up healthy on *that*, then our kids are sure to be fine.

Does Tim read any of the baby books about development and stuff? Around here it seems that every question about Anna is directed at me; that is, no one expects David to have a clue about when she's going to roll over or sit up or eat cereal. And of course he *doesn't* have a clue because he's never taken the initiative to read anything. Someone gave him a book on being a father and he never even opened it. (If you're detecting a bad attitude, yes, he's on my list tonight.)

I've been busting my butt just to keep our household together (including paying the bills and keeping clean underwear in his dresser). Now I have some freelance work, and I need a little extra help from him: His response is, "If you feel overwhelmed, just don't freelance." It never occurs to him that it might be about more than the money. Then he tells me he wants to train for a triathlon! And of course when I get upset, he has no clue why. I'm so tired of having to *explain* everything to him. Aren't you glad we had girls?

On a brighter note, Anna laughed three times today! It was so funny because she couldn't figure out how she did it, so when she tried to do it again, it came out like a cough. Of course I was singing, dancing, making funny faces and noises—everything but standing on my head—to try to get her to do it again. I tell ya, things are so much better now. It makes such a difference when the baby starts interacting with you—even just a little. For two months she was just a little blob, and a *demanding* blob at that. It's like you're doing all this work and getting nothing back. That first smile is like finally getting a reward!

I bet Sara will do great on the plane. I know what you mean, though; the first time we take Anna somewhere, it will really bother me. David and I are flying to Acapulco next month, and I'm already imagining that we're going to die in a plane crash and leave her orphaned.

March 10

From: Stephanie
To: Sara
Subject: Real men don't read books

I get so excited when I see a message from you! I don't know where to start: Acapulco, David's non-reading, dying in plane crashes, leaving orphans behind. . . . I guess I'll go with the tri-athlon.

I feel that it's my job to lead you to the silver lining of this husband cloud. Keep in mind that we all started having babies kind of late in life. Tim and I feel very strongly about the need to make time to take care of our bodies so that we're not totally decrepit by the time our kids are in college. It's gonna be kind of tough to bail them out of jail at three in the morning if our arthritis is acting up.

Of course I haven't exactly figured out when I'm supposed to find the time to exercise, but it *is* something to consider. So it's pretty cool that David's taking an interest in keeping his body healthy. On the other hand—sheesh, that's quite a goal! Maybe he should start with "I'm going to run a mile twice a week." Him saying, "I want to be in a triathlon" is right up there with me saying, "I'm going to grow breasts like Tyra Banks by July."

(Although with the help of my trusty breast pump, maybe that's not out of the question. Except for the fact that they'll look like used socks by the time Victoria's Secret discovers me!) Anyway, you don't have to be a palm reader to determine where I'm going here. I say to you, my wise and faithful girlfriend, "This too shall pass." Don't forget: He's a guy . . . it won't last. (David, if you're reading my e-mails again, sorry. The only thing Tim can do with discipline for more than three days in a row is crack open a beer after work.)

I think we try to plan too much, and guys just don't need all that advance notice. If I need to go to the mall, Tim doesn't need to know the day before. When he comes home, I hand him the baby and say, "I have to go to the mall—will you be okay for a couple hours?" It pretty much always works. Of course I'm rushing to get back to my child the entire time, so even shopping isn't the same anymore. Sometimes I think it's probably a healthy thing for me to be going back to work—a balance is a good thing. Anyway, my point is, just do what *you* need to do, and it will all work out, even if it cuts into David's kickboxing matches.

Okay, now on to David and books. This is not uncommon: Men just don't feel the need to educate themselves on child care like we do. I think it's partly because they know we'll do it for them, and partly because they're not the ones who have to squeeze something the size of a watermelon out of a hole the size of a lemon (at least that's how Carol Burnett described it). I think it's just utter shock and fear that drives us to read and educate ourselves. Men don't have those worries to motivate them.

Tim has exactly three books and two videotapes on fatherhood—and nope, he hasn't read or watched a single thing. I don't think he even bothered to look at the pictures (if only he knew about all the pictures of naked breasts in those books . . . of course they all have a baby attached to them, so I guess that may take something away). Anyway, he did *great* with Sara while I was away, in spite of not reading the books. Yes, I fully educated him, but what else do I have to talk about, other than who Dr. Phil interrogated today?

Tim does have an Internet program that pulls info from news publications related to child care, and he's always coming home with interesting stories and facts. Of course, it's not useful things like how Sara and Anna are supposed to start eating cereal next month when they can't even sit up yet. (Have you figured

that one out yet? Can *you* swallow Cream of Wheat while lying down?) Yesterday's news brief was about the ideal time to have your second child, which is supposedly 18 to 23 months after giving birth to your first—apparently it takes your body that long to recover and recharge for the next round. Yet that will make me 36 or 37 for the second child. I'm not sure which is worse.

Don't worry about David's lack of information. After all, he knows important stuff like how to score in Ping-Pong and who won the game between the Bears and the Giants in 1943. Tim is a *wonderful* father, better than I ever imagined. Sara adores him, and I know that he'll always do everything in his power to take good care of her (even if it isn't exactly the way I'd do it). When David's watching Anna, you just have to surrender to this motto: "As long as she isn't maimed, bleeding, or scarred, and no one had to go the ER, it means everything went well."

What the hell are you going to Acapulco for? Vacation? (There are no vacations in parenthood! Didn't you read that in the manual they gave you when you left the hospital?) Have you thought about how much bottled water and formula you'll have to bring to feed Anna? Do you know how heavy water is? How are you going to pack enough diapers? Sorry, just bringing you down because of my jealousy. Actually, that sounds awesome! I've thought a lot about a vacation with my little family. It's just so hard to plan anything—after all, once you're a parent, *everything* is tentative.

Gotta go. Sara just spit up on the love seat.

March 11

From: Sara
To: Stephanie
Subject: "Romance"

We're going to Acapulco because David won a trip for being in the "President's Council" (which basically means he sold a lot of phones). My parents will keep Anna, so it really *will* be a vacation! Aren't you jealous? I'm already dreading the flight and wondering what I was thinking deciding to go. On the one hand, I'm *so* excited to get a break, yet on the other I keep thinking of every worst-case scenario. (What is it about being a parent that makes you think about things like that?)

You're right—men are full of other information that comes in handy from time to time. David will be the one who teaches Anna how to drive the boat and water-ski and fish. God knows I wouldn't be able to teach her how to bait a hook or tell a bluegill from a bass. Yet the thing that still gets me is how sexist our society still is, even in the 21st century. People don't expect David to know the answers to the baby questions, so they don't even ask him. When the subject of Anna's development comes up in conversation, it's like he's not even in the room. I've noticed that this is especially true with our parents and people of that generation. People our age are a little different, but not much. I don't get it—I mean, David and I are *both* responsible for Anna's well-being. It's not like carrying her for nine months gave me some lightning bolt of wisdom about this whole deal that enables me to know at what age she's supposed to sit up!

As for all that maternal-instinct stuff they talk about, that's crap. Everyone says, "Oh, you'll know what to do." Like hell! I feel clueless most of the time. I can't tell one cry from another—they all sound the same to me. I'm starting to know what she needs, but that's from two and a half months of practice and simply getting to know her. I'm realizing more and more that motherhood is a lot like marriage: It's way over-romanticized, and nobody talks about how much work it is!

March 12

From: Stephanie
To: Sara
Subject: Back to work

Well, it's finally arrived: Today is my first day back to the old grind . . . and I cried all the way here. I was sobbing so hard when I left the house this morning that I could barely see to drive, which is a little dangerous in Atlanta traffic.

There are photos of Sara all over my new office—it looks like a shrine. I have to try to bring something else to hang up in here so that it looks like I have a life. On the other hand, my new office [Stephanie's office changed while she was on maternity leave] is *awesome!* I'm on the 16th floor, and I have a wall of windows overlooking the city. It's the office I've always dreamed of having . . . except now that I have it, all I can think of is that I wish someone would come in and fire me so that I could go home and sit on the couch and hold my little baby. I miss her like crazy!

It's terrible—it physically aches. Of course I'm still breastfeeding her, since I don't want to give that up yet . . . so that means I get to pump milk at work. Since there are only about seven of us in the office, things are a little close, and I'm concerned that the whole breast-milk thing is going to really weird people out. I've done everything I can think of to ease the tension: First, I always put the milk I've pumped inside a cooler before I leave the privacy of my office. (It just doesn't feel right to walk down the hall to the kitchen with a bag of freshly pumped breast milk in my hand. What if someone stops me to make conversation? Can you imagine standing there in the hallway, holding a bag of breast milk and discussing last night's prime-time ratings?) And since other people use the freezer, I put the entire cooler in there so that my milk is never in plain sight.

To make things even more complicated, my office door doesn't lock. So to ensure that no one will ever walk in on me, I made a little sign for my doorknob when I'm pumping. I thought a little humor might help "un-weird" the situation, so the sign has a cow-print background and states in large letters: "MAKING BABY FOOD. PLEASE COME BACK." My boss had a good laugh about it, and it seems to work well. I'm the only mom in my office (one other lady has two grown children), but that means that the other girls have no idea what I'm going through. Suddenly, I have nothing in common with them, and there's really no way to bring them up to speed, unless I can drive them to a sperm bank and speed up the process. So I'm quite sure that it must seem like I'm from another planet, what with all the breast-pump noises coming from my office, the frequent calls to day care, the tears, and the fact that I have but one topic on my mind from dusk till dawn. I've become a member of the exclusive club of parent: The admission isn't cheap, it has more membership benefits than any club that ever existed, and those who aren't fortunate enough to belong can't even begin to imagine how wonderful it is to be a member.

My co-workers are being so sweet, though: They decorated my office with big welcome-back signs, brought me plants and photo frames, and are taking me out to lunch. All that helps a little, but I still can't believe that I'm not going to see my baby for another six hours! Ugh. I've been so upset that I lost four pounds in two days (which is the only upside to all this).

Have fun with Anna today . . . I'm very, very jealous.

March 12

From: Sara
To: Stephanie
Subject: Pumping at work

I thought about you last night and wondered how you were holding up. I know it has to suck—there's just no two ways about it, so I'm not going to try to tell you otherwise. However, I will say that it's going to get easier, and little Sara will be fine. Hang in there. I don't think I've ever uttered this sentence before, but—I'll pray for you to get fired!

I can't believe how much you have to go through to pump at work. I swear, I want to go back to the hospital and crash one of those breast-feeding classes I took and tell all those moms-to-be what it's really like. If one more person tells me how "convenient" it is, I'm going to punch them right in the face. Sure it is—if you like living behind a closed door all the time. I guess it *is* convenient in the middle of the night, as there's no bottle to heat up or formula to mix, but that's about the only time. And there are still so few places to breast-feed in public, in spite of the fact that it's supposed to be the ideal way to nourish your child. People still look at you like you're a freak. I wasn't even comfortable doing it in the hospital, because I never knew if someone was going to walk in unexpectedly. Of course that's just me—it's obviously working great for you. It also sounds like you came up with the ideal solution to maintain your privacy while pumping at work.

Call me if you need a shoulder to cry on. Oh, I will say one thing in regard to going back to work: I think it's important to remember that not only will our daughters look to us for mothering and nurturing, but they'll also look to us for an example of what kind of woman to be. And to have a life and career of your own is never a bad thing to show your daughter. Women have a tendency to put their needs behind everyone else's, and I want

Anna to know that she should never feel guilty for doing something for herself. I think that's a wonderful gift to give a child. Hope that helps a little.

March 13
From: Stephanie
To: Sara
Subject: Fear of flying

Hey, woman! I wanted to talk to you about the whole fear-of-flying issue. Apparently, lots of women become afraid of this once they've become mothers. Believe me, I feel your pain! Here are some things that help me:

1. Try to think about *all* the thousands of planes and millions of passengers that take off and land safely every single day. The chances of your actually having a problem are about like winning the lottery.

2. Our good friend Jeff Sabol is a pilot for a commercial airline, so Tim and I always ask him lots of questions. He said that there are only about three seconds during a flight that a pilot is even concerned, and that's during takeoff. He won't tell me exactly *when* those three seconds occur—but I usually sit there in my seat and count *one-one thousand, two-one thousand, three-one thousand,* and then I feel better.

3. Jeff also explained that turbulence *cannot* cause a plane to crash, no matter how rough it is. It's just like hitting bumps in the car, or waves on the boat: It's simply currents of air going up and down instead of horizontally, so there's no reason to be afraid of turbulence.

4. He also told us that pilots are trained to handle every emergency. They even simulate getting the plane right-side-up if it should flip over for some weird reason. I know that this is twice as scary for you since David's mishap last year—but even then, remember that they *did* land the plane safely.

5. Take some deep breaths and try to relax. Think about all the pilots and flight attendants who work on these planes and take off and land hundreds of times every month—they're still alive and well.

You know, it's very normal and quite common for you as a new mother to fear flying more than you used to. While I was pregnant, I hated it. Maybe it's our hormones, but I also think that it's just more evidence of how much value we now put on our lives, since as mothers, we have a little someone who needs us so much. On one trip a flight attendant sat next to me, and I told her that since I'd become pregnant I was so much more afraid than before. She told me that it was quite common, and many flight attendants that she knew had quit their jobs when they became pregnant because they were suddenly afraid to fly.

So there you have it! You're not alone. You'll be fine.

March 19

From: Sara
To: Stephanie
Subject: *What?*

Flip the plane over? *Planes have actually flipped over?* Your strategies are great, but I've already got one of my own. It's called "vodka."

March 21

From: Stephanie
To: Sara
Subject: I curse day care!

Well, once again the day-care center called at 11:30 A.M. and told me to come and get Sara because they couldn't get her to eat anything all morning. This means that she hasn't had anything to eat for more than five hours!

Tim and I worked with her all weekend to take the bottle. By Sunday, she took it all day with no complaint, and we were so relieved . . . until that evening, when she reverted back to her old ways and would have nothing to do with a bottle. Tim has a trick where he calms her down with the pacifier and then switches it out for the bottle. But, of course, even though he thoroughly explained that to the day-care workers, they'd seemingly rather administer an IV due to severe dehydration than bend their ridiculous no-pacifier rule and use it to urge Sara to eat. They're idiots.

My sister always told me that you didn't know what true anger was until you had to deal with someone messing with your child. And she's so right. I'm so pissed off right now that it's actually affecting my vision. I cannot believe that they waited *five* hours to call and tell me! That poor little baby hasn't eaten since I fed her before work this morning. When I went to pick her up she was crying, and I could tell that she'd been doing so for a very, very long time. Her face and eyes were all red, and she did that gasping thing (you know, the one kids always do after they've been crying hard) for 45 minutes after I took her home! That tells me that she'd been really upset for quite a while.

I asked the day-care workers if they'd tried to give her the pacifier (which always calms her immediately), and they said no because it's against their stupid policy. I've explained to them that we're going to try to wean her off the pacifier gradually, but if they could just give it to her long enough to calm her down, she'll then take the bottle more willingly. I realize that she's a pain to try to bottle-feed because she's used to being breast-fed. But my God—they're *the* most expensive day care in the area. I'd think that they'd be able to handle this issue, which I'm sure is very common. Yet they keep giving me these lame, narrow-minded, old-fashioned excuses about how they're so "development oriented," and giving her a pacifier will slow her development. I'm sorry, but I think they're totally full of shit.

The assistant director was so condescending, too: She tried to make me feel like *I* was the one doing something wrong. There's just no reason to make a little baby cry like that. Tomorrow I'm going to call the owner and tell her that we need to have what I like to call a "coming home to Jesus" meeting with her and her little assistant.

And as if things weren't bad enough . . . I was sitting here on the couch with Sara, thinking about how stressed out I was about missing work, and what kind of torture the day care would be inflicting upon us tomorrow. Suddenly, there's this huge explosion and the whole house started shaking! I was thinking it was either a tornado or an earthquake, and I wasn't sure whether to run outside or stay in. But since the house had shaken, I ran outside with the baby—I didn't want to be trapped under a collapsed house. That's when I saw the source of the explosion: Two huge trees from our neighbors' yard had fallen. They landed on *both* of our cars and part of the house. Both cars were smashed *completely flat*—even the tires!—and the roof had a gigantic hole in it where the trees were still lying (part of them ended up in our bedroom). The car alarms were going off, there was glass and debris and limbs everywhere, and I was shaking from the shock of it all. The sound of it was unbelievable!

I called Tim and with a quivery voice told him that somehow he needed to come home immediately. I then called the fire department to make sure that nothing was going to explode and that the fallen power lines weren't dangerous. I'm so thankful that Sara and I weren't sitting in the car for some reason. We would have been killed—there's no doubt about it. What a freaking nightmare! (Like I needed one more disaster this week.)

March 22

From: Sara
To: Stephanie
Subject: A can of whup-ass

Did you open one up on the day-care bitch? Some people say that once you have children you gain a better understanding of the Mafia's protection of family. So I have visions of you with this woman's shirt collar twisted in your fist, saying through clenched teeth, "You mess wit' my family, you mess wit' me, capeesh?" (Since I'm not Italian, I have no idea how to spell "capeesh," but you get the idea. Of course, being Southern, I *do* know how to spell "whup-ass.")

I've discussed your situation with the two smartest people I know (my mother and David), and we all agree that this woman's behavior is worthy of the little "prayer meeting" you were thinking of having with her. So did she see the light and "come home to Jesus"? You know, even Jesus wasn't above breaking bad on somebody when the occasion called for it—remember the money changers? I'm sure that even the highest authority would agree that what this lady needs is a good old-fashioned ass-chewing. After you're done, you can tell her it was for *her* "development."

(As for the tree incident, thank God those things didn't fall right when you pulled into the driveway or when you were getting out of the car. Nevertheless, I know the whole thing had to be incredibly scary.)

March 23
From: Stephanie
To: Sara
Subject: Nipple confusion

Yes, a can of whup-ass for her "development" is exactly what she got. Although I have to admit that Sara *is* a nightmare to give a bottle to lately. It all started when we took the pacifier away—I'm not sure why the two are connected, but we've seen a *huge* change in her temperament since then. She screams when trying to bottle-feed, and it's really become a battle. (She obviously has my strong temper and determination.) We've tried everything you can imagine, including warming the nipple, so our plan is to give her *only* the bottle all weekend (including at the 3 A.M. feeding). But it sucks for me, too, because I've grown really attached to feeding her. I love being that close to her. It's so hard to hold her and listen to her scream when I know that I could just open my shirt and make us both feel better.

My advice to all the future mothers I know is to *start feeding your baby with a bottle as well as the breast from the very beginning.* The lactation nurses at the hospital tried to convince me that this was a bad thing because it causes "nipple confusion." I'm here to tell you that "nipple *refusal*" is much worse! I can promise you that the next time I have a baby, the first lactation nurse who dares to step one foot into my hospital room is going to find herself tossed back into the hallway on her clipboard! Don't get me wrong, I think every mother-to-be should attend a breast-feeding class . . . 'cause the bottom line is that there's *nothing* "natural" about it! (Not to mention the fact that pumping, freezing, and storing breast milk is a science unto itself.)

I remember once seeing an episode of *Murphy Brown* in which Murphy was struggling with all the changes her body was going through after she had her baby. As she sat in her hospital bed, she said, "Oh, great—now my body's making milk. It's like you go through your whole life and suddenly bacon starts coming out of your elbow!" That's about the best description I've ever heard. It's too weird!

Anyway, the classes do help tremendously because you have to know how to latch the baby on properly so that your nipples don't get so sore. There are dozens of little tricks that made breast-feeding much easier, like sticking your finger in the baby's mouth to break the suction before removing her from sucking (that can really hurt). The problem is that some lactation nurses tend to put way too much pressure on new moms. Once the baby is born, it's really hard to tell how much she's eating—or if she's eating at all, because the milk doesn't come in for days, and for some like me, even weeks.

Once we started supplementing with formula and a bottle, Sara began to gain weight and cry a lot less. She just couldn't get satisfied on breast milk alone, at least not until my milk stabilized itself. Plus, the fact that your little baby can drink from a bottle is a *huge* benefit because it means that you can get a break and let Dad or the babysitter take over for a few hours. (And, just for the record, Sara never had a problem with switching back and forth from breast to bottle in the very beginning.) The other, and very important, benefit to supplementing with a bottle is that many breast-fed babies are lacking in iron, while most formulas are fortified with it. So, based on my own experience and current knowledge, the very best situation is to breast-feed *and* supplement with a bottle. It makes everyone's life better and healthier.

I spent $60 at the bookstore yesterday buying all these baby-psychology books—the next time the day care gives me a reason why they won't do what I ask, I'm going to be educated enough to argue with facts. I bought *The Baby Book* by Dr. Sears (he's a doctor who recommends co-sleeping and has actually done studies on it), and that *Baby Whisperer* book (which is surprisingly very good), *and* I found a book with ideas for playing with Sara according to her age. We're having a ball with it!

So we'll see how it goes. But I can tell you that it isn't easy dropping her off at day care. I feel like I'm taking her for a root canal every morning. And despite what everyone says, it's not getting any easier.

As for our tree incident, both cars were deemed total losses. So now we have to go shop for a new car (yuk!). Of course we didn't make money on the deal, so we have to lay out a big fat down payment. It really sucks. All I can say is, thank God it's Friday!

March 23
From: Sara
To: Stephanie
Subject: Nipple *preference*

I totally agree with you on that nipple-confusion BS. I went to see a lactation consultant at Anna's pediatrician's office when she was about two weeks old because I wanted to be able to give her the bottle and breast so badly. They'd completely brain-washed me in the breast-feeding class that supplementing was a sin right up there with child abuse. Fortunately, the lactation consultant said that was ridiculous. She said there is no such thing as nipple confusion. "There may be nipple *preference*," she explained, "but not confusion."

The other thing that they don't bother to mention is that most breast-fed babies don't gain weight as quickly and, there-fore, don't sleep through the night as fast. Plus, formula takes longer for them to digest, so if you give them a bottle in the night, everyone may get an extra hour of sleep. I think these Nipple Nazis forget how important sleep is during this time!

The bottom line is that everything can't just be about the baby: You have to do what works for *everyone* in the household or you'll go insane, and who does that help? I've made that old say-ing my motto: "If mama ain't happy, ain't *nobody* happy."

And yes, did those breast-feeding teachers ever mention the iron thing? Nooooo. I finally inquired one day at the pediatri-cian's office why they always asked me if Anna had been exclu-sively breast-fed from birth, and they told me about the iron thing, which was news to me. So I agree with you that the best idea is a combination. I'm going to try that with my next baby—maybe then I'll last longer than two weeks.

Thinking back to that day with the lactation consultant, I so badly wanted to quit breast-feeding, but I was just guilt-ridden because of it. It was like I wanted her to give me permission to quit. Next time I'm going to be able to give myself that permission on my own if I need to, because I see that it certainly wasn't detrimental to Anna to switch to formula—but at the time, breast-feeding was detrimental to *my* mental health. The bottom line is that you just have to find what works for you.

I can't believe the photos of your cars. No doubt car shopping with an infant is *just* what you feel like doing, right?

March 25
From: Stephanie
To: Sara
Subject: Time to make a change

I've decided to make a change—after once again picking up a child from day care who's displaying red eyes and irritated skin, I really want to stay at home.

Her doctor told me today regarding the whole pacifier battle that it's "highly inappropriate" to take it away from her at this age. Not just from the standpoint that *we* are her parents and the day care should do what we feel is right for her, but also thanks to the fact that babies have the need to suck because it's very comforting to them. She said, "Anyone who knows anything about child care knows that."

So we have an appointment with a new day-care place tomorrow morning. And I found a lady who's looking for another baby to care for in her home. If those two things don't work out, then screw the mortgage: I quit!

It's really too bad, because I'm doing so well with the whole going-back-to-work thing. It's my second week back and my house is spick-and-span, everyone has clean underwear, there are groceries in the cupboards, I managed to cook supper three days this week (and I'm talking *real* food, not Hamburger Helper); and, despite the fact that I'm sensing people want my job (I really think they were surprised that I came back), I'm doing really well at work. If only I could feel good about Sara's day care, everything would be pretty hunky-dory. I'm hoping that we'll have it all straightened out here, because I have a day trip out of state coming up this week. I have to go take a client to lunch—in Texas (I love my job).

Hope all is well with you! Have you heard the country song called "Just Another Day in Paradise"? It's about the phone ringing, the kids crying, the washing machine breaking, bills to pay, and somebody crawling into bed with Daddy after a bad dream . . . and all the singer prays for is just another day in paradise. Sound familiar? It makes me cry every time I hear it. Damn these hormones.

March 26

From: Sara
To: Stephanie
Subject: Pacifier ammunition

I totally agree with your doctor that it's highly inappropriate to take away Sara's pacifier. I ran across an article today in *American Baby* magazine that I thought you might appreciate. It's about thumb vs. pacifier, but it says that you shouldn't take a pacifier away from a child before six months of age because before that time sucking is a necessary reflex. The doctor quoted says that society associates sucking with immaturity and lack of intelligence, but neither is true. Sucking is perfectly normal for babies—they even do it in the uterus. It's probably a reflex that's built in to teach us how to eat. In fact, sucking not only provides comfort, but it also lowers the baby's heart rate and helps the brain to focus.

So it *is* good for Sara's development! It makes sense: It doesn't take a rocket scientist to figure out that a baby can't do much developing when it's not eating and just crying all the time. After reading that article, it sounds like this day care's rules are almost sadistic. And just because they've been doing it for 15 years doesn't mean that they know the only right way. After all, 15 years ago doctors were telling mothers to put babies to sleep on their stomachs and that formula was better than breast milk, too.

It seems that a little open-mindedness would be good for these people.

One other note: The article also says that most babies give up the pacifier when they start on solid food, and are off it completely by the time they're a year old. Most of them will start spitting it out at six months, and if the parent doesn't keep giving it back, they give it up on their own. Interesting! I can fax or mail you a copy of this article if it would help give you some ammunition.

I hope that the other day-care places you're looking at are more flexible. Surely there are others out there that don't object to a pacifier. I feel so sorry for you and Sara. I hope you can get this resolved soon. And I can't believe that people are after your job! Scumsuckers!

On that bright note, let me know how everything goes tomorrow. Good luck!

April 2

From: Stephanie
To: Sara
Subject: Husband points

Tim's been getting big points lately, and making the other day-care Mommies a little jealous. I go to visit little Sara at her new day care every day on my lunch hour, and (on most days) Tim comes with me! It's so awesome to have our little family together every day at lunch, even though it's only for an hour. The new place has a little "nursing room" with two rocking chairs, and since no one else breast-feeds their baby, we have it all to ourselves. It's perfect.

Sara smiles when I come to pick her up now, which I think means that she recognizes me. I don't think she's cognizant enough yet to know that we leave her, visit her, leave again, and then come get her at the end of the day—it probably just all runs together in "baby time." But I do know that she has a good time during the hour she's with us. We carry her around outside and show her the pretty flowers, and then we sit on a park bench and sing songs and play with her. When we go to leave again, she's usually so interested in the other babies that she doesn't even notice our leaving. This morning she was sitting in her bouncy seat with all the other babies in a circle. I was trying to kiss her good-bye, and she was giving me the old "get out of my face, crazy lady" look. It was funny. And I'm thrilled that she's so happy there.

This place is everything a day care should be, including being extremely clean and organized. It's part of a church, and I can see the steeple from my office window. The two ladies who take care of the baby room have been there for 14 years—they know everything there is to know about little babies and have been so helpful in giving me advice so far. I think I've learned more from them than I have from my pediatrician. They hold Sara, rock her, and play with her; and they gradually worked her into the schedule that the rest of the class follows. It took a lot of extra attention in the beginning, but she's fitting right in now. I feel a hundred times better. It's like a thousand-pound weight has been lifted off my shoulders. And I love the fact that it's only two blocks from my office, and I can go visit her whenever I need to. It's just a great situation—so much better than the original day care, *and* almost half the price!

There was a big announcement made at work today: My boss offered me the chance to switch jobs with a co-worker whose job requires less travel. Since Tim travels so much, too, it was going to be really hard to juggle Sara around between our schedules, especially with no family members in town. I get to keep my office and salary, and I'll still be in contact with most of my clients. Although I'm so thankful that my boss suggested this, I'm still struggling with it. It's been a hard decision for me, because even though my income will stay the same, the title is sort of a demotion. But that's just my ego talking—this really is a great solution for my family. I guess it's just the kind of thing that mothers have to do sometimes.

Nothing in life gives you more perspective than having a baby. No matter how stressed out you are, you just go home and look into that adorable, innocent, smiling face, and nothing else matters anymore. I don't know when life has ever been as sweet as it is right now, or when I've ever felt more comfortable in my own skin.

April 4

From: Sara
To: Stephanie
Subject: Finding our way

I'm so glad to hear that things are falling into place. This new day care sounds awesome, and it seems like Sara sure likes it. I love that they have their bouncy seats in a circle—I can just see that! You know, the more I think about going back to work part-time, the more I think that it would be really healthy for Anna to have some social time like that.

David and I had a Nextel dinner to go to last night, so friends of ours came over and kept her. It was the first time that someone other than our parents had watched her for us. (Of course, my friend Veronica happens to have a doctorate in neonatal nursing—how's that for a dream babysitter?!) But when Veronica tried to feed her at first, she'd cry every time until I took her. I thought, *Oh no!* But I actually think she's teething. Anyway, it just made me think that I don't want her to grow up clingy and scared of other people. So it's good to get them used to a social scene early, I think.

That's so great that you and Tim are meeting at Sara's day care a lot. It must be great to be so close. We really do have great husbands don't we? David is so into Anna now, too.

Yes, parenthood certainly gives you perspective. I'm glad that you're so comfortable. I'm so much more comfortable being a mother now myself, but I'm still trying to find my place in the world. I think that motherhood really was a big "What do you want to do with your life?" wake-up call for me. My marriage is good, I have purpose as a mother, but there's one more piece I still need to find.

I sent you something I tore out of an *O* magazine the other day. (If you haven't gotten it yet, you will soon.) It mentions what we always talk about—doing what's right for yourself without worrying what other people think about you. I'm still struggling with that—trying to get everyone to approve of me. So much so that I wonder if I even know what *I* want sometimes. Anyway, the article is a good reminder, and I hope you enjoy reading it as much as I did. It's been such a blessing to share these experiences with you—a real joy. Thanks for being a wonderful friend.

April 4

From: Stephanie
To: Sara
Subject: Frenzy at work

You know, it really surprises me to hear you say that you struggle so much with other people's approval. As your "wonderful friend" (thanks for saying so), I have to tell you that I admire *everything* you do! There isn't an *inch* of your home that couldn't be photographed for a magazine (even if, like my own, it suffers from the clutter of baby paraphernalia at times). You have amazing taste and good judgment in everything you say, do, wear, dress your baby in, write, read, and think. You're one of the most solid people I know. So quit kidding yourself: People approve of you when you're not even trying.

Anyway, my point is that you just need to be yourself. You've got approval from everyone you need approval from—just work on getting that into your thick head!

Just when I thought things were calming down at work, the girl I'm switching positions with has the whole office whipped into a big frenzy. Apparently, even though she's getting a better job and title and more experience, she found out that my salary is $5,000 per year more than hers. So she's on a campaign to discredit me in order to prove how bad they need her in my position. I feel so sorry for my boss, because I heard this girl yelling at him in her office today. He was trying to do a nice thing for us both, and it's turned into a big fat nightmare for him. She's so negative that it's really stressful to be at work in the middle of all this mess. I just want things to get back to normal again. I'm willing to do whatever we need to do to get past this and get back to work—I even told my boss to take the money for her raise out of my paycheck. I think that made him want to keep my salary as is even more.

In my opinion, she's making a huge mistake. She's letting a small amount of money get in the way because it's that whole "It's not fair" thing. People would be so much happier and better off in the business world if they just worried about themselves instead of comparing themselves to everyone else. If I ever have the chance to manage a business, I'm going to get a big sign printed that reads: "JUST WORRY ABOUT YOURSELF." I swear, if it weren't for the fact that I don't want to travel, I'd march into my boss's office and say, "Forget it. I'll just keep the job I have and she can keep hers." So, it's total Weirdville here. Politics—ugh.

It's hard enough to adjust to leaving your baby and coming back to work, since it's nothing short of having *two* full-time jobs. And if you happen to be the only parent in the workplace, it's even harder. They just don't get it around here. I'm definitely feeling the effects of being a parent . . . you know, people glancing at their watches when I walk out the door at *exactly* 5:29 P.M.

My boss is cool, though. I'm blessed that he believes that family comes first. I told him that I wanted all the days that I missed during my first two weeks back (during the day-care and smashed-cars escapade) to be counted against my vacation time so that no one would have to worry about my getting special treatment as a "parent" (which has actually been verbalized by a co-worker, believe it or not). He told me to forget about it, that it all comes out in the wash, and it was better to take a few days and get it all behind me than to take an hour a day and have it drag on for a month. And that it wasn't anybody else's business, because he's done the same thing for the others. (Gotta love him!) As long as I know that, those who are against me can all kiss my shiny white hiney, right through the maternity underwear that I'm wearing today because nothing else was clean. (And yes, for the record, they're baggy.)

April 5
From: Sara
To: Stephanie
Subject: Thank you

Thank you for your kind words. I'll keep reading them over and over, and maybe they'll stick! That was really nice to hear, especially coming from someone as capable as you are.

I can't believe your co-worker is making a big deal out of this. She's getting a good deal—why on earth would she insist on a raise, too? That's really bizarre. If she's trying to prove that she's more capable than you are, she certainly isn't getting off to a very good start, is she? Some people just don't get it. She sounds like one of those people who will wind up hanging herself if you give her enough rope.

But it's great that you won't have to take a pay cut! Sounds like you have a terrific boss, and that he knows who his good employees are. I'm sure that you're worth everything he's doing for you. Smart bosses know how to take care of their good people. And while all those other people at your office may not understand what it's like to be a parent, at least the most important person does (your boss). You just can't worry about what the rest of them think. You have a daughter to be there for when the workday is done. And I'd think that most *decent* people, even if they don't have children, could certainly respect that; if they can't, then obviously they're not decent people.

Hang in there!

April 6

From: Stephanie
To: Sara
Subject: Bitch session

I need to start the day with a quick bitch session. And guess who's at the core: *Tim, of course!* He's an awesome dad—better than I ever expected—but as a helpmate, everything I ask him to do is either forgotten or done halfway. Permit me to share some examples:

1. I asked him to vacuum the upstairs on Sunday. Then I reminded him again on Monday. Today is Friday, and it still hasn't been done.

2. I asked him to take some of my clothes with him to the dry cleaner, and one pair of my pants needed to be hemmed, so I asked him to have the cleaner do it. Today, the cleaning came back, and my pants aren't hemmed. (Luckily I didn't need them today—it's my only business suit that fits with my pregnancy-butt still in existence.) And one of my shirts was missing, so he has to go back again. What a waste of time.

3. I've been late for work every day because there's just too much to do in the morning to get Sara and myself out the door. So I gave Tim bottle duty: He has to wash her bottles from the day before, label them with that day's date, and fill them with formula (three bottles total—no big deal). When I opened her little cooler at day care today, the nipples weren't screwed on and there were no lids on the bottles. The formula was leaking everywhere, which means that when I get home I have to wash out the cooler, too. Luckily, I had some extra dry formula stored at the day care in case of an emergency, or she would have starved!

4. Last night was "bath night" for Sara, so I was running around like a maniac trying to get the daily load of laundry done, cook supper, straighten up a little, etc. I was actually sweating. Meanwhile, Tim's surfing the Net. So I asked him to do three things before he came to bed. Two out of the three were done—and only one out of the three was done correctly (I'll spare you the details).

Why is it that every time I ask him to help me, I would have saved time just doing it myself? I know it's not just me because I hear other women saying the same thing. Personally, I think this is a scam that men have been playing on women for a long time. It's the old "If I don't do a good job, she won't ask me to do it again" trick. Why else do we allow them to sit and watch sports on the weekends while we clean toilets? Well, I'm on to them.

I'd really like to know how to get Tim to help out more. It's too hard to pick up the slack now that I'm back at work. I'm very tired, but I admit that I'm too cheap to hire a maid. What we need is a solution that will stick, not just a nasty fight that motivates him for a few days and then goes away. Oh, if only Dr. Phil were here! Right now I think he'd kick Tim around the room for a good ten minutes and then give him the Comet and a toilet brush and put him to work. And he'd say, "How's that workin' for ya?"

Okay, I'm done. Got work to do.

April 6

From: Sara
To: Stephanie
Subject: Bathrobe bitch session

In response to your e-mail, let me first say that I don't know how you do it all! I'm still in my bathrobe as I type this. Of course, in my defense, this morning I've already conducted a phone interview, read the paper, given two feedings, done numerous diaper changes, and performed stirring renditions of both "Row, Row, Row Your Boat" and "Twinkle, Twinkle Little Star." But I can't imagine having to get to work on time. It's got to be tough, and by God, you need some help. That's part of the reason we got married, right? So we wouldn't be single parents?

And (sorry, Tim) how does anyone with a lick of sense pack bottles filled with formula in a cooler without putting lids on them? That's so pathetic it's downright funny (for me at least—I didn't have to clean it up). Would he have made that same mistake with freshly mixed Bloody Marys? I doubt it. You know what it is? Distraction. Men are in a constant state of it, so their minds aren't focused on what they're doing—at least when it's something *we* want them to do. That's why it's usually a half-assed job. They need to tune in . . . to engage . . . to be punched between the eyes. Or as Dr. Phil says, "be hit over the head with a two-by-four."

One thing that really helps David "see the light" is spending time with Anna on his own. Then he appreciates how much is involved in taking care of an infant. I know that Tim's had Sara on his own, like when you went to Texas, but sometimes they need frequent reminders, lest they forget. It's our nature as women and mothers to just do everything rather than have it done wrong or fight about it. It's an easy trap to fall into. But we don't want to do that, because we'll burn out in a hurry.

I advise that this Saturday or Sunday, you go out and have some "Stephanie time" and leave Tim with Sara *on his own*. You have to physically leave, too, so he can't say, "Will you hand me a bottle" or whatever. And not just for an hour or two, but for at least four hours or more. Give him a good dose.

Another word of advice is to just let him do things wrong and then bear the consequences. This is a tough one—I mean, it kills me to even see the towels folded any way other than the way I like them in the closet. But I think this is a good lesson for us as mothers, because soon we're going to have to allow our children to do things wrong and mess them up so that they can learn, and gain confidence in their ability. So it's good practice to do this with our husbands, who, in many ways, resemble children. Make Tim wash out the cooler if that was his fault, and get him to drop Sara off at day care and prepare all the stuff.

You can also do what I did once and go on strike: Just stop doing things that you don't want to do. Now I must preface this by saying that you have to pick things that have a consequence, like washing his underwear or paying the bills—something he'll *have* to do eventually. This takes a lot of willpower.

I have a fussy infant in my lap, and that was about all my advice anyway. I hope some of it helps. You can also try just having a heart-to-heart discussion about it (when you aren't trying to get Tim to do something) and tell him that you really need his help. And maybe start phrasing requests for help as "Can you help me, please?" instead of "Would you get your butt up off the couch and do something, you slack-ass?" In other words, say it in a way that will make him feel like a heel if he says no.

Okay, the fussy infant is now just plain ticked off. Typing an e-mail isn't fun for her anymore. Gotta run—good luck!

April 11
From: Stephanie
To: Sara
Subject: Justifiable homicide

I'm going to murder or at least severely maim my husband today.

I'm exhausted from working and taking care of the baby, which also doesn't help my mental state. I worked like a dog this weekend, and Tim didn't lift a finger except to play video games the *entire* time. I know that this is his getaway and that he's stressed out and needs some downtime, but I don't think he realizes that you don't get that much downtime once you become a parent. I need to clean the house tonight because we have guests arriving tomorrow. I've been so organized in preparing for our busy weekends—doing the grocery shopping one night, getting the beds ready another night, etc. Last night was bath night for Sara, and by the time I got back from the grocery store and made dinner, I just had nothing left. And just at that moment, I opened the freezer.

Tim had spilled coffee grounds all over the freezer more than a week ago, and it was still there. When I asked him, not very nicely, to clean it *now*, he had the nerve to mention some glasses that I'd left in the bedroom. That was the last straw. I exploded.

I can't live like this. I'm running myself into the ground. It's taking a toll on my mood and on me physically. I'm tired all the time, and my neck and back hurt. I'm miserable. Please don't get me wrong: I love him dearly, marrying him is the best decision I ever made, and he's the most wonderful father I've ever imagined. It's just that becoming a parent means a lot more work has to be done, and I feel like I'm the only one who's made the adjustment. All these little things add up to a lot of resentment on my part.

I was so proud of myself this first month for actually holding down a full-time, demanding job *and* having a new baby *and* running a home. But the way it makes me feel tells me that it's not worth it. I've made the executive decision to hire a maid, which I think will take a huge load off my shoulders. When Tim starts vacuuming and cleaning toilets on a weekly basis, I'll fire her.

Based on past performance, I'd say she'll have great job security.

Chapter 7

Motherhood Potpourri

April 23

From: Stephanie
To: Sara
Subject: Co-payment award show

Hey there! I imagine you've been as slammed as I have, and that's why I haven't heard a peep out of you. How was your trip? Did you mind leaving Anna? Tell me all about it!

I thought I was having the week from hell the last time we spoke. I was wrong: *This* is the week from hell. Sara and I are both sick with colds or allergies or something. Plus, Tim's out of town—and Sara and I have to fly up to Massachusetts to meet him on Friday for his grandmother's 90th birthday party/family-reunion thing. Which means that I'm trying to pack and prepare for a baby and myself, with no one to help take care of said baby, so needless to say, it's a slow process.

Sara's not sleeping well at night because she can't breathe, so I'm exhausted. Oh, and somehow I opened my big fat mouth and volunteered to make favors for the party guests (I have an infant and a full-time job—what was I thinking?). And then I get to come to work and battle all the bad attitudes and office politics.

But you'll be so proud of me . . . I finally broke down and hired some help! Yippee! I was in Nashville on business all day on Saturday, so the house is a pigsty. It's so bad that there are actually tufts of cat fur in the hallway (ick!). Before I left, I told Tim that the floors had to be cleaned and that I felt it was time to hire a maid; he said he'd take care of it. He was home alone all day with Sara and accomplished nothing other than taking care of a baby . . . typical Dad behavior. The condition of the house is stressing me out, so enough is enough. I'm interviewing my new housekeepers at lunchtime today. They're a husband-and-wife team, and I can hardly wait to meet my two new best friends!

Poor Sara is afflicted with what I like to call "first-time-parents disorder." Last week, we took her to the doctor because she had a fever and a cold (I figured that she was getting the virus I had). He told us to continue giving her Tylenol, but that because I was breast-feeding her, she probably wouldn't get my virus because I was passing all the antibodies to her through the milk.

Well, on Monday night, her hand looked a little swollen, and when I picked her up on Tuesday, it still looked swollen and she seemed feverish. No wonder: Her temperature was 102.4! The telephone-advice nurse told us to bring her in, so Tim and I brought her to the after-hours care facility. They gave her Tylenol again (a lot of it in a syringe this time), and the swelling in her hand disappeared—probably because we couldn't even remember which hand it was once we got there.

On the way home, we stopped for dinner and then went home to go to bed. But Sara was acting like she'd drunk 12 cups of coffee! She was so wired that I was sure they'd overdosed her. When we called them back, the nurse pissed Tim off because she asked him if this was his first child (sarcasm is *not* what you want to hear when you're accusing someone of overdosing your child). We took the baby's heart rate, and it was 185 (normal is 120 to 150). So we threw on clothes and rushed her to the emergency room . . . of course, by the time we got there, she was sleeping peacefully and her heart rate had dropped back to normal.

Tim assured the doctor that (having once been addicted to physical fitness) we knew how to take a heart rate, and we'd checked and double-checked it. The doctor's response was that a baby's heart rate can climb due to a fever. So, as we're walking out of the ER at 1:30 in the morning (with Sara peacefully sleeping in her car seat), disheveled and frustrated, Tim looks at me and says, "So, did we cover *every* co-payment on the insurance card today? Let's see, regular visit: $10; pharmacy: $15; after-hours care: $25; and ER: $50. . . . Yep, got 'em all!" That's got to be some kind of record.

Here's the moral of the story: If your infant is running a fever under 103, don't worry—just give her Infants' Tylenol. The only fevers you have to worry about in babies are the ones that don't respond to Tylenol or are over 103. I thought that one of 102 was pretty serious, but I guess a fever in babies is different.

Moral #2: If the people in the ER laugh at you, they're probably right—you're being ignorant. And as if we weren't feeling stupid enough, while we were at the ER, a lady hurried in with a tiny newborn and said that it was having trouble breathing. They rushed her to the back and grabbed oxygen masks on the way . . . and they weren't laughing at her. Ugh. It made me a little sick to my stomach, and extremely thankful at the same time.

Gotta go for now—at least I'll be coming home to a clean house and floors that don't make crunching sounds when we walk on them. Please give little Anna a big kiss for me. Isn't she just the most huggable little thing ever?

April 24

From: Sara
To: Stephanie
Subject: I need a third arm

My goodness—and I thought *my* life was a whirlwind! I'm so glad Sara's okay. Yeah, those ER people may laugh at you, but better safe than sorry in my book. I would have freaked out just like you guys did: It just means that you're good parents. Anna hasn't gotten sick with anything, so when she does, I'm sure I'll be a basket case. I have no experience whatsoever in this department.

God, aren't these babies of ours at a cute age? They truly are so kissable—I'm surprised Anna's cheeks aren't raw. She's so funny. We make that vibrating-lip noise at her all the time, and now she's trying to imitate us (but mostly she just spits). Sometimes she tries so hard that she just makes a noise to sound like the vibration. It's hilarious. She's also laughing more and more now. For example, the other day I started singing along with a Jolly Rancher commercial, and she got so cracked up. After 30 seconds, though, she was over it. I nearly killed myself making noises, singing and doing stunts trying to get her to do it again, but she just gave me this look like, "That's not funny." She's a tough audience.

It sure was difficult leaving her that morning we flew to Acapulco. David and I looked in on her as she slept in her crib, and of course I cried. I got a little teary on the plane, too, but once I talked to my mom and knew that all was going fine, I was okay. And surprisingly, I was fine flying this time—much better than I've been the past few times. (Maybe it was the double screwdriver and two glasses of wine, I don't know.)

I took your advice and wrote Anna a letter in a pretty little keepsake book, which I can add to over the years and give to her someday. I was writing it in bed, and David asked me what I was doing. I expected him to make fun of me, but instead he said, "Let me see it when you're finished," and then he wrote her, too!

Right now he's in Illinois visiting his grandpa. He's making the same journey that scared us last year with his plane incident. I told him that I hoped everything went well because I wasn't ready to get pregnant again. (Thankfully, he made it up there with no problems.)

I *finally* got Anna's birth announcements today. The factory said that they never received the order, so they were a week late—as if I wasn't already late enough. It's almost embarrassing to send them out now, but I'm going to. I was so frustrated after making my third trip to the stationery store and lugging Anna upstairs (the baby-announcement area is upstairs—how stupid!) that I told them to forget the ones I ordered and just do something that they could print right there. I feel like attaching an explanation to the announcements that says: "This announcement is late because I had postpartum depression and the stationery store screwed up. And yes, I realize that she looks nothing like this photo anymore, so please don't mention it to me . . . for your own good."

As well as God designed the female body to have babies, I think he forgot something very important: While the baby's growing inside her tummy, every mom should also grow a third arm! Think how much easier it would be to shop, write a check, and drive while finding the pacifier and looking for things in your pocketbook! It could wither up and fall off after a while—like the belly-button stump.

Anyway, let me know how your plane trip with Sara was, and how the party went. I hope you had fun. In regard to the party favors, we really need to learn to say no, don't we? I heard Oprah say something great about that the other day. She said if someone asks her to do something she doesn't want to, she says, "Let me pray about it." Then the next day she tells them, "Jesus said no." Isn't that awesome?

May 1
From: Stephanie
To: Sara
Subject: Babies and airplanes

Hey! The family reunion went great! Sara was an absolute angel: She let people hold her and pass her around all day, and never cried, not even once. Tim's grandmother kept asking me if this girl was real because she'd never seen a baby who didn't cry before (and at 90, she's seen a lot of babies!). The truth is, Sara loves the activity. One of the only things that makes her cry is being bored. Also, I think she got Tim's "social" gene—she really loves people. (We'll see if that changes when she's nine months old, which is when they're supposed to go through that "I hate strangers and I want my Mommy" stage.)

As for the airplane, it went great. I was so concerned about her crying and disturbing everyone around us, but when I got to our seat, the guy sitting next to me had just become a grandfather twice within the last two weeks; the people behind me had a small baby with them who *did* cry the entire trip, so they spent the entire flight walking her up and down the aisle so that everyone aboard could enjoy her act; and the guy next to them had an eight-month-old, so he was showing us photos and discussing breast-feeding and potty training right along with the rest of us. (I called it the "nursery section.") The bottom line is, people understand. And if they don't, they either will one day or they're just plain jerks, so who cares what they think?

The airline has it all worked out, though: You can check the stroller at the door of the airplane! So I was able to wheel her and all her belongings right up to the plane. Going through the airport was too funny: As I walked through, the crowd would part for me, and all I heard was "Ahh" and "Ooooh, she's so cute."

You definitely need to have them sucking (on a bottle, pacifier, or breast) during takeoff and descent, as it helps relieve the ear pressure. Also, I'd followed the advice of a magazine article and bought Sara her own seat so that I could strap her in her car seat. That's the only thing I'd do differently, because she stayed in my lap the whole time. It was nice to have the extra space, but I think that I would have rather had the money we spent on her ticket. The only pitfall was the x-ray lane in Atlanta: They made me collapse the stroller and put it on the conveyer belt, take the baby out of the car seat, put the seat on the conveyer belt, and walk through holding her. This sounds much easier than it is when you have a baby in one hand, your diaper bag and all your belongings in the other, and no one to help you. Luckily, there were two gentlemen who helped me all the way through. I don't know how I would have done it without them—I'd still be there trying to cram everything back underneath the stroller!

The return flight was the adventure, though (Tim was with us this time). Sometime over the course of the weekend, little Sara learned to squeal—you know, the kind that breaks glass and sends dogs running for cover. She was fed up with being in one place for two hours, so it didn't take much to set her off. As she's squealing in displeasure, Tim's looking at me like, "Can't you shut her up?!" and then, for some reason, the whole thing strikes me as hilarious! I couldn't stop giggling. There we were—all these people having to contend with my squealing baby—and there was absolutely nothing anyone could do about it except sit there.

Then, ten minutes after we took off, I realized that she'd made "stinky pants." I was afraid that I couldn't change her in our seats without activating the oxygen masks in the cabin. So I had to go to the lavatory and change her, which was an experience in itself. Lavatories, you see, are strategically placed in the tail of the plane (the part that moves around the most)—I think the airlines did this on purpose to deter passengers from using it. I'm sitting on the toilet seat, balancing a baby in my lap, trying my very best not to get any poopy on my sleeves or pants. Of course I only had ten inches to move my arms, so I had to do everything with my elbows bent. What a feat!

But what I've been dying to tell you about was my trip to Nashville last weekend. My company had an event at a mall that I had to attend, so I just flew up and back the same day. Since I'm still breast-feeding, I brought my trusty pump with me to relieve myself during my journey. However, when I reached the airport, I realized that I'd left the power cord at my office. Oh well, no turning back now.

By the late afternoon, I was extremely engorged and in pain. My breasts were huge! Since the event I had to attend was over and I had two hours to kill before my flight, what would any self-respecting normally small-breasted woman do in this situation?

I went to Victoria's Secret and tried on every push-up bra in the store! It was so much fun!

Since I've spent the majority of my life with the chest of a nine-year-old boy, you can imagine how entertaining this was for me. It was like I rented out Pamela Anderson's chest for an afternoon. They were beautiful! What a hoot! (Or should I say "hooters"?)

I guess I'm definitely a candidate for implants when I'm done birthin' babies. The only reason I'm determined to breast-feed for six months is so I can go through one summer with a bikini full of boobies. It really has nothing to do with the health or well-being of my child.

May 4
From: Sara
To: Stephanie
Subject: Is this 1950?

Why in the hell don't they put changing tables in airplane bathrooms? I mean, people *do* occasionally travel with babies. This stuff makes me so mad. And don't get me started on how rare it is to find a changing table in men's restrooms. (I can't tell you how many times David has taken Anna to the bathroom to change her, only to come back and hand her off to me because there was no place to change her.) Why isn't the world more accommodating to parents? I was at the beach this week with my mom, and trying to push Anna around in a stroller was a challenge. Aisles in the stores aren't wide enough, and if you have to go to a second floor, the ramp or elevator is always in the back of the building (if there even *is* a ramp or an elevator). Thank goodness for those disability laws that made businesses become wheelchair accessible, or we mothers would be up the creek.

I can't believe you in Victoria's Secret: You're sick and you need help, there's no doubt about it. I wouldn't have Pamela Anderson's chest if you paid me. But then again I've spent a lifetime (well, part of a lifetime anyway) trying to make mine look smaller. Weren't you just miserable being engorged? I can't imagine dealing with that all the time. It was so painful right after I had Anna.

Anna went for her four-month visit the other day, and she weighs 14 pounds, 4 ounces. (The doctor said that she had thunder thighs!) She started eating her rice cereal yesterday and she took right to it. She actually got mad when we stopped feeding it to her and gave her the bottle! How's Sara doing on cereal?

It's interesting that you mention the whole stranger-anxiety thing because Anna seems to be showing some of that already. She's freaked out a couple times when we've taken her to my parents' house: She kept looking around with this panicked look on her face, like she knew she wasn't at home. And she fusses now when someone holds her whom she doesn't know. The doctor said it's early for her to be doing this, so I hope she'll snap out of it soon.

May 4
From: Stephanie
To: Sara
Subject: Sara #2 hates cereal

Sara isn't doing well with cereal. I've tried everything: mixing in apple juice or applesauce; the wheat kind flavored with yogurt; making it warmer, runnier, or thicker—you name it. And the antics that I perform while trying to get her to eat . . . let's just say that if there wasn't a baby in the room, Tim would have me committed. Sara does laugh at me, but as soon as I stick the spoon in her mouth, she starts to cry and spits it all back out. If you remember, we went through this with the bottle, too. I have a feeling that we just have a "bad eater" on our hands. I figure it's okay—maybe it will help her stay thin later in life. I also think that I just have to keep offering it to her, and eventually she'll acquire a taste for it. But I tell ya, if I had the time, I'd like to make my own baby food—there are so many recipes and good information on that. (I also bought a baby-massage video last week, and she loves it!)

Ms. Catherine and Ms. Brenda, her day-care teachers, asked me this morning if I wanted them to work on the whole cereal thing (they're the ones who got Sara to drink from a bottle, which she does quite nicely now—what a stress reliever for me!). So, I guess I'll let them try. They're so awesome! They kiss and hug her before they hand her over to me every afternoon. They've made such an impact in Sara's life, and she just adores them. They're my heroes! It makes it so much easier on me to know that she truly enjoys being there.

So, Sara #1, you and I have a big holiday coming up—our *first* Mother's Day. I'm not taking any chances with Tim to figure it out on his own: I cut out a coupon for a local day spa and gave it to him with my choices highlighted. I've been told that men like it when you just tell them what to do: Don't make 'em think too much—they're not used to it. I just want to be greased up, massaged, and have someone rub my feet and hands. I used to get a manicure and pedicure almost every week, but now there's no way I'd give up my lunch hour with Sara to have my nails painted.

I saw some photos of myself from Easter weekend, and it drove me to spend an hour (and 150 bucks) at the Estée Lauder counter this weekend. I just felt like I needed an update, since my makeup and hair rituals got a little scaled back due to pregnancy and motherhood. Yeah, I may have been 20 minutes late for work this morning, but *my makeup looked great!* It's really hard to do all that beauty stuff in the morning and get a baby ready, too. But I think it's really important for Tim's sake *and* to set a good example for Sara as well. The long hair, on the other hand, is quite a struggle: Tim begs me not to cut it, but what a pain in the butt it's becoming.

We're having a family portrait made this Saturday. I want to capture all of us since Sara is at such a cute age right now. *I can't believe she's five months old already!* Where did the time go? I feel like I just brought her home from the hospital last week. I keep hugging her every morning and thinking about how great it is that I can pick her up to hug her. You're only able to do that for a couple years out of their life! I keep telling her to stop growing so fast because I'm going to miss having a little baby to cuddle. Guess we'll just have to make more. . . .

May 5
From: Sara
To: Stephanie
Subject: I come from a long line of swine

I think Anna has unfortunately inherited my eating gene.
(Of course, David's a hearty eater, too.) David's said things to her
like, "Hey, chubby girl," and alarms immediately went off in my
head. I told him not to start that: I went into the whole girls-and-
their-weight thing and how you might be able to get away with
saying that to a boy, but not a girl. (Being one of three boys, he
doesn't realize some of these things.) We discussed how so much
of a girl's self-esteem and future relationship with men is determined on her relationship with her dad. I told him that I don't
ever want us to make her self-conscious about her weight. I even
made him read an article I'd torn out of a magazine (I'm the kind
of woman who really likes to drive a point home!). Anyway, he
got it—and he hasn't said anything like that since (probably for
fear of what I'd do to him).

I'm not sure what I'm going to get for my first Mother's Day.
I haven't made any suggestions, but now that you mention it,
that whole massage thing sounds pretty nice. And I know what
you mean about updating your look: I have the same desire—
a new haircut, *something*. I'm still trying to make sense of my
whole life (I'm reading Dr. Phil's book *Self Matters*). Let's see, read
an entire book and analyze every facet of my life, or go get a
makeover? Hmm . . .

May 7
From: Stephanie
To: Sara
Subject: Mommy-vision

One of the things I love most about being a mom is how differently you see things now, and how much you notice things
that you never noticed before. For example, I went to the crafts
store last night, and I can't wait to come up with little projects
for Sara and me to do together. There's so much in that store for

little hands to do. If only her motor skills were developed beyond grabbing her toes.

Every day I spend my lunch hour with her, and it's the best hour of my day. No TV, no housework, nothing cooking on the stove, no distractions—just one hour of pure togetherness. I feed her in the nursing room, and then we walk around the church grounds admiring the flowers and birds. She's so cute, because when we first started our walks, I'd bend down and show her the "pretty flowers," take her hand in mine, and gently touch the petals with her fingers. Now when I bend down to show her, she stretches out her little arm and gently touches them all by herself. It's so cute—it's like she knows that this is what she's supposed to do.

She's such a great little buddy. Some people are amazed that I see her every day during lunch. They say things like, "Wow, you're really dedicated—that takes discipline." Frankly, I have no idea what they're talking about. I absolutely *love* spending that hour with her. We walk around outside and sit on a park bench and sing songs. That one hour gets me through the entire day.

I got such a kick out of the other mothers at day care today because they were all in the hallway discussing tips for potty training. It's really such a short time in your life that you get the privilege of mothering a small child. I always think about how this is going to be such a brief period in our lives—they grow so fast.

It's "teacher-appreciation week" at day care. To me, this is an opportunity to butter up those teachers, so I've really outdone myself. On Monday, they got little gift bags of pretty candles and a card with Sara's photo on the front; on Tuesday, I filled a little gift bag with Hershey's Kisses and put Sara's Valentine photo on the front with a caption that read "Kisses from Sara," and rubber-stamped the outside of the bag with red lips. For today, I found a three-foot-tall windmill of flowers with a frog in the middle. I took a photo of each baby in her class with my digital camera, cut out their faces, and glued them to the center of each flower on the windmill. Then I used plaster to fasten it into a terra-cotta pot, and did a bubble coming out of the frog's mouth that reads, "We Love Our Teachers." They loved it, and so did the other parents. I'll probably be updating it for months, because it's now a permanent part of their classroom. I figure that by the end of the week I'll go to pick her up and she'll be sitting on a throne wearing a tiara, while they massage her feet and rub Rogaine on her head (she's still so bald).

So I'm feelin' all good about life when I ran into an acquaintance back at the office. She's one of those people who can't see the good in anything and never stops complaining. As usual, she was going on and on about something trivial. She should have a baby: Being elbow-deep in baby shit at 3 A.M. with a new package of diapers (that you can't open one-handed) in one hand, and the legs of a kicking and screaming baby in the other, when you realize that you can't reach the diaper-rash lotion . . . now *that's* the kind of stuff that gives you perspective.

May 14
From: Sara
To: Stephanie
Subject: Get crazy with the glue gun

What a refreshing e-mail to find in my inbox between e-Business Daily and "50 percent off at Amazon.com" (except for that part about being elbow-deep in poop). I don't know how you do everything you do. All those things you made for the day care—I don't feel like I have time to do any of that and I don't work! What's your secret?

Did you ever think you'd be so maternal? I remember the Stephanie I first met, who wasn't even sure she wanted to have kids. Obviously, you were *meant* to. You've taken to it like a duck to water. A duck with a glue gun.

I got so many nice Mother's Day cards (and thank you so much for yours!). My mom sent me a wonderful one with a photo she'd taken of Anna while we were in Mexico: She's naked in the middle of her basket of stuffed animals, with a huge grin on her face. It's absolutely adorable.

Isn't it cute how they're grabbing at everything now? I can't hold Anna and have a drink in my hand anymore because she's trying to get into everything. And she's so fascinated by the dogs: She laughs and smiles when they're around and grabs handfuls of their fur. I'm coaching both her and the dogs on how to handle this.

Have you heard of Creative Memories? Have you ever done anything with it? I'm going to check it out next week. A friend of mine is doing a scrapbook for her daughter, and it's beautiful. I have all these different little books with things in them—it would be really nice to do one big book with everything.

I know what you mean about perspective—children definitely give you that. They make you think about your own life totally differently as well. Being a mother definitely makes me want to be a better person. I think that that's where some of this life reevaluation stuff comes from—I mean, I thought I'd have it so much more together by this point in my life. I want to be someone Anna will strive to be like, and I want her to be proud of me.

Well, I better go. Anna's asleep upstairs napping in Mommy and Daddy's bed, and it's about time for her to wake up. Wouldn't want her to try to land a dismount out of an adult bed!

May 15
From: Stephanie
To: Sara
Subject: Lunchtime, starring your favorite puppets

We're still having trouble getting Sara to eat cereal. Her beloved day-care teachers told me to bring it in, and they'd teach her. You would not believe the act I put on to get her through two tablespoons of cereal, but I confess that it does involve puppets.

To answer your question about how I get all that stuff done—well, first, I'm tired . . . very, very tired. Second, my company is up on the auction block again, so I have a total of two things to do most days at the office now. It's really bizarre.

Sara is grabbing at the cats, just like Anna's grabbing at the dogs. She's mesmerized by them. Thank God I had them declawed—I'm constantly prying cat fur out of her fists. We're enjoying her so much. She smiles all the time now, and she's doing that spitting thing that you were telling me Anna does.

Well, gotta go feed the kid.

May 24
From: Stephanie
To: Sara
Subject: The latest Triplett family health update

Okay, so I finally recovered from whatever cold/sore-throat virus Sara brought home to us from day care last week, and Tim's over his bout with pinkeye. However, now I've injured my back (I suspect from carrying the car seat around). I'm in extreme pain (let's just say that I could use one of those epidurals right now). And as of yesterday, Sara contracted a diarrhea virus that's been going around . . . so I have that to look forward to. With our luck, it will probably hit right around next weekend, since we're going to a NASCAR race. That means we'll be spending a lot of time in the delightful bathrooms at Lowe's Motor Speedway.

I just want to be well again: Either Tim or I have suffered some sort of ailment *every* week for the past six. Now we disinfect Sara when she comes home every night (put on new clothes, wash her hands and face, etc.). This is one of the many disadvantages of having a child in day care.

As for the scrapbook hobby, of course I'm all over it. And it's not been a good thing for our bank account. Let's just say that I'm already a member of the "lifetime 20 percent discount" at the local scrapbook store. I wouldn't dare confess to you how much you have to spend to reach that level, but suffice it to say, Tim would not be happy. He'll appreciate it when we're 80, and Sara's all grown up, right?

May 25
From: Sara
To: Stephanie
Subject: Haircut, and life evaluation

I'm sorry I'm just getting back to you. I had so much more time to e-mail when I was working!

You're in the Creative Memories cult, too? That's so cool! I wish I'd started this years ago—now I have the daunting task of going through hundreds—no, thousands—of photos.

How's Sara doing with her cereal? Have you tried any vegetables? Holding true to her family heritage (on both sides of the tree), Anna's eating anything and everything that's put in front of her.

I can't believe you guys have been so sick. How frustrating. I'm amazed that you actually like Atlanta: Since you've been there, you've been sick constantly and had a tree fall on both your cars. And that's in less than a year's time, right? Are you sure you haven't done something to tick off the Almighty?

You're thinking of cutting your hair? I did, and I really like it (at least the maintenance part). I went for the messy Meg Ryan look, and it takes me all of about five minutes to dry and style it. I was ready for something different, since I'd had the same style forever. I thought I'd miss my long hair, but I really don't. Besides, I can always grow it back if I want.

The haircut is part of reevaluating my life (only a woman could say that). I bought an audio book by Cheryl Richardson, and I'm trying to take some of her advice. I'm "eliminating the energy drains" in my life by clearing out all the clutter and trying to wrap up unfinished business like setting up Anna's college fund, etc. My freelancing load has been thankfully light of late. I'm still not sure what I want to do as far as work. I know the perfect solution—it's just that it doesn't exist (co-working, and co-parenting).

Wouldn't it be awesome if David and I could each work fewer hours and trade off working and being with the kids? Then they'd never have to be in day care, and both of us could have our careers. It would probably involve a pay cut, but we're taking that by me quitting work anyway. I guess the only way we'll ever be able to do that is if we own our own business. And I'm not sure that David's all that keen on trading work for Daddy-duty anyway.

Sometimes it's hard not to be resentful of him. Dads get it all: They get to have children without missing a beat in their career, interact with adults all day and eat a decent lunch without feeding anyone but themselves, and then come home to kids who light up when they walk in the room. They can become dads without losing themselves. It's harder for us moms to not get lost in the shuffle, but I refuse to. Somehow I know that I'll find the balance.

I guess that finding a way to offset mommyhood with individuality is relatively new ground, since there are pressures on both sides. My parents expected me to go to college; there was no question about that. They wanted me to have a career and be successful, and I knew that they wanted me to have kids someday. But no one ever told me how I was supposed to balance doing both. You know, I bet if men were the ones who had babies, the workplace would be a lot more family friendly.

May 30

From: Stephanie
To: Sara
Subject: Mommy and the ER

You haven't heard from me because I spent most of the other morning in the ER. I went to the chiropractor to try to help my back, but that seemed to make it worse. I've been in a drug-induced coma for the past two days, and of course, I can't breast-feed due to all the narcotics in me. So I've been pumping, and we've been bottle-feeding Sara at night (what a pain in the ass—how'd you guys get through that?)

Anyway, it's a little better today. I stopped taking the pain pills and muscle relaxants so I could feed her again (I'm afraid my milk will dry up, and I don't want this to be the reason I stop breast-feeding). But it still hurts a lot, and I can't lift anything.

You cut your hair—that means you've graduated to true Mommyhood! I've been battling the idea. I don't look good with short hair; I just don't have the face for it. And Tim hates the thought of me cutting it. But little Sara's grip is getting better and better, and she sure loves my hair. The first thing I do when I get home is put it in a ponytail, so I'll probably break down and cut it this month. Well, gotta go for now!

Chapter 8

Ruling the World with an Iron Underwire

June 4

From: Stephanie
To: Sara
Subject: Boobies are power

If you recall, my breast-feeding efforts have been dwindling due to my need for two days of muscle relaxants, brought on from a back injury last week. Well, my body has now begun to wean itself against my will, and it's put me into a state of pure panic.

Today I wish to follow up on our phone discussion of boobies and breast-feeding. I believe that after you completed your breast-feeding stint, your exact words to me, were, "You just wait . . ." Well, I feel the need to make a point here. At least you *have* boobs when you're not breast-feeding. Okay, so maybe they're a little droopier now—well, get over it. Think about *me* . . . I'm about to leave the euphoria of cleavage and go back to my reality, which is much like life as a nine-year-old boy!

No more dinners with Tim (not to mention other hungry patrons) staring down my shirt. Now I'm going to be reduced to having eye contact like everyone else. I don't want eye contact—I want to be looked at, ogled, and thought of in ways so disrespectful that a well-seasoned porn star would blush.

After having led a life of flat-chestedness, I've basked in the glory of full, beautiful breasts. I can't pass a Victoria's Secret without trying on the latest push-up bra (what those things can do in repositioning human tissue is a mystery in physics—at which even Einstein himself would marvel).

For months, I've spent time every morning bending over in front of the mirror, admiring my newfound gifts from the mammary goddesses and thoroughly enjoying my good fortune. (And I've thought that "Le Leche" was French for "Nice boobs, madame.") For the first time in my life, I've understood the "jogging jokes," what an underwire was for, and how many heads you can turn when you enter a chilly room. My breasts actually *touched* for the first time in my life, for God's sake! Yet somehow my family didn't appreciate the celebratory phone calls that day.

I haven't wasted a single opportunity to flaunt, jiggle, unbutton, or lean over for the sake of admiration of my two new friends. My efforts in dressing, sleeping, showering, and even walking have all changed as a result of my newfound voluptuousness. I've even been tempted to "sit" them on a counter of appropriate height now and then—you know . . . the bank-teller's window, the box office at the theater . . . the nice man at the DMV even moved me right to the front of the line—gosh, he was thoughtful; I guess their new training programs have really paid off.

I look forward to sauntering from the pool to my lounge chair this summer without worrying about who's looking at my ass. When you have big boobies, who *cares* about your ass? Your butt could be as big as Mount Rushmore and no one would ever know—as long as you're wearing one of those skimpy Jennifer Lopez-type bikini tops that leaves them wondering, "Was that part of her nipple I just saw?"

No, my dedication to breast-feeding has had nothing to do with the nourishment of my precious child—that's just a bonus. This is strictly about my own vanity. Face it, honey: Droopy or not, boobies are power. I love 'em. If I would have had them when I was single, I'd have ruled the world with an iron underwire. Anyway, I think I've made my point. So shut up and go buy yourself a push-up bra from Victoria (she has really cute matching panties, too). Gravity's no match for Vickie!

I remain (for now) yours in cleavage. . . .

June 8

From: Sara
To: Stephanie
Subject: Big guns

You're definitely not going to get that Mother of the Year award now.

But at least you have the benefit of my experience. No one told me that my breasts would turn into flabby mush and lose a cup size as soon as I stopped breast-feeding, or I might not have stopped so quickly (no, I still would have). Just blow up a balloon and then deflate it to find out what's going to happen when you stop nursing.

Life with breasts isn't all it's cracked up to be. Sure, you can appreciate being ogled now because you have the self-esteem based on a lifetime of actually being appreciated for your brains and having people look you in the eye when they talked to you. But had you dealt with this since age 14, it would have gotten *really* old by, oh, say age 16. Plus, it's a lot harder to look skinny with big boobs: You have to be pencil-thin because boobs just tend to make you look fat, especially in those big, chunky winter sweaters. Ever notice how all those J.Crew models are flat-chested?

And I'm sure you never had to endure hearing your brother-in-law announce to everyone as you arrived in your swimsuit the first day of family vacation: "Here she comes with the big guns!"

So there.

June 11

From: Stephanie
To: Sara
Subject: ERs and beauty salons

Well, we ended up in the ER again last week. Day care called around 4:30 and said that Sara was vomiting nonstop. I happened to be sitting in the chair at the beauty salon getting my hair highlighted at the time. Just as the stylist walked out with the dye and aluminum foil, the phone rang. Luckily I stopped her (can you imagine me showing up at the ER with my hair full of foil?). Anyway, Tim met me at the day care and we went straight to the ER.

It was the most pitiful thing I've ever seen: Sara vomited about six times in two hours. And it was so sad to see her that sick because it was like it came from her toes! Her whole head turned red (of course it's easy to see since she still doesn't have any hair).

They couldn't figure out what was wrong, so they did x-rays and some blood work. They gave her an IV for about an hour, and that seemed to do the trick. Of course she wouldn't drink any Pedialyte, even though we tried everything: putting it in her bottle, heating it, flavoring it with apple juice, etc. So they told me to give her breast milk only (no formula), which is easier said than done these days. I'm only feeding her about twice a day and a couple times during the night, so I didn't have enough milk to feed her for the next 24 hours. I kept explaining that to the doctor and the nurse, and they still kept giving me the same instructions.

Finally, I lost it: "Look! I keep telling you that I'm weaning her!" I snapped. "I only feed her twice a day! I can't just snap my fingers and have milk appear! Don't you people know *anything* about breast-feeding? Or are you just not listening?!" I was really concerned about Sara getting dehydrated. Anyway, the IV helped, and the nurse came to release us at midnight. She said, "Okay, Sara is diagnosed with vomiting." I thought Tim was going to rip her head off. *Um, thanks—we didn't need to spend the last six hours in the ER to figure that out.* Basically, they couldn't tell us why. "Probably a virus" was their best answer.

Little Sara was so awesome at the hospital. As you can imagine, it's not easy trying to put an IV into an infant's vein—they had to use a light in a dark room just to find one. She didn't cry when they put it in, and even the nurse was amazed. She told Sara to go out and show the big kids how to take an IV. She's such a good baby, which makes it even worse when she's sick.

Anyway, Tim left for a training meeting in Virginia Beach the next morning. Sara and I joined him over the weekend, but now he's supposed to go out of town again this week. So I can't get anything done because I don't get a break when I'm alone. I honestly don't understand how single parents survive! I was rushing around the house like a maniac last night trying to get everything unpacked, washed, and organized because I can't get anything done when Tim's gone except take care of Sara.

Our trip really messed up her schedule. She's having a fit trying to eat baby food again, and she's been so fussy (from being tired, I'm sure). She's also going through that "Mommy thing": She cries every time I leave the room. I call it "Mommy-itis." I don't know what's changed, but she won't go to just anyone anymore either. She's suddenly developed a fear of strangers out of nowhere.

Anyway, I wanted to tell you that we "sucked the marrow" out of the weekend on Sunday. We decided to skip our first flight at 4 P.M. and take a later one so that we could play some more. *I can't begin to tell you what a colossal mistake that was!* The next flight was full, so we didn't get out of Virginia Beach until 8:45 P.M., which means that we didn't get home until midnight. It was too much for me and little Sara . . . and I paid for it last night. Sucking the marrow out of the weekend isn't such a good idea with an infant.

June 12

From: Sara
To: Stephanie
Subject: Sucking the marrow out of life

I can't believe you were in the ER again! You must be the baby-illness expert by now. I know nothing, because Anna's never been sick. When she does get sick, we're going to panic— hell, we don't even own a thermometer!

I wonder what made Sara that ill. It's so hard when they feel bad because they can't tell you anything. Did you end up giving her formula? Are you having any luck getting her to eat solids? I've noticed that Anna is pooping a lot more: I wonder if that's good or bad.

I'm afraid that I committed a big no-no with her the other day: I gave her a chocolate-chip cookie. Can you believe that? I've got no excuse—I know better. It's just that I was eating some of those little Famous Amos cookies, and she was staring at each one as I ate it. Her eyes would follow the cookie from my hand to my mouth, and she had this look of intense longing . . . so I caved. I put one in her little hand, and she immediately jammed it in her mouth. Stephanie, if her eyes could have talked, I swear they would have said, "Thank you, Mommy. This is what I've been waiting for my whole little life." She managed to gum about a fourth of it and smear it all over her face, clothes, and hands. The cookie was no bigger than a quarter to start out with, yet with just a little piece of it, she was able to create a huge mess. And she pooped four times the next day. My mom said to give her a sugar cookie next time.

Sucking the marrow out of life is good, as long as it doesn't suck the marrow out of *you*. I don't know how you do what you do *and* work full-time. Speaking of work, how are things there? As for me, I'm really starting to enjoy being at home. I love being a mother and reading books to Anna and playing with her. I'm never bored: There's always something to do (or something I want to do). I'm even thinking about taking up sewing. I realize that I've gotten a lot of my self-worth in the past from working— actually from making money. Well, I'm starting to realize more and more that money isn't the point. Not that I wouldn't like to make some, especially with my shopping habits of late. But it doesn't define who I am anymore. It's like you said awhile back: Being a parent really puts things in perspective for you. It makes the things we used to agonize over seem pointless now.

Yet I still want to do something for *me* (something in addition to being a mother). I don't think it's writing advertising copy, although it's giving me some extra cash at the moment. After I had Anna, I felt like the world was shut off from me—as if so many possibilities were off-limits because I had a baby. Now I realize it's just the opposite: This is the perfect time in my life to explore what I really want to do, to discover what really makes me happy. There aren't fewer possibilities now; in fact, there are more. The only thing limiting me is my brain. I'm learning how easy it is for my own mind to put me in a box with thoughts like *You can't do that . . .* or *What would your mother say?*

There are so many things I want to give Anna, none of which are tangible. I want to give her a strong sense of independence; I want her to know that it's great to be a woman—an honor; I want her to believe in herself; I want her to never feel that she can't do something just because she's a woman; I want her to have the freedom of knowing that David and I will always love her, no matter what path in life she chooses; and I want her to know that other people's opinions really don't matter.

One thing's for sure: Kids need to know that their parents love them and are proud of them their whole lives through. So we can never stop telling them so, even when they're grown up and have kids of their own. Okay, I'm done.

Well, we're off to my sister's wedding this weekend. Family visits have a whole new meaning now: babysitters!

June 12

From: Stephanie
To: Sara
Subject: Grr . . . I've become an adult

I don't feel like we had a vacation at all. We just ran and ran—poor Sara is still trying to recover (she took a three-hour nap yesterday). You know, I realize that I've become an adult, and it's made me as mean as a snake. More about that later—I want to respond to your e-mail first.

First and foremost: *Go buy a digital baby thermometer, you freak!* Don't you know by now that it's an essential piece of baby equipment?! Take it from the "sick-baby expert"—the first thing the doctor will ask you is the baby's temperature. And if you don't have a definite answer, you've lost credibility with him in seconds.

Also remember that temperatures in babies are different from adults. They don't really take it seriously unless it's over 103 and doesn't respond to Infants' Tylenol or Motrin. Anna's not sick because she's not in day care—just wait till you start exposing her to other babies. By the way, also purchase a vaporizer (*not* a humidifier) for her first cold—it works miracles! The vaporizer is hot steam and lets you put some Vicks inhaler stuff in it. It made a *huge* difference for Sara's cold symptoms. (They're under 20 bucks, too.)

And no, Sara still isn't eating baby food well—there's *no way* I could get her to eat a cookie! The only thing she'll put in her mouth are the "un-edibles": you know, car keys, her clothes and toys, and pretty much anything that will fit into her mouth that *isn't* food. Tim and I didn't help the situation either, because we didn't try to feed her baby food all weekend—it was just too easy to give her a bottle.

I really appreciate and agree with everything you said about what you want to teach Anna. I think the same things so often—I'm just afraid that when we get to the point that it's time to teach them that stuff, we'll have forgotten how to say it!

But back to the main topic of the day. Here's evidence of my plight: Tim just called me to let me know that he missed his flight out of town. Why, you ask? Well, first of all, he waited until this morning to pack (his flight left at 10 A.M.). In my opinion, that was his first mistake because you never know what's going to occur when you wait until the last minute. He proceeds to tell me that the reason he was late is because while he was packing, he decided to sterilize some of Sara's nipples. He forgot they were boiling on the stove, so he caught the stove on fire; consequently, the house is filled with smoke and fire-extinguisher solution. While the fire alarm was going off, he threw his cell phone down on the bed. I had some clean, folded towels lying there, and his phone landed underneath them. It took him another 30 minutes to find the phone (because, being a man, he'd never think to look *under* something). He called me to tell me to stop and buy more nipples because all of Sara's are scorched.

Of course all this comes after last night's fight. Now please keep in mind that Tim's *only* baby duty is the bottles. The problem is that he'll wash them one at a time (just what he needs at the moment)—so every time poor Sara's hungry, she has to sit and wait (and cry) until we wash a bottle. I asked him to please wash *all* the dirty ones at once (except I didn't ask that nice).

Anyway, I've come to the conclusion that as an adult, I'm a complete bitch. I'm in "get it done" mode all the time, and it's made me lose all my joy. I found myself at the beach this weekend scolding Tim like a two-year-old because he didn't spread the blanket out on the sand the way I wanted him to. (Of course, I also asked him three times not to put Sara's chair in the sand because I didn't want little grains all over my suitcase, but he plopped it right down anyway.) One of our friends told him that he didn't know how Tim put up with me. While I'm very embarrassed about the way I behaved, I wish that these people could understand that Tim, while loads of fun at a party, is extremely frustrating to live with at times.

For the next eight weeks he's traveling at least three days a week—that makes it very hard, because I don't get a break. Plus, I have to prepare for his absence and try to get everything done in the few days he's here because I have to take care of Sara without any help while he's gone. He never thinks ahead to try to make things easier for me in his absence (like wash the bottles)—he's too busy getting ready for his next trip.

So, I'm working and dealing with the office politics (which are still going on) all day, and then trying to be a good Mommy at night, and quite frankly, I don't think I can do both. It's making me mean. I resent Tim because I do so much more than he does. He sat and talked on the phone for over an hour on Monday night, while I literally *ran* around the house unpacking the baby and me, getting laundry done, preparing for his trip, and trying to recover from the weekend.

I have so much resentment in me because I never stop working, and I *never* get to do anything *I* want to do (like work on Sara's scrapbook or write). My house is so unorganized, and that's the last thing on my list, so naturally I'm stressing over that, too. The maids are a tremendous help, but they only come every other week, so there's still plenty of housework to be done.

I went to the chiropractor and massage therapist last night for an hour (still trying to recover from injuring my back two weeks ago), but I couldn't relax. My mind just kept thinking of everything that had to be done at home and at work (I have a big presentation coming up).

Tim told me last night that he hates the way I talk to him. I don't even know that I sound so terrible, but I *do* know that I'm annoyed with him. All his little mistakes add up to a lot of resentment and more work. So you see, I envy your staying home. But as hard as it all is, I still can't justify giving up my income. Plus, Tim is totally against my quitting work. I hate where I am right now because I don't think I'm doing anything well. I'm paddling upstream as hard as I can, but the boat isn't moving. And the marriage oar isn't quite in the water right now. I'm putting so much effort into Mommyhood and work that I just don't have enough left over to be a good wife, too.

There just isn't a clear answer here. I'm living day-to-day, and you and I both know that's no good. If I didn't work full-time, I wouldn't expect so much from Tim—but the fact that we both have jobs is why I don't understand how I get stuck with all the chores at home. I can't make him see that, because he can't think for himself about what has to be done. I have to tell him everything (and he willingly admits that). I suppose that once his traveling stint is over, things will calm down a little. I need to clone myself.

June 13
From: Sara
To: Stephanie
Subject: Falling into roles

I know that this e-mail is the last thing you have time for right now, but I have to write when I can. Anna's sleeping right now, sideways in her crib (her new trick of late). So read this later if you need to.

I feel for you, and can understand some of your pain. I get frustrated with David and feel overwhelmed—and I don't have an eight-to-five job! Don't you realize now why women are mothers? Although I do think that some of this simply comes from necessity as we fall into our roles. But while men know that someone will be there to pick up their slack, women don't have that luxury.

You're talking to Tim that way because you're so frustrated and resent him for taking advantage of you. That's natural, but it doesn't help things (I know because I've done the same thing). Something has to give: If you don't want to quit working, hire someone to help you. You can't do everything. And that way you could spend your time at home with Sara, not doing laundry.

It's not fair that you have to do so much more—Tim should help you equally. Maybe you can find a time to talk to him about it when you aren't upset. Maybe he'd be more responsive if you guys were *talking* about it instead of *arguing* about it. And remember, marriage, like everything else in life, has its cycles: It's not going to be hunky-dory all the time. You're having a tough time right now—babies are demanding little things, and you and Tim both have demanding jobs. It *will* get better as Sara gets older, but right now life is all about the division of labor. Plus, you and Tim have been traveling so much that it doesn't give you that time to regroup and take care of things at home on the weekend.

It sounds like your life is out of balance. *You need some time for yourself.* You need to get away for a few hours at night or on the weekend to decompress, so go out by yourself and see a movie or something. But whatever you do, don't take the baby, and *don't feel guilty!*

Well, Anna's waking up, so I've gotta go. I know I haven't given you much wisdom, but if I had the answer to this issue, I'd be rich and have lots of free time!

June 14

From: Stephanie
To: Sara
Subject: Another theory gone awry

Here's a shocker: Until I had Sara, I was always so awkward around babies. I didn't know how to hold them, or really know anything about them. I always thought that once I had one of my own, holding other babies would come easy. Well, my theory has been proven wrong today. A co-worker and his wife just had a baby, and she brought their five-week-old in today for us to see. I asked to hold him, washed my hands (of course), and thought it would be a breeze. Wrong! I'm so used to holding a six-month-old that holding a newborn was really strange. His head had to be held, and his back wasn't stiff—he just kind of melted into my hands like a sack of potatoes. It really surprised me!

Gosh, I can't even remember when it was that much work to hold Sara—now I just tuck her under one arm and go. I have to admit that I'm not willing to trade: She's so much more fun than that little newborn who can't look at you and has no expression. I came back to my office and looked at her photo when she was five days old, and if I weren't the one holding her, I'd swear it was someone else's child.

It makes me realize how priceless photos and videos are—and those scrapbooks we're working on are going to be like gold. I loathe the fact that it goes by so quickly. It's not fair. And I feel like I'm missing so much when I'm working.

I'm only breast-feeding Sara a couple times a day now, so my milk supply is starting to diminish. I'm really not ready to stop it, though. It's a stage that's ending, and I think that's what's really bothering me. I love that we can be that close. And she's so funny now that she can roll over and move better. When she wakes up at night, she rolls over with her head bent upward and her mouth opened as wide as she can—as if she's hoping that a nipple will just happen to fall in there. It cracks me up. She looks like a baby bird begging for a worm. Isn't it great to be so deeply in love with such a little someone?

Remember when Sara was sleeping through the night and I was so happy—and Anna had you up several times during the night and you were miserable? And I told you that times might change . . . well, that time is now. Sara is such a poor eater that we can't get enough formula or baby food in her to last through the night. So now *I'm* the one getting up to make bottles twice every night.

Ever since she had that vomiting virus and had to go to the ER, she'll only take about two or three ounces of formula at a time. Which means that we're back to feeding her every two and a half to three hours again. And since the breast-milk supply is dwindling, I can't just pull her over to me and latch her on while we both snooze. It sucks.

I'm so tired that I'm thinking about volunteering for a work-related overnight trip just so I can sleep through an entire night for the first time in seven months! Maybe it's time for Daddy to take over for one or two of those late-night feedings, huh? In fact, this Sunday (Father's Day or not), Daddy gets to babysit. I'm planning on working on her scrapbook and reading and painting my toenails and getting in some "me" time. I spent every minute with Sara last night: I got out my baby-massage video and spent about 45 minutes rubbing down a little naked baby, all covered in lotion. She *loved* it. (Of course she did pee on the towel, but that's to be expected).

Okay, I'm signing off for now. Gotta get some work done.

June 18
From: Sara
To: Stephanie
Subject: How quickly we forget

My friend Jen called the other day to ask me when David and I first put Anna in her crib, when we started a feeding schedule, etc., and I could hardly remember any of it! I know that she thought I'd lost my mind, but it seems like another lifetime. Motherhood is so much easier and more enjoyable now.

Anna is sitting up great now. It's so cute to see her little belly lapping over her fat little legs as she gnaws on her toy of choice. By the way, she has her first little tooth! I've been feeling it for a week, and now I can see it. It looks like it's coming in crooked, though. I fear she's inherited my teeth (braces, four pulled teeth, retainer, surgery to remove four wisdom teeth, a zillion cavities, and permanent teeth so crooked I could have eaten corn on the cob through a picket fence) and not David's (no braces, no wisdom teeth, a cavity here or there). I guess time will tell.

Hell yes, it's time for Daddy to be doing the late-night feedings. You mean that you're the only one getting up? This doesn't sound like the Stephanie I know! Crack that whip, woman. If you have to be a Mommy *and* do housework *and* make half the income, then he can at least do half the feedings!

But back to your lack of sleep: What the heck is going on? Have you asked the doctor why Sara will only take a few ounces? That must be so frustrating. In order to help us through those late-night feedings, David and I would pre-make plenty of bottles in the fridge and then pop them in the microwave (with the nipple off) for 20 seconds, put the nipple back on, and shake. (I realize that they tell you not to do this, but come on.) Turn the television to HBO or MSNBC and you're in business. (I've seen more TV this year than in the last five combined . . . what *did* our parents do without cable?)

Have you tried giving Sara a biter biscuit? They're great! They make a terrible mess, but she'll be in heaven (and so will you) for at least 30 minutes. And the little face smeared with biscuit goo is well worth the effort of cleaning up.

Is Sara using her ExerSaucer now? I'd love to personally thank the person who invented that most wonderful piece of baby equipment. I can put Anna in hers near the kitchen and eat my lunch, empty the dishwasher, read the paper—it's wonderful. The only problem is that hers is a used one so it doesn't have a lot of play contraptions on it like the new ones do. I just lay various toys and teethers around it for her to pick up and then drop on the floor. So I'm picking up things constantly. But if I load enough stuff on there, it takes her at least ten minutes before they're all on the floor, so it's not that bad. It's like a little cycle:

ten minutes of play, pick up all toys on the floor, put back on the ExerSaucer; repeat.

Well, I hear Miss Anna broadcasting her hunger over the baby monitor, so I better sign off for the moment. Talk to you soon.

Chapter 9

Kiss My Metabolism

June 19

From: Stephanie
To: Sara
Subject: Baby weight

Since I've been breast-feeding, I've kept about ten pounds of "baby weight," which really sucks because I still can't fit into any of my old clothes. (Not that I'd wear them anyway—they're two years old and out of fashion by now.)

Anyway, I read somewhere that our body sort of "holds on" to some fat stores while we breast-feed, just like when we're pregnant (I guess that's in case some famine hits Atlanta or something). So I haven't really been too worried about it: I figured that once I stopped breast-feeding, my old metabolism would kick in again, and the weight would come off. I felt my theory was pretty accurate because when I hurt my back, I didn't eat anything except toast for about two days, and when I stepped on the scale at the end of those two days I hadn't lost a single pound (in the good old days, I would have seen a noticeable difference). That told me that my breast-feeding body was doing its job.

Well, as I was explaining my theory to a friend at a party last weekend, her (quite snooty) response to me was, "Oh no, honey, that's just that the dreaded 'last ten pounds.' It's the hardest to lose." This left me really doubting myself and what I thought my body was telling me. And then there's my sister, who gets that "You're so full of crap" look on her face when I tell her my theories.

Well, I'd like to proclaim to all those doubting Thomases that I stand by my theory. Now that I'm breast-feeding only twice a day, I've dropped five pounds in a week! And I've been eating pizza, pasta, cookies, ice cream . . . whatever my little heart desires. I haven't stepped on a treadmill or stair-climber, or even looked at a weight bench. In fact, the most I've exercised is a trip around the mall looking for a pair of shoes to match a uniquely colored dress for Tim's brother's wedding this weekend. (Unsuccessful effort, by the way—I'm having some dyed at lunch.)

Now I'm certainly no supermodel, and I've got another five or six pounds to go to make it back to pre-baby weight (and I'm convinced that four pounds of the weight I lost came from what's left over of my beautiful breasts), but I'd like those marathon breast-feeders out there to know that your body needs to have a little extra energy (fat) stored up to keep making milk efficiently. I have several girlfriends who didn't lose the last of their pregnancy weight until they were done breast-feeding. That's just the way it works.

And I'd like to say the following to those who doubted my theory and my ability to listen to my own body, those who thought that I was just making excuses: *"Kiss my metabolism."* Go put your running shoes on and drink your can of Slim-Fast for lunch . . . I'm ordering a pizza.

June 20
From: Sara
To: Stephanie
Subject: "Kiss my metabolism"

Although my breast-feeding stint was short-lived, I experienced the same thing . . . but simply getting back to pre-pregnancy weight isn't everything. I've managed to do so, but it's not all in the same place anymore—somehow about three pounds slid from my chest to my ass. Yet even though I still care what I look like in a bathing suit, I'm not like I used to be. Now I'm more concerned about being healthy: I want to feel good as I get older, and I want to be around to see Anna get married and have a baby, too.

By the way, another great weight-loss secret (one I don't recommend, however) is postpartum depression. A week after Anna was born, I had absolutely no appetite. I had to force myself to eat, and with my typical hearty habits, that was a big red flag waving that something was wrong. I'm sure I lost a good five pounds that one week. Make that a *bad* five pounds—it was hell.

On a different note, how's Sara sleeping these days? Do you have a bedtime ritual, which most of the books seem to recommend? Anna and I have one, and it seems to work well: I rock her and read a book, and then I sing lullabies to her till she goes to sleep or until I lay her down. If she's still awake, then I put on a lullaby CD very low and let her fall asleep to it. The music has worked wonders with her. And if she gets fussy in the car, I just start singing "The Itsy Bitsy Spider," and she quiets right down.

Also, have you thought about when you're going to put Sara in her own crib? That may help, too, although it's probably going to be an adjustment at first. I *love* having Anna in her own room. I treasure the time in bed with David before we go to sleep—we're relaxed and can talk about our day, or watch TV or read, or anything else that comes to mind. Speaking of that, *how* have you maintained a sex life with your child in the bed with you? Sofa, kitchen counters? Not that it's any of my business, but I couldn't help asking.

July 2

From: Stephanie
To: Sara
Subject: Sleeping through the night

Question: How do you get a baby who's been breast-feeding to sleep through the night?
Answer: Stop feeding her when she wakes up and let her go back to sleep, for crying out loud!

All this time I've been worried about how to get Sara to sleep through the night, so I spoke to her doctor about it, and she gave me some great advice. She said to give little Sara a bottle of warm water in the night instead of milk. If she doesn't get what she wants (milk), she'll soon figure out that it's not worth waking up. The *real* problem here is that it wasn't Sara who was conditioned to wake up and feed at night—it was her *parents*. I really got into the habit of getting up and making a bottle when she stirred (to prevent her from crying). Well, she's already sleeping through the night—all I had to do was stop giving her a bottle and let her fall back to sleep. Simple, huh? It just proves once again that Sara's "parent-handicapped." There are times when she'd just be better off without us.

Tim and I are feeding her as much as we can at 9 P.M. to hold her for the night, and it seems to be going very well (and Mommy is *much* more rested now). I'm very pleasantly surprised, because I thought that we were going to have to "train" her to do this. It's wonderful! She's the best little baby—she always amazes me at how easygoing she is. We take her everywhere, and she just rides along with no complaints, no matter how much we push her.

July 3
From: Sara
To: Stephanie
Subject: Sleep, baby, sleep

I don't know how you've gone this long without getting a full night's sleep. People say your body adjusts to it, but mine never did—12 weeks seemed like an eternity to me. We did have to let Anna cry it out a few times, though: It was tough, but I think it was the best thing we ever did, since it taught her to fall asleep on her own. And although it seemed like a lot longer at the time, it really only took five or ten minutes before she quieted down. I used to think I wouldn't be able to do things like that—I thought I'd keep her in the room with us for months. Shoot, she was out of there in less than two weeks! I never thought I'd be able to let her cry, but one morning I woke up to discover that David had put a blanket at the bottom of her door to muffle the noise. How bad is that? (There goes his Father of the Year award.) But we *did* get a good night's sleep.

So I guess you're not going to answer my sex question. You're probably just too polite to say, "None of your damn business!"

July 6
From: Stephanie
To: Sara
Subject: Sleeping like a baby

Okay, okay, to answer your question about our sex life with a child sleeping in our bed, all I can say is: *We have a really big bed.* And Sara is one of those babies who you can vacuum around and she'd never wake up. If we don't want to risk waking her, a blanket and a few pillows in front of the fireplace is always an option. I suppose it does make things a little more complicated, but Tim and I enjoy sleeping with her so much that it's totally worth it. It really helps me reconnect after being away from her all day. I can't tell you how much it means to me to be able to cuddle with her all night long. And now that Dr. Sears's book has educated me, allow me to share with you why this worked so well for us (and for so many parents).

Did you know that having a separate room and bed for your infant is a strange concept in most other countries? It really is the most natural thing in the world to sleep with your baby. I'm not sure why some American parents have turned it into yet another parenting competition, like you're going to win a prize if your baby sleeps through the night. So what? They're babies—they're *supposed* to have needs. Yes, it sucks to lose sleep . . . but you knew that going in to this parenthood thing.

There are also many physiological as well as psychological advantages here. For example, studies have shown that the risk of SIDS [sudden infant death syndrome] is lower in babies who sleep with their parents. Dr. Sears describes it as "Mother as a breathing pacemaker," because the mother's warm body and breath help stimulate the baby to breathe during the early months of life when Baby's self-start mechanisms are immature. Mother and Baby develop a sleep harmony—I know this is true because I'd often wake up just seconds before Sara would.

Some people have asked me if I'm ever afraid that I might roll over on her in my sleep. But as long as you're not under the influence of drugs or alcohol, this is highly unlikely. As Dr. Sears says: "Mother sleeps like a baby (babies are poor sleepers) until baby is mature enough to sleep like an adult." And of course, you have to be smart about not smothering your baby with heavy comforters or pillows or "sinky" surfaces.

I just can't imagine abiding by the whole "cry it out" thing. To Tim and me, that's such a cruel thing to do to a tiny, needy baby. How will she ever learn to count on you if you're not there for her when she's so upset? Why do people have such unrealistic expectations when it comes to babies and sleep? As you know, when Sara was first born, I was reading that book *Babywise*—and I can't tell you how many times I literally threw that book across the room! Everything it recommended seemed so cruel and unnatural to me, but I followed it because that's what I thought I was supposed to do. Of course I finally learned to get rid of the book and start doing what felt right to me as a mother.

Tim and I both love sleeping with Sara and wouldn't trade it for anything. We lie there at night with her between us and just stare at our little sleeping angel. I'm the most well-rested working mom because it makes feeding her so easy at night. And I'm really convinced that it makes our bond so much stronger.

Okay, I'll get off my soapbox now. I know that you and David don't like the idea of sleeping with Anna, and that's fine, too. I think this is just another one of those "You have to do what's right for you" lessons again.

To change the subject, my daughter is the biggest *ham* you've ever met! Her day care had a Fourth of July parade this week, and she was in her glory! The teachers decorated all the kids' strollers with red, white, and blue crepe paper and streamers and made little hats for them to wear. And then all the classes lined up for a parade through the church hallways and outside to the parking lot. Of course *all* the parents were there, lining the halls with cameras and camcorders in hand (it's really *quite* the event).

Some of the babies cried; some of them slept; some of them lay there, looking around . . . and then there was Sara: fake exaggerated smiles for everyone; cooing, laughing and engaging all the onlookers. I have a photo of her with both arms stretched out widely, as if presenting herself to her public, and all the parents around her are cracking up. Tim and I laughed until we cried. We often have the old nature vs. nurture debate over how much of one's personality is inherent at birth and how much is learned from parents, environment, and other children. Sara *loves* a crowd, as does Tim. There's no way, at this age, that she could possibly have learned that behavior from him—it's *got* to be a "trait."

I consider all these characteristics she has, and I can't wait to see who she'll grow up to be. If only she'd grow some hair so people would stop calling her "he." (I refuse to torture her with those elastic headbands on a daily basis. They look so uncomfortable!)

I have to go to California from July 22 to 24 . . . *three days* away from my baby! And what's worse, Tim's going to be away at the same time, so my mom's coming to care for Sara. It sucks because I leave Sunday morning, but Mom won't get there until Sunday afternoon. Tim leaves on Monday, so I have to count on him to train my mother in the ways of Sara. I've already started an instruction sheet and checklist. I know, I'm a freak—but I know he won't tell her things like, "Before you go to bed at night, get a bottle ready, because she wakes up hungry and cries like she's in pain until you feed her." Moms like that kind of information.

I'm sure she'll survive—I just want her to survive in *comfort*.

July 8
From: Sara
To: Stephanie
Subject: Handbag babies

Yes, David and I have one of those babies you can take everywhere, just like a handbag—and it's wonderful. I'm thankful that Anna has such a good disposition, but I wonder if it's because we kind of trained her to be that way—to just go anywhere, I mean. Anna has been out to restaurants quite a bit. As I mentioned earlier, it started when she was just a couple weeks old and I was going stir-crazy. I called my mom and asked her if she thought it would be okay if we took Anna out to a restaurant (for some reason I'd told myself that I couldn't take her out of the house until she was eight weeks old). When Mom said yes, we were off.

It went well the first time we took her out, so almost every night when David got home I'd greet him with, "Do you want to go out to eat?" It got expensive, but it maintained what sanity I had left at the time just to be able to get out of the house for a little while. So going out to eat is nothing new to Anna. Needless to say, I'll never again turn my nose up when I see a mother out with a newborn like I used to.

Good luck showing Tim how to instruct your mother. Fathers definitely don't think about the same details we do (I guess because they don't have to). And God forbid they should actually *prepare* for something. Women are equipped to think about seven or eight steps ahead: We can see an entire scenario unfolding in our minds before it actually ever does. For some reason, men just don't think that way. David sometimes waits until the absolute last minute to squeal across four lanes of traffic to make his exit instead of thinking about it a couple miles back. It drives me crazy! He even took Anna somewhere the other night and had to come right back home because he forgot to take any bottles. *Hello!* I hope he learned from that. I try not to do too much for him so he'll figure it out for himself. I wonder if they act that way on purpose. Like the old Bill Cosby philosophy: "If I screw it up bad enough, she won't ask me to do it again."

As for the whole co-sleeping thing, the reason I can't do so with Anna is because I *am* under the influence of alcohol every night! Seriously, I think I'd feel the same way you do if I was at work all day, but since I'm with her, I really need that space at night. I say if it works for you, then do it. And don't worry about what anyone else thinks.

I have to go now—time for my nightly glass of wine.

July 18
From: Stephanie
To: Sara
Subject: The end is near

I fear the end is near . . . of my job, that is.

I've been getting some weird vibes from our VP. Usually when I bring something to his attention that needs to be changed, he's ready for the fight. Lately, he's been in a bad mood and gives me the "Well, that's the just the way it is and it's not going to change" answer—which is surely evidence of our impending doom. I don't know whether to run out and buy Sara a high chair and all the baby equipment she's going to need for the next six months or just start socking away some extra cash. It's all very unsettling.

And to add to my problems, I've been out with a stomach virus for the past two days. It was awful—I've never been so sick in all my life! I wasn't aware that the human body could store so much fluid until I saw how much I was able to eliminate and still have blood pumping through my veins. I will say that I've developed quite an impressive technique for sitting on the toilet while balancing a trash can between my knees. (I know, I know—too much information. Sorry.)

We had Sara back in the ER on Saturday (of course she never gets sick Monday through Friday, nine to five, when the regular doctors are available) because she was throwing up everything we fed her. It turns out she had another virus—and then, of course, I got it, too. The doctor said that sometimes babies get a mild version of an illness, and then the adults get it ten times worse. So Tim had to be the Mommy *and* Daddy for a couple days. But that's always great for their relationship—and it's good for him to see what I have on my hands from day to day. It's sort of entertaining to sit back and watch somebody else struggle through the battles of caring for an infant. I think it must be an impossibility for men to think five minutes into the future, and completely inconceivable for them to do more than one thing at a time (I'm referring, of course, to an activity other than drinking a beer).

July 19
From: Sara
To: Stephanie
Subject: The big dunk

I'm so sorry you've been sick, and sorry about all the job turmoil. You're probably stressed and run-down from that drama, which made you more susceptible to Sara's virus. I really believe that when things are out of balance in our lives, we get sick. It's like a sign that we need a change. There's my cosmic thought for the day. (But why in the world does nature make the parents sicker than the child? I guess we can muddle through better than they can.) Anyway, I hope you can get some freelance work that allows you to stay home with Sara. Surely in Atlanta, with all the agencies there, you should be able to find some business. You sure have a lot on your shoulders right now—are you doing okay with all this?

I was very busy last week with Anna's baptism . . . then I just kind of went on vacation this week because I was so wiped out. We had 20 people here for lunch Sunday, and about 10 here on Friday night. Plus we had another houseguest during the week and a big cookout. I was also nervous about the baptism because I didn't know what to expect—since Anna was going to be completely naked (that's right, no diaper) when she was immersed.

Thankfully, everything went well, and there were no embarrassing moments. There was one near-disaster when she made a swipe for the priest's dish of anointing oil, but he was experienced enough to move it out of her reach and never miss a beat in the service. Anna wore the dress my grandmother was christened in, so that was another concern. It's so old it could tear very easily; and of course, I didn't want her to spit up or poop on it (fortunately, she didn't). Mom keeps the dress in a glass case, so I was relieved when I could give it safely back to her. I felt like I was holding on to something priceless, which I guess I was. I think it was neat for Anna to wear it, though, and Mom certainly would have understood if anything had happened. It was a really beautiful baptism—wish you could have been there.

July 24
From: Stephanie
To: Sara
Subject: Career vs. baby

I'm glad to hear that the priest was the only one who did any "christening" at Anna's ceremony. You know, you Catholics could take a few notes from us Baptists on this one: We keep 'em fully clothed and sprinkle a little water on their foreheads, and then everybody goes out to have fried chicken and iced tea. That whole naked-baptism thing is way too much pressure if you ask me. Hell, I'm in my 30s, and I can't help but "make wee-wee" when my feet touch cold water. (Okay, so you guys get to drink without going to hell, I'll give you that one. But the Pope needs to seriously rethink that whole dripping-naked-babies thing before the holy water starts looking a little too yellow to be considered "holy"!)

A pregnant girlfriend of mine keeps talking to me about whether or not she should return to work after the baby's born. She's an executive at a bank, and she and her husband are trying to decide whether or not to buy a new home, which would require her to keep working. If they don't buy the house, she could very comfortably stay at home with the baby.

After leaving day care yesterday and watching my child cry as I left, I've finalized my answer for her and all those trying to decide whether to be a stay-at-home mom or a workforce mom. Here's the cold, hard truth:

- If you decide to go back to work, you'll have more money to spend on the baby; you'll be able to save faster for the college fund; you'll live and pay your bills more comfortably—but you won't have as close a relationship with her. When you're with your baby, a part of your mind will be thinking about your work, just like when you're at work, a part of your mind is on your baby.

- If you go back to work, you'll be tired all the time, physically and mentally. You'll watch your baby sit up for the first time and wonder if that really *was* the first time—or if it happened at day care the day before and they just didn't tell you.

- Each time you take a vacation that allows you to spend a few days with your baby, bringing her back to day care will be like the first time you ever dropped her off all over again. After I'd been with Sara continuously for *four* glorious days at Tim's brother's wedding, as I walked down the hall from her classroom, my arms felt so empty that I swear they actually ached. I'm not sure what hurt worse: my heart or my arms.

- You'll miss your little baby. And you'll wonder if she's crying, and if so, if anyone is comforting her—immediately—the way you do. You'll wonder if she feels alone, sad, or happy. And most of all, you'll experience more pure guilt than you ever imagined: guilt about putting her in day care and missing so much time with her. And guilt about your job when she's sick with a fever for the fourth day in a row and has to stay at home, or when you have to leave work early or come in late *again* because of a doctor's appointment.

- So, my answer is: If you can afford to stay at home, do it!

Now, having said all that, as a workforce mom, here's what you have to do to keep your sanity and your relationship with your baby: Quality time is key; chores wait until the weekend. I try to spend every night on a big blanket with little Sara. No television, no telephone, no doorbells; I just concentrate on her and play with her. I figure I have three good hours with her at night before she falls asleep. Everything else can wait until after 9 P.M.—I *have* to reconnect with my baby again each night. During those three hours in the evening, we play, we have bath time, I use a baby-massage video, and next week I'm going to try working in a Mommy & Me exercise video (only if she's very involved in the workout).

I don't think there's anything one can do about the guilt. No matter how I try to stay focused on what's really important, I still have to deal with the personalities at work (usually those without kids) who don't understand the huge responsibility of being a parent. It gets really difficult sometimes, but as soon as I get to day care and see that little smile, none of the other stuff matters.

The other thing to remember, whether you're working or not, is that everything is a stage. In a few years, your baby will be required to go to school. This is the only advantage to not staying at home, because if you've continued to work, then you won't have to play catch-up to the business world.

I have to go for now—it's time for my midday visit, which is the *best* part of my workday! I miss her so much.

July 24

From: Sara
To: Stephanie
Subject: Making time

Well said—so well that after I read your message I picked up Anna and headed down to the lake with her to throw sticks for the dogs. Then I rocked her to sleep, hugging and kissing her as much as I could while I still can. Before I know it she'll be too big to rock to sleep, or she won't want me to anymore. You just erased every doubt I ever had about staying at home with her. And no child will look back on their youth and say, "Gosh, I'm glad Mom and Dad worked longer hours so we could live in this really big house!" (If they do, then congratulations, you've raised a materialistic brat.)

I want to tell you about something I witnessed at my sister's rehearsal dinner last month. The woman seated next to me, named Helen, had seven-year-old twin boys, who were with a babysitter. She talked to me about them all through dinner—then she got a call from the babysitter. It seems that recently a woman in their neighborhood had gone out to run an errand and was shot and raped. Helen hadn't told her sons about it, but they'd heard the story at school. Ever since, one of the boys hadn't wanted his mom to go anywhere without him. The babysitter said that he was upset and wanted to come be with his mom at the rehearsal dinner. A few minutes later he was curled up in her lap next to me.

Helen's father came over later when the boy was playing to ask if he was okay. I heard him tell his daughter, "You did the right thing, honey." My heart just melted. She was parenting her son, but she was also receiving some parenting herself. Her dad was supporting her and being proud of her . . . and I want to be that kind of parent to Anna. You can never, ever assume that your kids "just know" something. Everyone needs to be told the important things. And often.

No matter how old Anna and Sara are, they'll always be our daughters and will always want and need the love and protection of their parents.

July 26

From: Stephanie
To: Sara
Subject: Now what?

Well, the sale of my company was finalized last week, and it doesn't look good for us. There are quotes throughout all the news pubs that say they plan on eliminating all the sales and marketing positions to make a dent in their debts. Great . . . I'll be hanging on as long as I can because Sara's in that outstanding day care just three blocks away. It makes me sick because she loves it there and I've become so involved in the parent-teacher organization (I'm even chairing a committee for publishing a cookbook as a fund-raiser). And I hate the thought of having to move her (the chances of my finding another job this close to her day care are very slim).

We don't really know anything for sure yet, and that's the hardest part. I'm pretty sure I'm going to get canned; the big question is *when?* The company that bought us did have an Atlanta office, but they recently fired everyone last month (with only two weeks' notice) and closed the entire office down. So I think our fate has already been sealed. I'm going to pursue free-lance copywriting, but it makes Tim very nervous because it's nice to have that steady paycheck every two weeks. I figure I can start now and get some momentum until they get rid of us.

Tim's been out of town last week *and* this one, so my mom came to visit to give me some help with the baby. I took the last two days off, and it was so wonderful being with little Sara. She's so much fun right now: She just started giving hugs, and it's the *best.* She smiles, laughs, and plays all the time—it's such a joy to be with her. I hated coming to work today (especially under the circumstances). I just want to be with her all the time.

Have you listened to the song "Just the Two of Us" by Will Smith? If not, go buy the CD. He wrote it for his son, and it's just awesome. It's another testament to how having a child changes your view on everything. Before Sara, I liked that song because it was about a father giving good, loving advice to his son—but now that she's in my life, I can relate to every verse. I was listening to it in the car this morning for the first time in a long time, and the tears were streaming down my face so bad that I couldn't see to drive! I was fumbling around for tissues, and all I could find was a panty liner (hey—it's paper *and* it's absorbent . . . at times like that, you have to be open-minded). Anyway, I hope you get a chance to hear that song soon.

Tim's job stress is really putting a strain on our relationship. He's been traveling constantly, and when he *is* home, his mind is elsewhere or he's preparing for his next trip/class. So he's become very, very distant. I asked my mom to please stay an extra night so that he and I could have a date when he got back. I told him about it last week, and I've been looking forward to it ever since. But when he called last night, he was upset that I'd even suggest going out without Sara. He said, "I've been away from my daughter for two weeks! Why would I want to go out to dinner and leave her?" Nice. *Guess what, you big jerk—you've been away from your wife for two weeks, too. You know, the one who cares for your daughter while you're away?*

I get so frustrated, too, because everything seems to take a backseat to his job. For example, our lawn looks awful right now (there's so much debris in the backyard from when the trees fell), and he doesn't seem to care. And there are so many little things around the house that I've asked him to do, and even though he says okay, they never get done. I'm beginning to think "okay" means "I'll just agree for now to get you off my back." I know he's busy, but no matter how busy or tired *I* get, I still have a baby and a house to care for. Is it just me, or have you noticed that women have twice the workload as men? I think I just have higher standards for the way I want the house and yard to look.

It's funny, because I used to see all those articles about "baby-proofing your marriage," and I thought they were so silly. As Tim and I would lie in bed at night—gazing at our sleeping baby and each other, and having pillow talk about her and our family and our future—I thought the whole baby-proofing thing was crap. But every now and then, I'm starting to think otherwise.

I really want to come see you and David and Anna soon. I hope we can get together. Sara and I are taking swimming classes at the Y every Saturday morning. It's so much fun! I'll tell you all about it another time—gotta go get some work done.

July 28
From: Sara
To: Stephanie
Subject: Outsourcing

That's too bad about your company. Do you think there's any chance they'll keep you on? If you get laid off, will you at least get a severance?

As for your yard, didn't I hear Tim say once that he was a big fan of outsourcing? I think you should take him at his word and hire some help. I have the same issues here. David does keep up the front yard pretty well, except he doesn't touch the flower beds—those are my responsibility. And I think hell will freeze over before he edges the lawn. I've asked him a hundred times, and he always says yes . . . yet still no edging. Lately I've just said to hell with it and either done it myself or had it done. I kept thinking about what Dr. Phil says: that you can only improve your relationship by working on yourself. And to my surprise, it's working. The last few weeks I've been breaking my back working in the yard, planting, landscaping, watering, fertilizing, etc. I bought a bunch of shrubs and plants for the front beds, and when David saw how much I had to plant, he offered to help. Then I hired someone to spread pine needles, and he didn't even get mad about the money!

The next day I planted some monkey grass and other ground covers in the back and spread the pine needles myself. He was so impressed that he started watering them for me and also replanted one of the beds that the dogs dug up. I'd been asking him to move a bird feeder for weeks (the birds were pooping all over the deck), and he just got up and did it that Saturday morning without my saying anything. Then I started wiping down the billions of spiderwebs on the back of our house, when he took over and started doing it. I had to work really hard to conceal my amazement! This strategy does work!

However, I've got a story for you that's along the same lines as Tim blowing off your date night. (And no offense, but I think I've got you topped here.) David and I recently discussed that we're going to reserve furniture and other big purchases for birthdays and Christmases. My birthday was last week, so I told him that I wanted him and our families to go in together and get me a nice wicker sofa for the screened porch. He kept asking me what kind of sofa I wanted, and I told him that I didn't know—I'd just have to go look and pick it out. He said that he was asking me all these questions because he wanted to surprise me, but if I wanted to pick it out, then I should just go and get whatever I wanted.

At this point I hadn't priced all-weather wicker and didn't know that it's insanely expensive (however, it does last a lifetime). So when I told him how much it cost, he freaked out. Of course he couldn't be polite and say, "I know you really want this, but maybe we should hold off." No, he started interrogating me, demanding to know what I thought "a reasonable amount to spend on a birthday gift" was. This, from someone who suggested that we get major purchases for special occasions! Happy birthday to me.

Unfortunately, the story doesn't end there. I have a good friend here whose fiancé has the same birthday as me, so she invited us to come over for pizza and cake and celebrate with them. By the time we got in the car to come home that night, I was in tears: Not only did I have no present to unwrap, I didn't even get a card from my husband. Now wouldn't you think he would give a little honor to this, the most life-changing year of my entire life, the year I gave birth to our daughter? At the very least, I could have gotten a card from Anna (especially since he didn't give me anything, not even a card, when she was born).

I didn't get mad; I was too hurt. I knew he didn't do it on purpose, but I felt so taken for granted. While we were at my friend's house, David even left me to eat dinner by myself and watch Anna! So, other than whipping out the old Visa card to buy the sofa, he made no effort for my birthday at all. The sad thing is that he didn't even realize it until we were driving home . . . and then he felt really bad. And to make it up to me, he went out and bought the matching chairs to my sofa. While I'm thrilled to get the chairs, something a little more sentimental would have been nice. So, although he got the point, he didn't *totally* get it, if you know what I mean. Oh well, marriage is a continual work in progress—and it helps to have a short memory.

Chapter 10

Will You Marry Me?

August 2

From: Stephanie
To: Sara
Subject: Wanna get married?

My biggest problem is that I have a permanent chip on my shoulder . . . I just don't like men. I find them ineffective and self-centered. But I think I have the solution to all our problems: Let's divorce Tim and David and marry each other! You can stay home with the girls and write; I'll get another cushy, overpaid job in the cable-TV industry; and we'll live happily ever after. (Maybe we can even arrange conjugal visits along with the child support.)

I'm reading a book about love languages, and the overall message is that what I require of Tim to feel loved is probably different from what he needs from me to feel loved. (I'm sure you've heard this theory before.) Tony Robbins describes it along the lines of, "You love tomato soup, so you give your spouse tomato soup thinking that he'll love it as much as you do. But your spouse doesn't like tomato soup—he prefers chicken noodle. So you have to figure out what your spouse likes and then give him the flavor he likes best."

Based on your story, I think that you need to realize that tomato soup (i.e., big gifts for holidays) is *not* what's going to make you happy. I think the "giving big gifts for holidays" idea isn't a good idea for you. You obviously need something else to make you happy (as would I), so you should get rid of that rule. Why on earth would you eliminate the two or three times per year that they're forced to *think* about doing something nice for us? Dr. Phil also says that men need to be hit over the head with a two-by-four, so do what I do: I tell my darling husband what I want a week or so before the big day. You can try leaving hints, but I highly recommend that you forget being subtle. Besides, David's going to sit his ass on that sofa, too, so why should it be for *your* birthday? (Which, by the way, I'm so sorry I missed!)

It always makes me feel better when I know that it's not just Tim . . . they're *all* like that. I hate 'em.

Wanna get married?

August 3

From: Sara
To: Stephanie
Subject: Platonic lesbians

That's just about the most romantic proposal I've ever received!

Maybe we should just become platonic lesbians—some days it seems like a really good idea. I often wonder if two women living together have the same issues as a man and a woman do, or if it's different having a relationship with the same sex. You and I would probably work great together except for one area: decorating. It'd be a disaster because we'd both want control. That's one benefit of living with men—for the most part, they just don't care. And who would unscrew the lid off a new jar of jelly or grapefruit juice? And I don't know about you, but I don't plan on mowing the yard anytime soon. However, if you find a job that would let me stay home with the girls *and* allow us to hire a beefy yardman named Sven, give me a call.

As far as the gifts go, I want the big honking piece of furniture *and* something sentimental. (You see, if I don't go along with this system, those big purchases will *never* happen.) It doesn't have to be something expensive, just something that shows some thought. Although it *is* a true expression of love for David, tight-wad that he is, to part with that much cash for the chairs (they were not cheap). And the sofa really is more for me than him. I know he'll use it, but this is going to be my reading and lounging room. So I guess that makes me sentimental *and* materialistic.

August 16
From: Stephanie
To: Sara
Subject: The epitome

A picture is worth a thousand words, and I wish someone had taken mine this morning—I was the epitome of a working mother. I dragged my laptop out of my trunk, hurrying because I was late as usual. I got into the elevator and walked through the lobby of my huge office building, which was buzzing with busi-nesspeople. By the time I got to the second set of crowded eleva-tors, I realized that I had one of Sara's diapers hanging out of my briefcase! (I keep diapers in my trunk for day-care reloads—one less thing I have to remember when leaving the house in the morning.) What a picture!

I'm so sad because I have to go on a business trip today, and I don't get back till tomorrow night. I *hate* being away from little Sara. And I'm *so* glad I changed jobs so that I don't have to do the travel thing more often. One of the girls in my office just quit (I expect there will be more), and for a moment, I fantasized about getting my old job back—but after saying good-bye to my little baby this morning, I'm not going to have that thought ever again!

I must be really sappy, because my "business trip" is to West Palm Beach to stay in the Ritz-Carlton and have dinner with a client tonight and a meeting tomorrow morning. So I guess there *is* a small part of me that's looking forward to it. It could cer-tainly be much worse.

August 18
From: Sara
To: Stephanie
Subject: The Ritz?!

Hey, at least it was a diaper hanging out of your briefcase and not that panty liner you were wiping your eyes with a while back.

Quit your crying—right now I'd kill for a night in a Ritz-Carlton.

August 20
From: Stephanie
To: Sara
Subject: A dilemma

Okay, here's my latest dilemma . . . my husband washed and waxed my car for me yesterday. He used a special chemical to remove all the built-up road residue, cleaned the wheels, and applied tire shine—it's gorgeous! I'm so thankful.

So what's the issue? Well, on Saturday morning at around 9 A.M., he disappeared. He didn't say where he was going, didn't ask if I minded, and didn't say when he was going to come back. He was gone for over four and a half hours. (He did his own car, too.)

I'd just returned from two trips and a business dinner that week. So you can imagine my "To Do" list: six loads of laundry, two suitcases to unpack, yada, yada, yada. It's not that I don't appreciate having a clean car, it's just not a priority in my life. I didn't even get to take a shower until four that afternoon, since Sara wasn't feeling well and was fussier than usual.

I was so stressed out from my house being a mess—it was a terrible day, and I couldn't have cared less about my car. See, I've come to the conclusion that men do what I call "fun work." Tim enjoys washing and waxing the cars . . . far more than he enjoys changing the kitty litter and folding 32 pairs of tighty whities (how many times *does* he change underwear in a day?!). But when I became upset because he'd spent four and a half hours on the cars, he acted like he'd been working his white hiney off all day. It's such a scam!

August 28

From: Sara
To: Stephanie
Subject: Men do the fun work—we do toilets

I know this dilemma. It *is* a scam—men have a very well-coordinated system. However, I actually took some cues from David while we were at the beach and used some of his best tricks on him. Like when he started taking care of Anna for a second, I just disappeared . . . and then I got some *me* time!

The whole thing of Tim doing the cars is, yes, it's work, but he's not taking care of a baby at the same time. He doesn't have to get her down for a nap; take the baby monitor outside, plug it in, and make sure it's working right; and *then* start on the cars—he just goes outside. Whenever we moms go outside, we have to make sure our husbands know so that they won't just ignore the baby and leave or something. When do men ever say, "I've got to go outside for a minute, can you watch the baby"? Never. They just leave and assume we'll take care of the kid.

Also, whenever we work, we're usually doing it while taking care of a child at the same time. For men, it's one or the other: Either they're taking care of the child *or* doing work, not both. I had to go somewhere the other night and David was to watch Anna. When he got home from work, he actually asked me to stay another minute so that he could go to the bathroom. I said no. His response was, "I can't go to the bathroom with her!" *What* does he think I do all day—hold it until she takes a nap? And the scary thing was, he was serious. You'll be proud to know that I told him to figure it out, and then I left.

I get frustrated because I take care of everything through the week, and then David gets to enjoy the boat all weekend with little or no responsibility. I want us to somehow change our lives so that we can both work and parent more equally. Lately I still have this burning need to "do something" with my life. David always says, "You *are* doing something—you're raising our daughter." Yes, that's true, and it really is a great thing to do with my life, but I've lost something of myself in the process that I need to get back. I'm just not sure how to do it yet.

I think I'll be a better mother if I get a little break every now and then. I feel like I get burnt out sometimes—if I can just get away for a little bit, I come back renewed and with a better attitude, which makes me a better mother. I want both David and me to think creatively about what it means to be a family and about our division of labor. Who says we women have to take on these traditional roles?

August 28
From: Stephanie
To: Sara
Subject: Getting a life

Those so-called traditional roles are for the birds (or should I say "for the slaves"?). I don't know what our mothers were thinking with that whole *Stepford Wives* routine. I remember seeing this article once from the '50s about how to be a good wife. It said that a gal should take time to make sure the children are clean, always touch up her makeup, and have cookies baking in the oven so that the house smells good when her husband comes home from his hard day at work. Wives were servants, and I don't know how men got away with it!

Now, regarding your "search" to figure out what you want to be when you grow up, you want to know what I think? (Too bad, I'm telling you anyway.) There's *plenty* of time to find and do that other thing we're supposed to do. For the next few years, I think we're just supposed to be great mothers to our children—after all, they won't need us forever. No one ever looks back on their life and wishes they spent more time at the office; and if, God forbid, you found out you were sick and only had a short time to live, I doubt you'd be struggling so much to find your place. You'd be spending every minute you could with the people you love—you'd want to memorize the color of Anna's eyes and the softness of her cheeks and her chubby little hands and feet . . . you know, the things we so easily take for granted in our normal days. In the whole span of our lifetime, we only have the privilege of being the Mommy of a little child for a brief, fleeting period.

That's all I have to say.

August 29

From: Sara
To: Stephanie
Subject: Well said

Thank you—I needed to hear that, and it was a good reminder of just how brief this time is. It's just that taking care of a baby is so tedious that it sometimes feels like forever! It would break my heart not to be here with Anna, I know that. Even when I felt like the walls were closing in on me, I knew deep down that I really didn't want to go back to work (not on someone else's schedule anyway). I like knowing that I can be here for her all the time, yet I can't help but feel like I've put my life on hold in some ways. I heard my mom say the other day that being a stay-at-home mom is so different for me than it was for her. Even though she went to college, she wasn't giving up a great career to stay at home with her kids. I think it certainly is a more heart-wrenching choice for our generation.

I believe that the ideal solution for me is to work out of the house and occasionally go to the office for a meeting, etc.; or if David and I did a business together where we could share the workload—of course we might kill each other in the process, so that would kind of defeat the purpose.

But your point about this only being temporary is a good one. I have to remember that this isn't my entire life—it's only a part of it. I just need to find the right balance for me. I will say that as awful as it was, going through postpartum depression was very beneficial for me in that it made me step back and reassess my life. And now that I'm in my 30s, it's time to get on the stick. I think that was part of my depression: Suddenly I entered this new phase of my life, but I realized that I hadn't done everything I thought I was going to do in the previous phase. Postpartum depression was the big kick in the pants I needed. I guess everything we go through in life really does teach us something.

In a way, quitting my job and having a baby gave me a new freedom, too. After all, it's not like I wanted to do that job for the rest of my life! Now I can pursue a lot of the dreams I've always wanted to—I'm just going to have to juggle a little more. I know that I have something to offer the world, and it's high time I stopped talking about it and started doing something about it.

The key is balance. I know that in being here day in and day out, I sometimes take this time in my life (and Anna herself) for granted. I think that having something for myself, even if it's just a small something that doesn't take a lot of time, will help me appreciate more what I *do* have.

Well, I guess you can tell your e-mail inspired me! Thanks— I needed it. Okay, gotta go: Anna's spun off an entire roll of toilet paper!

September 5

From: Stephanie
To: Sara
Subject: Day-care side effects

What is it about paper?! I pry tiny little pieces of tissues, newsprint, magazines, etc., from Sara's fingers daily! She wants to eat it!

We've been battling another virus, but she's feeling better now. I swear, she's sick *every* two weeks—it's ridiculous. The doctors keep telling me, "At least she's getting everything now instead of when she starts school." I hope what they're telling me is true and it really is helping her immune system. Only time will tell, but I'd like to think that something good came of all this. I feel so bad for her. She just hasn't been herself for the last week or so, but she finally just got her "Sara smile" back.

The other scary part is the medicine she's on—it's for people with asthma. And the side effects are horrible: tremors in the hands, diarrhea, excitability. At ten o'clock last night she was *wired!* We couldn't get her to calm down and go to sleep. She just wanted to crawl on us *and* everything else in her path. It was hilarious, but the whole family is exhausted today.

Since she's still bald, I'm going to take advantage of it for our Halloween costumes. The two choices for her and me are Dopey and Snow White, or Dr. Evil and Mini-Me. What's your vote?

September 6
From: Sara
To: Stephanie
Subject: Vote for Dopey

Either way, your daughter is going to need major psychother-apy down the road. I guess I'll go with Dopey, since at least he's sweet and funny-looking; whereas Mini-Me is evil and funny-looking. (You guys are sick and twisted.)

By the way, isn't it hilarious how one day we're talking about dreams and the meaning of life and the next day it's Dopey and Mini-Me?

September 8
From: Stephanie
To: Sara
Subject: A good foot rubbin'

I'm physically tired from work today. We're selling these pro-motions all over the country, and we've been hustling to meet our goals before the deadline. We get paid a commission on how many we sell; otherwise, we really wouldn't give a crap, consider-ing that we're probably going to be canned in a couple months.

Yesterday was the same way, and so frustrating. I swear the people in our corporate office make *so* many mistakes and are so slow to respond to us. By the end of the day I was in a weird funk that I just couldn't talk myself out of. So I went and had a pedi-cure—I just had to have someone rub my feet.

Hey, keep December 8 free if you can—I think we're going to celebrate Sara's first birthday in Raleigh. There's been too much discussion about where to celebrate: My mom wants us to come to her house because my grandmother will be visiting; plus my sister, her husband, and their child are there, too. But I'm afraid that the last thing Tim's family and our friends want to do is go to Fayette-ville, sit on my mother's velour couch, sip sweet tea, and watch the latest church choir cantata video. So we decided that Raleigh might be a good compromise: We have some good friends there, and it's a short drive for pretty much everyone. (Of course, it's going to cost us a fortune, but it might be worth it in the end.)

Okay, gotta go pick up the baby from day care. She's finally almost over that last virus—whew! One more trip to the ER and they're going to name a wing after us. Have you heard of "RSV," which is what Sara had? Pray that Anna doesn't get it, because it's awful (you probably don't have to worry since she isn't in day care). Anyway, it stands for respiratory synctial virus (which is medical lingo for *inflammation of the lungs*). It's like bronchitis but much worse: It's highly contagious and very hard to get rid of. We've even had to treat her with an inhaler, like the kind people with asthma have to use. But of course a baby can't put her mouth around an inhaler, so there's this special one for infants that the children's hospital gave us. It's like a tube with a mask that fits over Sara's face, and the inhaler attaches to the other end. So we spray it, and then hold the mask over her face until she inhales. As you can imagine, it's not much fun. It's a scary virus, too, because she wheezes and at one point was even doing what the medical folks call "indrawing," which looked like she was gasping for air. Anyway, the whole ordeal has been a nightmare on top of working and no sleep. I'm so glad it's over.

Gotta run for now! Chat back when you can.

September 9
From: Sara
To: Stephanie
Subject: Neutral territory

Personally, I *need* to have some alcohol in my bloodstream to listen to a choir cantata. Growing up in a small town, I firmly came to believe that these productions should be left to large churches with professional choir directors who hold auditions, not small country churches who let anyone who shows up sing. Maybe your in-laws can stash some mini-bottles in their clothes so that they can doctor their iced tea.

These family events are kind of like court proceedings: You have to be on neutral territory; otherwise, you're showing bias. Good luck, and try to stay out of the ER. Of course, The Triplett Trauma Center has a nice ring to it. Might be confusing to people, though—sounds like a trauma center that only allows triplets.

Okay, it's obviously time for me to go to bed.

September 10

From: Stephanie
To: Sara
Subject: Baby menu

Actually, just for the record, the church choir is pretty large, and very good. And Mom only makes us watch the video on holidays.

Hey, I was thinking about how you once told me what a challenge it can be to find things that babies can eat (without teeth). Here are some things that I've picked up from "the girlfriends," as well as my own experiences:

- chicken noodle soup (drain most of the liquid out)
- vegetable soup (no meat)
- Lipton noodles (in the package)—chicken flavor is our favorite!
- potatoes
- peas
- green beans, boiled soft and diced
- spinach—especially the creamed, chopped kind
- baked beans
- cooked carrots
- cottage cheese
- oranges—(remove seeds, obviously)
- mandarin oranges in the can—another favorite
- macaroni—throw some spaghetti sauce or Alfredo sauce over the top
- Jell-O with fruit dices—mash it up because Jell-O can be a choking hazard
- good ol' Kraft mac and cheese in the box—love it!
- Sara loves fish sticks—just cut off the crunchy outside layer
- baked apples—you can actually put one in plastic wrap with a little water and place in the microwave for a few minutes until it gets soft

Hope this helps!

September 13

From: Sara
To: Stephanie
Subject: Baby buffet

Thanks for the ideas. I'll have to try the drained-soup thing—that's a really good idea. However, if you cut the bread off the fish sticks, doesn't that just leave fish mush? By the way, have you ever given Sara those "meat sticks" (lovely name) in a jar? Are those things disgusting or what? Anna won't eat them, and I can't say I blame her.

I think I was so paranoid (and clueless) about when to introduce certain foods that Anna's a little behind in the baby-meal game. At least it sounds like it, based on what Sara's eating. Your child is eating fish; mine's still gnawing on Gerber wagon wheels.

September 14

From: Stephanie
To: Sara
Subject: Interior decorating at its best

Last night I bought a cat bowl that was the *exact* same plum color as my kitchen curtains. Quick, call *Southern Living!*—'cause *that's* talent.

September 14

From: Sara
To: Stephanie
Subject: Cat bowl?

Is that a bowl to feed the cats, or a bowl with cats on it?

September 17

From: Stephanie
To: Sara
Subject: Thank God for antibiotics

It's a bowl that the cats drink from—it allows water to drain in as they drink, to ensure that their water is always fresh. However, they were so enamored with it that they just kept playing with it. Every morning I'd find the water dispenser in the middle of the kitchen floor with its entire contents all over the place—extremely dangerous on a ceramic tile floor. So I decided that they lost their "fresh-water privileges": It's back to the old plastic bowl, which will eventually be lined with slimy mold because I never bother to wash it out for them. Hey, ever since little Sara came along, they're lucky we let them sleep in the house, let alone eat or drink. I'm tired of the shedding and the kitty-litter pan—and if I find one more hairball on my kitchen floor, they're outta here. I can't keep up with all the housework as it is!

You know, my friend, it's not just us: Every mom I know is tired, flustered, and burnt out. I recently went to lunch with a friend of mine who has two very young children. One of them managed to find a tasty morsel of food on the floor under our table, and he put it right into his mouth. Now, we all know that caring for children in a restaurant is in itself a daunting task, but by this time she was so flustered that she didn't even try to fight the battle of prying it out of his mouth. She just looked at me, shrugged her shoulders, and said, "He's on antibiotics."

I thought I was going to fall out of my chair laughing. As if his antibiotics were going to fight whatever foreign bacteria was living on that piece of food. But sometimes Mommies are just too tired to fight the fight . . . sometimes it's just about survival.

September 18

From: Sara
To: Stephanie
Subject: Letting things slide

Good lord, something has to slide, doesn't it? For me it's been vacuuming. I had the dogs clipped so that the hair doesn't build up and I can stretch out the time between floor cleanings. This house is a bitch to vacuum.

I'm tired, too. I want to make a lot of money, be able to stay home with my daughter, and hire a maid—do you think that's possible? And I think I'm becoming an alcoholic. After running around all day, as soon as I get Anna down to sleep at night that glass of wine sure is nice. It's going to be a lot harder to give up coffee and wine the second time around. Do you ever think about what it's going to be like having two? I usually stop myself from thinking about it too much because it scares the crap out of me.

I went in to my old office today for a meeting. As usual, I now have four projects due in a little over a week, so I'll be working every night. I'm thinking of buying some investment property, a fixer-upper or something, and trying to make some money that way. I'm more confused now than ever about my life, and I'm hoping that some clarity will come soon. I do know that I don't want to go back to work full-time and that the free-lance money right now is nice. And I need to start getting Anna out with other babies—she's starving for interaction! She's very social, and being here with me all day just isn't cutting it. I'm going to enroll her in swimming classes, and the library here has some reading times for kids her age that I can take her to. I know there are tons of other things—I've gotta get on the ball. I think that damn postpartum stuff made me fall behind . . . or maybe I've simply been too absorbed with my own life.

I just have this need—this something in me that's searching. (I know I sound like a broken record.) I want to have that third aspect to my life other than wife and mother. I love mothering Anna: It's like you said about Sara once—you fall in love with them more every day. I finally know what that feels like. Anna is so full of personality now. She's so inquisitive and wants to discover everything. Tonight while I was giving her a bath, I saw her looking at her hand underwater, then out of the water. I wonder what she was thinking. I'm so thankful to have a daughter, but when I think about what I want for her, I also think about that missing third aspect . . . which I don't want her to miss. So if I want that for her, shouldn't I want it for me? Even if I wait until later to do it, what is that saying: "You *can* have it all, just not at the same time"?

Chapter 11

Here I Go Again!

October 12

From: Stephanie
To: Sara
Subject: Here I go again!

You *are not* going to believe the news I have for you today.

You know how I've been complaining about feeling so tired? And how I've been so sick from all the day-care viruses? Well, it turns out it wasn't a virus . . . I'm very pleased, happy, and a little freaked out to announce that *Triplett Baby Number Two is on the way!* Yep! I just took a pregnancy test yesterday morning and I couldn't believe my eyes.

I'm such an idiot: I've been pregnant for almost two months, but I was in complete denial. I've had *all* the signs—I've been exhausted, and I've been feeling a little nauseated, especially when I'm hungry—but I just didn't stop to think about it. I was casually telling my friend Laura that I'd puked that morning, and I was starting to think I should see a doctor because I might have caught another virus from day care. I heard laughter coming from the other end of the phone, and she said, "Stephanie, you're pregnant!"

Of course I gave the standard response: "No, you have to have *sex* to get pregnant." But then I started thinking about it . . . I already had a pregnancy test at home, left over from when I was pregnant with Sara. So the next morning, I decided, *What the hell, I'll pee on the stick.*

I was in complete shock when it turned pink. Actually, I'm not sure if my first reaction was joy or guilt about the fact that I'd be taking so much away from Sara so soon. I mean, by the time she's 17 months old, she'll have a new brother or sister to share all the attention with—I feel like I'm robbing her of her baby-hood somehow. But I've since become a little more rational, and I know that I'm giving her a wonderful, lifelong gift, who'll be there long after Tim and I are gone.

Anyway, I went to work this morning and proceeded to throw up in the public bathroom (yuck!). It's the first time I've ever stood up to puke, but let's face it—you just can't get down there and hug it like you do your own at home. It was really hard to have such a big secret—to run to the bathroom and vomit and sweat, and then stroll back to my desk trying to disguise my puke breath and watery eyes. I guess it's a good thing we're losing our jobs, because I'd hate telling my boss that I'm doing this again already.

I swear, Tim and I must be the two most fertile people on the face of the planet! I know this is more information than you need or probably want to know, but it's so mind-boggling, I just have to share. Tim traveled three weeks out of the month of September. The one week that he *was* home, I was sick with the flu. So, we had sex *one* time . . . and *bam!* I'm with child.

How can this be possible? I hear couples all the time talking about "trying" to have a baby. The only thing we have to "try" to do to get pregnant is not fall out of our bed. I'd just finished breast-feeding Sara, and I'd only had a period one time. Can my body really be ready for this so soon?

The story gets better. The morning I found out, Tim was already at work. Of course I wanted to tell him in person, and wanted to figure out some creative, memorable way to do it. So I had to go to work, puke, and keep my secret to myself. It's just not right for other people to know before your own husband.

Anyway, it was someone's birthday in our office, so we were all going out to lunch together to a swanky gourmet Mexican restaurant. (Just what you want to put in your stomach after puking: Mexican food. Perfect.) As the hostess sat us at our table, the nausea kicked in hard. I thought I was going to vomit again, so I excused myself and found the bathroom. I didn't throw up, but I was just so queasy. I went back to the table and ate some bread and water. Needless to say, I wasn't making much conversation—it was all I could manage to just sit upright. The food came, but I couldn't eat. I kept excusing myself to go to the bathroom. I couldn't throw up; by now, I couldn't even *stand*. I was so sick.

I was so desperate that I sat down on the bathroom floor with my head between my knees. Now, you know, germ freak that I am, I'd have to be knocking on death's door to find myself sitting on the floor of a public restroom, but I was trapped. I couldn't let my co-workers see me like this because I didn't want them to know. So I called Tim from the bathroom floor, and I asked him to come and get me because I was sick. He was having a lunch meeting with his boss and said, "I can't really leave—where are you?" I told him where I was. He said, "Isn't that four blocks from your office? Can't you just get someone to take you back there, and I'll come and get you as soon as I can get away?" I started to get a little upset, and he knew something was up. "Stephanie, you're not pregnant, are you?" I told him I didn't think so, but he knew. So that's the romantic way my husband found out about his second child: I announced it crouched on the floor of a public bathroom over my cell phone.

Somehow, I got it together enough to go back out to the table. But I was white as a sheet and so weak . . . and everyone was on to me! They asked me if I was okay, and I told them I just wasn't feeling well. One of them belted out, "She's pregnant again!" And of course everyone ran with it. My boss even threatened to buy a pregnancy test on the way back to the office. I told them I refused to pee on a stick for them—we're close, but not that close.

Before Tim got home, I took a bottle of Budweiser beer and made a new label on the computer. I tried to make it look like a Bud beer label, except it had a little photo of an embryo and said, "This bud's for you. Now you'll have two."

Here we go . . . *again!*

October 12

From: Sara
To: Stephanie
Subject: Fertile Myrtle

I *cannot* believe it. I don't even know what to say, I'm in such a state of shock! I guess the reality is that it only takes once! The good news is that you'll have your kids close together and then you can be done (if you want). It will be great for Sara to have a brother or sister that close. And since she really won't have time to get used to being the only child, maybe it will be an even easier adjustment.

You know, it's probably just typical that you made the announcement to Tim over the phone on the bathroom floor—it's the second child, after all! Everything can be well planned and coordinated for the first, but the second one has to be a whole different ball game. I guess that's why second children are usually so easygoing (hopefully yours will be, too)—they have to just go with the flow!

So . . . that puts you due in May? I think that's a great time to have a baby. (Remember what a pain it was to have to bundle up a little infant every time we went somewhere after Sara and Anna were born?) You'll be able to get outside and take walks—I think it will be great. Do you have a feeling about it being a boy or girl yet? This is all so exciting! What does Tim think? I bet he's excited, too (once the initial shock wore off, that is). I can't wait to tell David!

Congratulations, and keep me posted! I have to go take my birth-control pill now.

October 18

From: Stephanie
To: Sara
Subject: Hormones

I hate hormones!

I'm so tired that I can barely sit upright. Apparently, progesterone (the hormone that's made in mass quantities during your first trimester of pregnancy) is also a sleep-inducing hormone. I'm here to tell you, I have an abundance of it!

I'm also learning about the "pregnant mothers with a child in day care" curse: Every sickness that traverses day care is brought home and transferred to you by your child . . . guaranteed. There are only two differences: (1) Adults tend to have much worse symptoms than children with the same virus; and (2) your child can take medicine to combat the symptoms—pregnant women can take "NBT" (nothing but Tylenol). So, not only can I not sleep at night (having to pee every three hours), but I can't breathe through my nose either. It's like some weird, evil torture: "Let's pinch her nose shut, inject her with a sleep-inducing drug all day, and then see if she can sleep with a bowling ball on her bladder!"

This morning was the icing on the cake. I was feeling a little queasy and *very* weak; yet despite my ailments, I managed to get Sara and myself dressed (and coordinated, I might add). Her cold seemed worse today, so after giving her a bottle, I decided to give her some cold medicine. Well, if Sara doesn't like the taste of her medicine, she starts gagging and it comes right back up. Such was the case this morning, only along with the medicine came all five ounces of semi-ingested formula—she projectile-vomited all over both of us. I wish I would have paid more attention in that college physics class I took so that I could understand how five ounces of formula becomes equal to that of a gallon when your child regurgitates it all over your clothing. I'm sure they must have covered that during the second half of the trimester . . . er, I mean *semester*.

It's just a good thing that we love them so much—or there would be a lot of psychiatric wards just for parents. I just sat there on the kitchen chair with my kid in my lap, both of us covered in vomit, her crying and me swearing. Looking back, I feel like a terrible mother because I didn't comfort her for having just lost her entire breakfast. Instead, I asked her why she couldn't take medicine like a normal child, and then I told her that this was the first day I was ever glad to be dropping her off at day care. (A comment that, looking back, I hate myself for.)

So, I had to get us both dressed all over again, which was another dilemma, because I haven't done any laundry or been to the dry cleaner in a week. That means I had to fish around the dirty-clothes hamper to find the least revolting article of clothing available—anything that had a minute chance of passing for "clean." Oh well, nothing that a damp cloth, lint brush, and a hot iron couldn't cure.

Of course, then I had to listen to my husband criticize me for being upset with Sara: "She's ten months old—she can't help it." This is the man who slept in this morning while I got the baby dressed and prepared her lunch and bottles. I even got up and walked around the bed to turn the alarm clock off for him. This is the man who has been "out of town on business" for the last four days, eating at five-star restaurants every night and having the nice people from room service bring his breakfast every morning. The biggest crises he's had to face are his self-induced hangovers, or if the cook prepared his steak to the desired color. The nerve of him to stand there in his stain-free clothing and criticize me. Isn't it funny that the parent who *hasn't* been doing the caretaking recently can be so logical in a crisis?

I'm convinced that the first and last few weeks of pregnancy are the worst. But of the two, the first trimester of pregnancy is definitely the worst, hands down. Not only do you have to deal with morning sickness and fatigue, but you're not ready to let anyone know your little secret yet.

Sure, your feet swell, but at least during the last few weeks you're so huge and uncomfortable-looking that people are kind to you, and you can really milk it. And the clothing dilemma during the first trimester is the worst, too: Your regular clothes won't fit around your belly, but you're not quite big enough to wear maternity clothes without feeling silly. So you're forced to wear all your shirts untucked to conceal the rubber band (strategically looped around the buttons on your waist) that's holding your pants up. During the first pregnancy this was really cute, because it meant that your stomach (the baby) was growing. I can tell that this, my second time around, is going to be nothing but annoying. However, I'd still choose the rubber-band method over going out and buying "big girl" pants.

That's all for today's update. My boss went to play golf with a client (men have such sacrifices to make in the name of business), and I'm going to take a nap on his lovely Italian leather couch.

October 20

From: Sara
To: Stephanie
Subject: Four words for you . . .

. . . stay-at-home mother. Can you possibly work from home? I mean, it's so much easier for both you and your child (children) not to be on a major schedule in the mornings.

I must preface this all by saying that I can hardly type right now because I've consumed at least an entire bottle of wine. We hosted an engagement party for our friends Mick and Veronica tonight, and Anna is with the grandparents! Woo-hoo! And of course I've called a million times, to the point that Mom said, "Stop calling me! She's fine!"

October 22
From: Stephanie
To: Sara
Subject: Puppets and Saran Wrap

I was wishing *really* hard that we lived close to family members this past week. Tim was out of town again, and with me having morning sickness all day, it would have been such a blessing to have a little help.

It's so weird . . . all I want to do is sleep! I don't have anything challenging going on at work either, so being bored during the day isn't helping things. I could come home and go straight to bed and sleep through the night and still be tired the next day. I'll be happy when the first trimester is over.

Sara is so much fun right now—she's so much more interactive! She laughs at everything and wrestles around on the floor with Tim and me. Isn't it great that we can actually play *with* our girls now? Sara *loved* that *Baby Mozart* video you'd given me, so I upgraded her to *Baby Shakespeare*. It stars a dragon puppet that she liked a lot in the first video. She has a ball watching that crazy video. Every time the puppets come on, she squeals with delight and even laughs out loud sometimes.

You should have seen how happy she was when Tim came home last night. She couldn't *wait* for me to hand her over to him. Of course then she wanted to come immediately back to Mommy, but it was so sweet how she welcomed him home. Short of wrapping my naked self up in Saran Wrap and having porn playing in the living room, I don't think I could have topped her welcome. (Sure am glad she came along, 'cause that Saran Wrap is a bitch to clean up!)

October 23

From: Sara
To: Stephanie
Subject: Vomit morning

Well, since I was reveling in my free-parent weekend, I didn't really respond adequately to your "vomit morning" e-mail. I'm sure what you said to little Sara was a result of hormones and the stress of trying to get out the door on a schedule. Of course it's easier for the "other" parent to be logical in a crisis, because they aren't *dealing* with the crisis—they're just looking at it from outside (and in Tim's case, with the benefit of a full, restful night's sleep). He's lucky you didn't just sock him one for getting you into this condition again: "*You* did this to me!"

Yes, the kids are at a great stage now, and the interaction is great. By the way, Anna's going through that stranger-anxiety thing, too, so I don't think it's day care, it's just a stage. She used to go to anyone; now she's suddenly afraid to let anyone but David and me (or the grandparents) hold her. Makes you wonder what's going on in their little heads. Of course, obviously Anna didn't miss us one bit while she was with my parents. I'm glad, though: It makes it a lot easier to know that she's happy there (but it's good to have her back home).

October 24

From: Stephanie
To: Sara
Subject: Diet for relieving stress

This came my way today via the Internet. You know I only pass on the really good ones, so enjoy!

This Is a Special Diet Designed to
Help Mothers Cope with Stress:

Breakfast
1 grapefruit
1 slice whole-wheat bread
1 cup skim milk

Lunch
1 small portion lean, steamed chicken with a cup of spinach
1 cup herbal tea
1 Hershey's Kiss

Afternoon tea
The rest of the Hershey's Kisses in the bag
1 tub Häagen-Dazs ice cream with chocolate-chip topping

Dinner
4 bottles of wine (red or white)
2 loaves garlic bread
1 family-size supreme pizza
2 Snickers bars

Late-night snack
1 whole Sara Lee cheesecake (eaten directly from the freezer)

Remember, "stressed" spelled backwards is "desserts"!

October 24
From: Sara
To: Stephanie
Subject: Have you been spying on me?

Move one bottle of wine up to afternoon tea, and you have my daily meal plan.

October 25
From: Stephanie
To: Sara
Subject: Baby or pancakes?

Well, pregnancy is a wild mix of twists and turns. Last week I lost weight because I was so sick, and I couldn't even *smell* food without throwing up. But this week the only thing that makes me feel better is to keep food in my stomach. The downfall is that there's this little deli/grill in my building, which is extremely dangerous for a pregnant woman because it's convenient and it's cheap. I've had pancakes and bacon for breakfast for the past two days. Of course this is *after* the wake-up glass of chocolate milk (which I crave 24 hours a day) and a granola bar or two.

If I keep this up, I'm going to be huge. My stomach is already pooching—I can't tell if it's the pancakes or if it's the baby, since you start to show twice as fast with the second one. I'm hoping it's the baby—the pooch was there last week, and I was six pounds lighter than normal.

Well, the deal involving my company was finalized yesterday, but we still don't know what our fate will be. And I'm going through the same inner turmoil about continuing my career: I'll be having another baby in eight months, and I really don't want *two* of them in day care. It just seems ridiculous to keep having babies for someone else to raise eight hours a day, five days a week. I only see Sara for a couple hours every night before she goes to sleep, and it's really sad.

I'm in the process of creating a database with all the local ad agencies' addresses and phone numbers so that I can send out some letters and résumés to see if I can get this freelance-writing thing off the ground. I guess that would mean a *huge* lifestyle change for us . . . as we speak, the maids are scurrying around, cleaning my house. I love the maids.

I've never been so split right down the middle before: I want to be with the babies, but I'm not sure I can stay at home all the time and give up the restaurants, shopping, and maid service. I suppose it would just take some getting used to. I'm in work mode right now, and I know that I need to get back into Mommy mode.

But right now, I need to go eat some saltines.

October 29
From: Sara
To: Stephanie
Subject: Mental meltdown

Good God, I can't get anything done these days, since Anna is nonstop! Anyway, nothing like a company buyout and a pregnancy to keep your life interesting, huh? And here I was stressing out over hosting an engagement party. . . . How are you holding up?

Now you know what I mean about the struggle between working vs. staying at home. I'm enjoying being home more now, but I still long for something else for me. I still want to have it *all* . . . but I'm slowly becoming open to the idea that maybe I can have it all, just not at the same time.

I just see how fast Anna is growing and changing, and I'm starting to realize how true it is that "they grow up so fast." I'm really trying to cherish every moment I can.

Of course being at home you still have a million things to do during the day, so it often still feels like a rat race. I used to long for somewhere to go during the day—now I'm thankful when I don't have to go anywhere. I so need some domestic help. Right now I'd almost trade my husband for a good maid. If I ever get the money, I'll definitely hire someone to help with the major stuff. That would be such a relief. Hell, I have a full-time job picking up after Anna. And around here a neat house only exists after her bedtime, if at all anymore. These days I'm just happy when the place isn't a disaster.

October 30
From: Stephanie
To: Sara
Subject: Prince Charming and family

We're going to a Halloween party tonight: I'm Snow White, Sara's Dopey, and I finally talked Tim into being Prince Charming. Ha! He's *miserable*. He made me promise not to leave his side tonight. You should have seen him trying on all the costumes with big puffy sleeves and ruffled collars. Even the guy at the costume store was encouraging him, "C'mon, man! You'll be a chick magnet—what woman doesn't dream of Prince Charming?!" Poor Tim . . . I kept sticking my head behind the curtain of his dressing room to see, and he said, "Will you leave me alone?! What do you not understand about this? I told you to get out of here!" (Yeah, right—like I was going to miss *that!*) He finally found one that isn't so bad. It has pants instead of tights, which is a *huge* plus for a man of Tim's stature.

Sara's costume is hilarious! Tim's mom made her these little brown dwarf pants with a green ragged shirt and a little belt. I made her a brown floppy hat that sits perfectly behind her ears, so they stick out just like Dopey. Poor baby, she'll never forgive us. I'll be sure to send some photos.

As for the work/don't work dilemma, I keep thinking about what a different state of mind I was in when I stayed home with Sara those first three months. Now I'm kind of back in work mode, but after listening to you, you've confirmed my theory that I'd just get used to being at home again. It's like a new job— and I know I'll enjoy it so much more.

My house is a wreck right now. Between feeling sick and tired and traveling, I have *four* loads of laundry on my closet floor, and clutter everywhere. I surrender! I've been so chronically exhausted with this pregnancy that it's all I can do to get home, feed and bathe Sara, and get her into bed. I just want to sleep— I don't care about the house. The maids keep it from being condemned, but other than that, I don't expect *Southern Living* photographers to arrive on my doorstep anytime soon. I'm behind on everything—I'd love to have the time and energy to just clean out a couple of kitchen cabinets or do a few pages in Sara's scrapbook. But, hey, that's the first trimester, right? I just have to get through it.

The second pregnancy is *so much harder*. With the first one, when you were tired, you could just go lie down. Now you have someone who doesn't care if you're tired—she still needs to be fed, bathed, played with, have clean laundry, etc. Poor Tim has had to change *every* poopy diaper in the morning because my gag reflex is so sensitive that just the smell of a dirty diaper makes me throw up. It's crazy.

My first doctor's appointment is next Friday. I look forward to that, because they're going to give me a definite due date (yeah, right—definite) and help me get into "good pregnancy mode" again. So far, all I've eaten is junk food because I only crave greasy fried stuff. It's like having a permanent hangover. And I've had so much trouble getting food down that I just eat whatever doesn't make me puke. It's a matter of survival right now, not health. But that has to change or I'm going to gain 50 pounds! The problem is that when you're having morning sickness (which, as you know, is such a crock, because in reality you're sick *all day*), the only thing that makes you feel better is to have something heavy in your stomach. Yogurt and baby carrots don't cut it. I'm talking hamburgers, French fries, fried chicken, and bread . . . lots and lots of bread.

Okay, enough rambling for one day. I have to go have some more bread.

November 7

From: Sara
To: Stephanie
Subject: My new favorite word . . .

. . . is *babysitter!* We have one scheduled for Friday night, and she came over last night so she could meet Anna. I should have done this months ago. As you know, when you don't have family around, you don't get many breaks. And something this girl said made me think about you: She said she used to work as a mother's helper. In other words, she'd come to the house and watch the baby so that the mother could do some work. Maybe you could arrange a way to work for your company from home, at least part-time. More and more women are doing this now, and more companies have to look at it in order to keep good employees.

This babysitter came highly recommended from one of our neighbors, and after meeting her I feel really good about it. She's only 14 but seems so together. I took her around the house and showed her everything, like the room the dogs come in when we're not home, etc. At one point during the "tour," I said, "You know, I'm probably going overboard here." And she says, "Yeah, first baby." Can you believe that? A 14-year-old! Obviously this girl has babysat quite a few kids. I may be calling her for child-rearing advice before long.

Also, I just put Anna on a waiting list for preschool at a nearby church, and I've heard great things about it. It's either two or three days a week from 9:30 A.M. to 12:30 P.M., and it's only $100 a month! You could do something like that for Sara—it would give you some free time, but you'd still be able to be with her most of the day. Also, I do a lot of work at night, which, with Tim's travel schedule, would probably work out fine for you as well. Just some ideas.

Your Halloween costumes were hilarious! I have to say that Sara did make a cute little Dopey. I can't wait till she sees that picture in a few years . . . you better start formulating your explanation now. Of course, you can at least say, "Well, come on—look at your father and me!"

Anna was a cute white bunny rabbit for Halloween, although it took both David and me to hold her down so that I could draw the whiskers on her face. She just didn't understand that those whiskers were key in increasing her candy intake. Mommy knows best, after all.

November 7
From: Stephanie
To: Sara
Subject: No news is good news

So I'm just hoping to hang on to my job through the holidays. Everyone in my office keeps bitching, "I want to know! I need to know!" and I keep telling them they don't want to know *anything* until after the holidays. Don't they realize how bad it sucks to get fired at Christmastime? No news is good news, but they're so impatient—they must think that the new owner is going to give us two months' notice to find new jobs or something. *Right.* As soon as employees find out that they're going to be canned, all work stops. I know it, and the new company knows it. We'll get two weeks' notice if we're lucky—but I can't seem to convince anyone else of that.

In the meantime, I'm sending mailers out to the local ad agencies. I'm actually thinking about trying to get something full-time until the baby comes, and then scaling back to freelancing. That would give me more experience and more confidence. Plus, we could use the income. Sara's so happy at her little day care these days. She loves her friends, and although I miss her terribly, I don't feel as guilty leaving her there (if only it weren't for eight hours a day!). But that's all temporary—if my job goes away, I feel like I need to make as much money as I can, for as long as I can.

November 10

From: Sara
To: Stephanie
Subject: New possibilities

Wouldn't it be cool if someday when Sara and Anna are older we could all take a weekend trip together, just us girls? I'm so glad I had a little girl. If she only shares my love of shoes, then my life will be complete.

I'll keep my fingers crossed that your job lasts as long as possible. What a roller-coaster ride this whole year has been, with this buyout hanging over you for so long. However, I think you'd really enjoy freelancing, and you have the ideal personality to do it. Some people don't have the discipline to stay focused and work at home, while others don't have the sales skills you need to go out and drum up business—you have both! Plus, when you factor the cost of two kids in day care, I'm sure it starts becoming more feasible financially to work from home.

Let me know if I can help you in any way. And remember, whenever one door closes, a window opens. Maybe there's something even more exciting and rewarding waiting around the corner!

November 14

From: Stephanie
To: Sara
Subject: Biological warfare disguised as "day care"

Once again, I curse day care and those who invented it—and most of all, those who bring their sick children there! Sara brought home *yet another* stomach virus last Thursday. She seemed to feel fine, but then she vomited every single thing she ate. By Friday she was feeling fine, and we proceeded to Charlotte to visit Tim's mom. By Saturday, I was puking *my* brains out—at my mother-in-law's house. Perfect. It's miserable to be that sick and not be at your own home, not to mention that it took us *six* freakin' hours to drive back home because of traffic and detours. It was terrible. I haven't been able to keep anything down, not even water, *and* I've had to take Sara to day care every morning because Tim has trainees in town. It sucks not having any family around for these emergencies.

My doctor almost checked me into the hospital yesterday because I became so dehydrated that it started to affect the baby. We finally found a prescription that worked, and I was able to keep some toast and Gatorade down for the first time in three days. I was really worried because I started having horrible cramps and was spotting a little. All I could think of is how tragic it would be—and how pissed off I'd be—to lose a baby because of a stomach virus. Sara's still not feeling well, so I'm leaving work early today to take her to the doctor. I'm sure I have no sick days left, but hey—when you're sick, you're sick.

This morning I was feeling a little bit better, but in the process of getting Sara ready, she made a horrible, poopy diaper. So between my nausea from the virus, and the nausea from morning sickness . . . well, enough said.

Tim's been great through all this. Yesterday I told my mother, "Poor Tim, tonight he has to come home from work, pick up Sara, stop at the drugstore to pick up a prescription, go to the grocery store, and then feed her," and my mom shoots back, "What do you mean, 'poor Tim'? *You* do all that every day!" She's right! What was I thinking? I must be delirious with fever and lack of nourishment.

Looks like we're going to hold on to our jobs until first quarter, but I have to admit that I'm ready to move out of Atlanta now. We don't have any family here; plus, we're so busy with Sara and work that we haven't made any new friends. I hate leaving her with a babysitter—I just don't know anyone I trust, except for her teachers (who aren't always available). And besides, when I've been away from her Monday through Friday, the last thing I want to do is leave her with a sitter on a Friday night. So we usually take her with us, which is no fun for anyone but us, I imagine. Consequently, we've become quite the hermits. I'm sure that if I was with her every day, I'd look forward to the Saturday-night sitter, like every other normal parent.

Oh, damn! I just looked down, and I have a *huge* run in my tights. Probably caught them on the bathroom door while sprinting to get my face into the toilet.

It's not easy being me.

November 15

From: Sara
To: Stephanie
Subject: Tough jobs

I can't believe that you haven't had an emotional and mental breakdown after all you've been going through! Give yourself a pat on the back for being so strong—I don't know how you do it! The more I stay home with Anna, the more I love it . . . yet it's great to be able to leave her with a babysitter. And by getting a break, I'm a better mother: It recharges me to come back home with energy and enthusiasm again.

I know I'm fortunate to have the option to stay home. I've gotten into gardening, and I'm enjoying taking care of the house (scary)—it doesn't feel so much like drudgery anymore. I also have a lot of work from the agency right now, which is nice. It's a good balance for me to be able to stay at home and work there as well; I need the work to be able to handle the staying-at-home part. It makes me feel like I'm contributing to our income (even if it's only a little) and retaining part of myself that exists separately from being a wife and a mother. I need to hold on to *me*— at least some of me.

Did you get a due date from your doctor yet? I sure hope that you'll be past the nausea part soon. Do you have any gut instincts on the baby being a boy or a girl? How about names? I've started to think about names for number two a lot lately . . . but it's not quite time for that yet!

I know what you mean about living in Atlanta. That's how it was for us in Virginia Beach at first, until we met you guys and some other people. And when you have kids, it's even harder. We have a great circle of friends here in Charlotte, which is one of the reasons we moved back. It would be hard to leave that because it really takes years to establish. Any chance of you guys moving back here? You'd have instant friends *and* family!

November 16
From: Stephanie
To: Sara
Subject: Please—not Junior!

Actually, Charlotte is numero uno on our list of places to move. I'm sure that when the time comes for us to leave Atlanta, we'll move back to that area.

My due date is June 1, which seems like *years* from now. Tim and I haven't started thinking about names yet because we're going to find out the baby's sex this time. We had a really hard time with boy names last time—so I'm not looking forward to that task. Tim's family wants us to name a boy after Tim—but I have a really hard time imagining calling my baby the same name as my husband, and I *don't* want him called Junior (ugh).

You won't believe how quickly you'll start showing with baby number two. I can't button any of my pants already. I'm less than three months pregnant, yet I look like I did when I was at least four months last time—it's crazy! I just hope it doesn't mean that I'm going to be bigger this time. I just saw pictures of myself when I was nine months pregnant last year, and oh my God! I'm *so* not ready for that. My doctor prepared me by explaining that the second time is much different. She said that I'm older now, so I'm going to feel a lot more aches and pains and fatigue. When you're pregnant the first time, it takes a lot out of your body. I'm glad she prepared me—I'd rather plan for the worst and expect the best. Of course they want to do an amniocentesis this time because I'll be 35 when the baby's born. We're weighing our options, but I'm not sure what we'll decide. They also want us to go to a genetic counselor to review all the advantages and disadvantages of inserting a needle into my womb. I'll keep you posted.

It's great to hear that you're becoming happier being at home—I think it's just a transition period that you have to make. Remind me of that if I get lucky enough to make that situation happen, because I'm sure it will be a huge adjustment for me, too.

November 22
From: Sara
To: Stephanie
Subject: The second time around

I'm sure that the second time is tougher due to all the things your doctor mentioned, as well as the fact that you already have a child to take care of. It's not like you're just going to be able to sit down and relax whenever you feel a little tired. But the good thing is that you're getting all the pregnancy stuff over with in short order. And just think how close your kids are going to be since they'll be so close in age. I want to have mine close together, too—that way, I won't be completely old and decrepit when they're graduating from high school. You'll be fine, though. Look at all those women who have four and five kids. They're nuts in my book, but they're obviously physically able to do it.

That's so exciting that you're going to find out the baby's sex! It will make it more fun to shop. And it will be neat to have a different experience the second time around.

Gotta go—it's cocktail hour. I'll have one for you.

December 11
From: Stephanie
To: Sara
Subject: Amnio

How's it going? Well, we met with a doctor yesterday to discuss whether I should have an amniocentesis or not. Apparently, at 35 years of age, there's a 1 in 200 chance that the baby will have some type of abnormality. Tim and I went in thinking that we weren't going to opt for the amnio—really, what are the chances of *me* being that one?—but by the time we left, I was all for it. In a nutshell, I could get over the disappointment of a miscarriage after a while—but if the baby was born with a disability, that would be a lifetime of difficulties (which would affect Sara's life, too).

The chances of miscarriage due to an amnio are 2 in 1,000. Also, some of the things they may find can be corrected before the baby is even born. Which makes me think that if the baby *was* born with a defect that could have been corrected in utero, we'd be kicking ourselves for not having it done. Now, Part Two of the question is, "If they find anything wrong, would we terminate the pregnancy?" I'm not going to worry about that unless I need to.

Anyway, the amnio is next week. They'll do an ultrasound, and the whole procedure takes less than 30 minutes or so. Then I have to stay off my feet the rest of the day, and not run any marathons the following day. The risk is that the tiny hole made by the needle in the membranes sometimes doesn't close back up, which is what causes a miscarriage. The doctor says that it has nothing to do with the way the procedure is done, and everything to do with the individual woman and her membranes. It's a little scary, but if everything comes back normal, I can relax and enjoy the rest of the pregnancy with no worries. Also, we'll find out the baby's sex, which I'm really looking forward to.

December 15

From: Sara
To: Stephanie
Subject: The amnio question

I'd opt to do the amnio, too. It's kind of like that AFP [alpha-fetoprotein] test that you take regardless of your age, but which is also optional. I thought I wasn't going to do it, but when my doctor told me that they could tell if there was a problem so severe that the baby would die right after birth, I decided to do it. I think that as far as terminating the pregnancy goes, for me it would come down to what quality of life the child would have.

When I was going back to school for my English degree, I took some special-education courses, and we visited a facility for severely handicapped children. There were some whose heads had to be propped up with devices under their chins and who were confined to wheelchairs—and they basically just sat there and drooled on themselves all day. Their parents couldn't keep them at home because they needed such extensive care that they were in this facility. What quality of life is that? I think that would be the question I'd have to answer, because there are lots of people with milder disabilities who lead very fulfilling and meaningful lives. But the bottom line is that there's no point in crossing that bridge until you come to it—and hopefully and most likely, you won't.

I can't wait to find out whether you're having a boy or a girl. What's your guess? I think I'm going to have two girls for some reason. Anyway, good luck, and let me know what you find out!

December 18

From: Stephanie
To: Sara
Subject: Barbies and footballs!

Okay, here's how it went. The nurse started doing the ultrasound, checking out the baby and the amniotic fluid, etc. We could clearly see all the images on the screen, but of course she saved the sex for last. I saw almost immediately what I thought was evidence of a boy, but I needed to hear it from the medical professional. She said that she'd never admit to being 100 percent sure, but she was about 80 percent sure that this was a boy. We have a perfect ultrasound picture of a little penis. (Hopefully, for his sake, it will grow.)

I was so happy that I started clapping my hands and couldn't stop crying. This will be the first boy born on my side of the family in 74 years! I was so excited that I could barely stand to lie there on the table a minute longer. Tim was laughing at how emotional and thrilled I was about the news. It was a great, great moment. Just as great, I believe, as if we'd waited to find out at the baby's birth.

Here's my take on the whole amnio thing—it's really no big deal. I have to admit that I was really nervous: A needle that long would scare anybody! But the excitement of finding out the baby's sex lessened the fear. I had to lie very still while the doctor inserted the needle. I didn't really feel the prick, I just felt my stomach muscles tighten intensely, like a strong cramp. It only took a few seconds, and then it was all over.

The myths about miscarrying because the baby gets stuck by the needle are just that: myths. In fact, the doctor told me that although they use an ultrasound to avoid disturbing the baby, babies move and get stuck often—but they just get mad and move to the other side of the uterus. The reason women miscarry is usually because the little hole made by the needle in the uterus doesn't fill in and heal, but instead begins to leak amniotic fluid, and *that* causes a miscarriage. (It's funny, because once I knew the baby's sex, it made it seem so much more like a real person, more like I was risking his life—I even asked Tim if he still thought we should go through with the test.)

Anyway, I called both our moms on the way home from the doctor's office, and everyone is so thrilled. And then Tim treated me by taking me to the nearest Babies "R" Us, and we bought lots of *blue, blue, blue!* It was the best! Sara's going to have a baby brother—time to pick out some boy names.

We're so blessed to have the privilege of raising both a girl and a boy. Barbies *and* footballs! Yippee!

December 18
From: Sara
To: Stephanie
Subject: Yippee!

One of each—how much more in the world could you ask for? Congratulations! Now you finally get to go buy those G.I. Joes you've been wanting for so long! How much fun to know the baby's sex and be able to shop and decorate and think about names. Of course the good thing is that since you didn't know Sara's sex beforehand, you've probably got plenty of neutral clothes and baby stuff that you can still use for Baby Boy.

What a wonderful moment for you and Tim! I'm so happy for you, and relieved that everything went well with the amnio. Go put your feet up and relax—come May, you won't be able to again for five or six years!

December 20
From: Stephanie
To: Sara
Subject: Doing it our way

I was having one of those sentimental moments today (hormone-induced, I'm sure), about how different our experiences have been throughout all of this. Who knew that the whole having-a-baby thing could lead down so many uniquely different paths?

In the movies, everyone rushes to the hospital, driving like maniacs (yeah, like *that* happens), and then there's some yelling and sweating, and the next thing you know, a happy mom is holding a new baby in her hospital room, while the adoring father looks on. How are the media able to completely and consistently misrepresent this whole motherhood thing? Thank goodness for Oprah.

And as you read this e-mail, my dear friend, try to imagine Frank Sinatra's song "My Way" playing in the background (surely it's the theme song of mothers everywhere). I'm so proud of both of us for finding our own way through this whole motherhood thing, and even though our choices were different in so many ways, we never judged or criticized each other's decisions (well, hardly ever).

I think the only thing we had in common is that our first children were both girls. Everything else—from breast-feeding and sleeping arrangements to career choices and decorating—could not have been more opposite. But it was through those differences that we were able to encourage, support, and provide perspective for each other's individual struggles. I wish I could be like that all the time—to consistently overcome the primitive instinct to compete with other women and be more supportive instead. I've made the commitment to stop judging women based on how clean their house is or what designer shoes they're wearing. All I want to do these days is bask in the "motherhood club," which is the greatest club on earth. Initiation is the same for everyone: puking and crying and struggling and getting fat and being sleep deprived for years on end.

It's all so scary and so difficult—and immensely unpredictable—because each mother's experience is entirely her own. But *every* healthy and sane Mommy knows that the afterglow created by that little someone you adore so completely makes every stitch of pain and every ounce of difficulty so worthwhile.

In the end, no matter how different our choices might be, we mothers do love our children in exactly the same way: with our whole hearts.

December 22

From: Sara
To: Stephanie
Subject: What a year

I was just thinking back over this year as well, and it's pretty amazing. We've both gone through so much adjusting to motherhood, but I think we've done pretty well, all in all. And now you're going to experience it all over again! I'm sure it will be so much easier the second time around. There won't be the big learning curve that there was with the first baby.

I think what's interesting is that different things worked for both of us: You loved breast-feeding and I hated it; you went back to work and I stayed at home (neither of which is an easy choice, as we both know). But what that shows me is that there isn't just *one* way to be a good mom—every woman has to do what works for her and her family. I think it's good that you and I respected each other's choices (like you didn't try to preach breast-feeding to me even though it was so great for you).

Why *are* we women so competitive with each other? I guess it's just human nature. Men get to release their competitiveness when they play sports, whereas women use daily life as our arena. We can be pretty tough on each other, though: Our houses have to be cleaner, more beautiful, and more perfect than our neighbors. Reminds me of one of my favorite jokes:

> One Sunday in church, a minister asked his congregation how many of them could forgive their enemies. About half of the people sitting in the pews raised their hands. So he asked again, more emphatically, "How many of you can forgive your enemies?" This time about three quarters of the people raised their hands. So he asked again, raising his voice to a dramatic pitch, "How many of you can forgive your enemies?" Now every person but one raised their hand. The only person without a hand in the air was a little old lady in the back of the church. The minister asked her why she couldn't forgive her enemies. She replied that she didn't have any. "Ma'am, can I ask how old you are?" he said kindly. The little old lady answered that she was 93. "Would you mind sharing with our congregation how a 93-year-old woman can have not a single enemy?" the minister asked. "It's simple," the lady said, "I outlived the bitches."

Anyway, I'm so glad that you and I got through this without judging each other. Being a mother is hard enough without feeling like you have to live up to some impossible standard to boot. The bottom line is this: *As a mother, you just have to do what works for you.* It's such a huge adjustment that you have to get through it the best way you can. (I recommend lots of caffeine, wine, Advil, and a good antidepressant.) And you can't comprehend what it's like until you've been there yourself.

I realize now that the same thing that happens when you get married also happens when you have a baby. Most of us women get so wrapped up in planning the wedding, making sure every tiny detail is just perfect, that we aren't prepared for the marriage, which of course, is the really important thing. Having a baby can be the same way: There's all this focus on the pregnancy and labor and childbirth (and there's such a buildup for all that), that when you get home, it's kind of like the honeymoon's over. Yet that's the time we should prepare for most—that's when motherhood *really* begins. At least it did for me.

I certainly had a difficult time adjusting to being a mother. As for my bout with postpartum depression, I just wish I'd known that what was happening to me has also happened to millions of other women. Those few months were without a doubt the toughest thing I've been through in my life—but I'm so much better for it now. I've always known that I wanted to have children, and deep down I've always felt sure I'd be a good mom. I think that's why the depression threw me for such a loop: Coming home with a perfect baby was what I always wanted, so why did I hate my life? Of course I didn't; it was the depression affecting me.

I'm finally at peace with things. I just love being a Mommy now. There truly is nothing on earth like the love you have for your child—you just want everything for them. Having kids makes Christmas magical all over again: I've been waiting my whole life to be Santa . . . and now Anna's almost a year old. (What a year!) Sometimes I feel like my heart could explode.

I've learned that with the greatest happiness also comes the greatest risk. Someone said once that having a child is like walking around with your heart on the outside of your body. Stories you read in the paper or see on TV about something happening to a child affect you in a way you could have never imagined before. Being blessed with something so wonderful also means that you're more vulnerable than ever. But it's so, *so* incredibly worth it. It's like that scene from one of my all-time favorite movies, *Parenthood,* where the grandmother says that some people go to the amusement park and only want to ride the merry-go-round because it's safe and doesn't go too fast. But she said she preferred the roller coaster—oh, you might get sick and feel a little scared, but you sure got a lot more out of it.

Let's enjoy the ride.

December 31
From: Stephanie
To: Sara
Subject: The job of being a Mommy

Wow—today is Anna's first birthday! Look at how we've both changed—did you ever realize that the job of mother was actually a compilation of so many jobs (which you're expected to be *good* at)? I certainly didn't.

Think about it: We're teachers, chefs, maids, and entertainers. We're artists who make faces on pancakes and can turn celery, peanut butter, and raisins into ants on a log. We cook, clean, sew, and sing. We have to be physically and mentally fit, and still be able to fit into the "tunnel playgrounds" at all the fast-food restaurants (in case somebody gets stuck).

The workload has never been greater, and the salary has never been smaller . . . but the rewards are infinite. We get to play again, ride the water slides and the carousel. It's an excuse to color with crayons and squeeze paint between our fingers. It's a chance to imagine and pretend, and run through the sprinkler and sit in a one-foot-deep pool in the backyard and not be embarrassed. We get to buy new toys and wrap beautiful presents with great anticipation. It's hugs and squeezes and kisses and smiles, all on demand.

Motherhood brings the magic in everything back to the surface: Disney World, the petting zoo, the movie theater, Christmas, riding a bike, the smell of a swimming pool, the feel of tearing cotton candy from the stick, and how a Popsicle can be so cold and still taste so good. It's not just reliving it all; it's *living* it with more wisdom, more love, and so much more joy than you did the first time. Watching your child live and love is even better than experiencing it yourself. It's like adding a great seasoning that enhances the already great taste of life.

How sweet it is to just exist each day with someone you love so completely. We mothers have so much to look forward to.

I can hardly wait.

.

Afterword

From: Stephanie
Subject: I've become a domestic goddess

I was laid off from my job in the cable TV industry just two months before my son, Timothy, was born. My family moved into a new house on a golf course just north of Atlanta, and we had just enough time to get settled before baby number two came along. My son's birth was more complicated than Sara's and resulted in a C-section. Apparently, he had a huge head (a Triplett family trait), so he wasn't going to fit through my birth canal unassisted. In fact, I just had a conversation with Dr. Soundararajan (Dr. S) a few days ago, and she's still telling me facts about the births of both my children that I have absolutely no recollection of. Her memory is amazing (I guess that's why she's a doctor).

Today I'm a full-time, bona-fide, stay-at-home Mommy. I drive the children to preschool, ballet lessons, and play group. I'm a room mom during the school year, and the play-group moms call me "Julie McCoy, the cruise director" (you know, like from *The Love Boat*), because I love planning all our outings. I have a small garden with herbs and vegetables (or at least I hope there will be vegetables), I bake cookies (both varieties—slice 'n' bake and from scratch—depending on the occasion and the ingredients present in my pantry . . . yes, I *have* a pantry), I have pots with pretty flowers on my front porch and deck that I remember to water whenever they look droopy, and I'm known for throwing the best birthday parties in the neighborhood, complete with take-home CDs of theme music, over-the-top decorations, 3-D invitations, and an occasional appearance by a Disney Princess or two.

Honestly, I did get a little bored and lonely about six months into the "stay at home" thing, so I started doing some freelance writing and marketing consulting. I started a little business called "Writer's Block," with the hopes of channeling writing and marketing assignments to moms and my "block" of qualified writers who don't have the opportunity to get out and make the contacts necessary to keep the workload plentiful. I spend about eight to ten hours a week in my home office, while the kids play at a neighbor's house. My clients are very agreeable to working around my changing "kid schedule," and I love them for it.

I still find marriage challenging (who doesn't?), but Tim and I have discovered that our children have bonded us very deeply, and there's nothing more important to us than our family. Tim's an incredible dad. He's still thriving with AutoTrader.com, and in his spare time, he's now a certified stage hypnotist. I know, he's a little strange, but he's still very funny, especially now that the kids give him so much new material to work with. For the record, I'm planning on keeping him.

There are good days and bad days. Sometimes I struggle to find the patience to put up with the constant and seemingly never-ending demands and whining of a two- and three-year-old. But I landed in a great neighborhood full of wonderful stay-at-home moms who took me under their wing and taught me (along with Dr. Phil) that you have to get some time for yourself to recharge your batteries and your patience. So I go to the gym a few times a week, I schedule a few hours away from the kids *religiously* every weekend to catch a movie or have dinner with my girlfriends, and every Tuesday morning I take adult ballet classes. (Sara and I have the same teacher, and we both think that's pretty neat.)

Despite the bad days, I'm even more in love with my children: They're adorable and gorgeous, and I kiss them a hundred times a day (especially their perfect little feet and cheeks). My favorite hobby is dressing them. I love coordinating outfits: For example, last Halloween Sara was Cinderella, and I had a Prince Charming costume made for Timmy (I don't sew, and I never will).

My house is never clean enough: There are always at least two laundry baskets overflowing with dirty clothes in my closet, and still nobody helps me do any housework. I can't decide on a color to paint my living room. My office looks like there's been a high-wind advisory in there. And my garage currently smells like cat urine. But life is as sweet as it gets, and I think about that every single day.

From: Sara
Subject: I may drive a minivan, but I'm still me

I can remember the exact moment I fully embraced motherhood—when I was pregnant for the second time.

It was just before Christmas, and David and I had come to the realization that our Toyota Highlander (a fun little SUV that we loved) wasn't big enough to accommodate our holiday trip to Virginia. We needed a car with capacity for our luggage, all the Christmas gifts, Anna's birthday gifts, two large dogs, and the three of us (soon to be four). And after looking at quite a few large vehicles, I started to really appreciate the practicality of a minivan. You can fit amazing amounts of stuff into those cars; plus, they're built for our stage in life . . . you know, automatic sliding doors, a DVD player, 42 cup holders.

The real pivotal moment came when I heard Katie Couric talking about her minivan one morning on the *Today* show. I thought, *Well, she's successful, hip, stylish, and her own woman. If it's good enough for Katie, then it's good enough for me.* I, the woman who swore that she'd never, ever drive a minivan, found myself convincing my husband that we needed one. And here I am.

Several months later I gave birth to our son, Cade. Although I didn't have a C-section like Stephanie, I didn't have an easy birth either. (Unfortunately, I wasn't lucky enough for Dr. Beurskens, my favorite OB, to be on call this time.) I think Stephanie and I both disproved the theory that the second delivery is easier than the first. Let me just say this to all you expectant moms out there: If during labor your doctor suggests the "San Antonio method" of administering Pitocin, don't just say no, say *hell no*. They'll deserve it, because basically what they're suggesting is giving you about a day's worth of Pitocin in a matter of a few hours. Enough said?

But all's well that ends well, and we've completed our family with a beautiful, irresistible little boy who looks just like his

Daddy. David and I feel fortunate to get to experience raising both a daughter and a son. We're happy with two children (we prefer not being outnumbered). And I fear that if I had more than two I might spend most of the day saying, "Yes, that's a nice picture you colored, honey—now go get Mommy another martini."

Adjusting to the second child was much easier for me, but there *were* struggles. With the help of my doctor, I stopped taking my antidepressants since I wanted to get pregnant again. A couple months into the pregnancy, however, I started noticing the signs of postpartum depression again. So, guided by Dr. Beurskens, I decided to go back on the medication, but at a lower dosage. It wasn't as difficult a decision this time, because I had a two-year-old who needed her Mommy—her happy, normal Mommy. I'd hoped that I wouldn't have to take antidepressants during my pregnancy, but I absolutely knew that I didn't want to go through that dark time again.

A few days after Cade was born, I started to get weepy again, so I upped my dosage back to the non-pregnancy level. I wanted to enjoy those first few weeks and months this time in a way I hadn't before. And I did! Now I'm really enjoying both of my kids—and it feels so good to be able to. Yes, having two is more work, but it's also more fun. The best is when they interact together. No one can make Cade belly-laugh like Anna—she's the apple of his eye.

People say that you have to surrender to parenthood, but I disagree. I can't think of it in those terms. Right after I had Anna, I thought my own life had come to an end. I think that's part of what threw me into postpartum depression (well, that and the hormones). I thought I had to surrender, that I had to completely give my life over to my child for at least 10 or 15 years if I was going to be a good mother. It almost felt like a prison sentence.

People told me all sorts of things about motherhood: They said I'd stop wearing makeup and dressing nice, I wouldn't love my dogs as much, and I'd never have time to read anymore. None of it was true for me. You can make space in your life for the things that really matter. Dogs and books are part of who I am—I couldn't give those things up, or anything else that defined me. If I surrendered part of myself to parenthood, then I'd lose part of who I am, and so would those around me.

I want to give my family the whole me, so now I define motherhood for myself. I'm never going to be a woman who wears a purse with a picture of her kids on it or a Christmas sweater or jingle-bell earrings. Half the time I don't even carry pictures of my kids with me to show off on trips or nights out with the girls—but it doesn't mean that I don't love them or that I'm not a good mom. I am. I'm confident in that now. I know what to let slide and what not to: If Anna wants to wear her Thomas the Tank Engine T-shirt to preschool, then so be it. But what I'm absolutely constant about is empowering her: praising her, teaching her control, giving her free time to use her imagination, and always, *always* letting her know that she's loved. Even when she's in time-out, which is quite often lately. . . .

David is still keeping me entertained and nervous by doing things like falling out of his kayak into the lake, while holding a running chainsaw. (He still maintains he had a perfectly logical reason for being in the kayak with a chainsaw.) Between him and the kids, there's rarely a dull moment around our house. Of course, David continues to hound me about money, but not quite as bad—or maybe I've just gotten better at ignoring it. He has a new job with Verizon Wireless as National Accounts Manger, and he's doing great. He's fascinated by wireless technology and loves being able to use the latest and greatest. He's on the phone constantly, and if we ever have to actually pay for his bill, I'm sure we'll have to declare bankruptcy.

David has instilled in Anna a wonderful appreciation for wildlife and nature. She's one of the only three-year-olds I know who notices a sunset. His gift to our whole family is getting us to stop for a minute to watch the minnows darting in the lake or the osprey perched high in a tree. He's given Anna his love of the water and taught her to jump off the dock into his open arms.

And me? As the mom, I hold it all together. That's what we do—we're the glue, the tie that binds. I have so much more respect for my gender now than I ever did before. I look at women older than I am and can really imagine what they've been through. And I know for myself the strength that is our birthright. It still makes me mad that society doesn't value motherhood. Sure, it gets a lot of lip service, but it's still not really, truly respected. I hope that will change, and *soon*. I especially hope so for my daughter's sake.

My life isn't perfect, but it *is* rich with friends and family.
I'm fortunate to have a group of girlfriends who mean the world
to me, and I volunteer for the Golden Retriever Rescue Club of
Charlotte, a cause near and dear to me. My mom was recently
diagnosed with breast cancer, so I know I'll be doing volunteer work in that arena as well. I may even run in the Susan G.
Komen Race for the Cure next year.

I stay busy freelancing as a copywriter for the ad agency I
used to work for full-time, Corder Philips Wilson. I truly am fortunate to work with such great people. Working from home is
the right balance for me: It means a lot of late nights, but it's
worth it. I like to be able to financially contribute to our family,
and I like what I do. Thankfully, the partners at the agency have
embraced our arrangement, even though I know it makes things
difficult for them at times. In fact, one of them recently asked me
about coming back to the office part-time. I said no. As flattering
as it was, I know in my heart that I'm right where I want to be.

Appendix

Acknowledgments

To Tim, my favorite (and only) husband, my greatest competitor, my personal comedian, my nemesis, and my love—thanks for giving me so much material and for putting up with my bad attitude.

Thanks to my mom for forcing me to take Mr. Lope's ninth-grade typing class, despite my rants about not wanting to become a secretary. (Little did I know that the computer would be invented.) Thanks for teaching me to move fast and work harder.

Thanks to my grandmother, Mabel Deittrick, who taught me how to put my feelings on paper. The writing gene came from you, I'm convinced.

Thanks to my sister, Julie Bowen, who's actually much funnier than I am, but doesn't have time to write a book. I can only aspire to the level of smart-ass you've achieved.

Thanks to Lisa Burnette for all the free legal advice, without so much as even a thank-you note (we're so ashamed).

Many thanks to my boss, Bo LaMotte, whose understanding and patience saved my job and my sanity; and to another great boss, Kevin O'Brien, who got this party started.

Special thanks to my dad and my Uncle Jimmy. Neither one of them had anything to do with the writing of this book, but since they're both important parts of my life, both were pissed that their names didn't appear in it. Billy Emory. Jim Marchesani. There.

Huge thanks to my very own talented artist, Jaycen leBlanc, for all the promotional artsy stuff. I don't know how one person could exit the womb with so many diverse talents (nor do I think it's fair)—dancing, art, writing—and be gorgeous, too. It's just a good thing that you're not a woman or I'd hate your guts. Just remember, Jaycen, you are now, and forever will be, my bitch.

Thanks to Dr. Phil and Oprah for having shows that proved we moms weren't insane. (P.S. Since we acknowledged you in our book, can Sara and I please be on your shows?)

To my dear friend Laura DiGirolamo, known in some circles as "Dr. Laura," thanks for accepting stupid first-time-parent phone calls in the wee hours of the morning, and for all the useful advice. You're more accurate than any pregnancy test.

And finally, to my dear friend Sara, thanks for listening to my endless babble about the worst details of my life and still being able to laugh at me. I'm just glad we conceived at the same time so that we could share this amazing adventure. And yes, if it doesn't work out with David and Tim, I'll marry you.

— **Stephanie Triplett**

First I'd like to thank my husband, David Behnke, for being the best sport in the world, and for being able to laugh at all my wisecracks and jokes in this book—most of which were made at his expense. I love our life, and I love that we can both laugh at ourselves.

Without the support of David; my mother, Elizabeth Ellington; and my sisters, Laura Vassar and Jennifer Brugh; I don't know how I would have made it through postpartum depression. For the understanding, caring, and love they gave me during that time, I'm eternally grateful. You did for me what no one else could.

I'm especially thankful to Dr. Maureen Beurskens, who's been my doctor for nearly 15 years, and Dr. Craig Gourley, her colleague, for their understanding and support. You both knew how to heal me with words as well as medicine.

I thank Julie Power for being my personal cheerleader and giving me the kick in the pants I so often needed. Thank you for also making a date with me at least twice a month to go see a movie and have a peaceful dinner out. Those nights have been a saving grace. For your incomparable friendship, I'm forever grateful.

To Kristina Kuehnel, Veronica and Mick Feduniec, Christi Keller, the Book Club Girls, and "WPC" (you know who you are), I thank you all for sharing in my dream and my joy. Thank you Ron Wehrli and Chris Barickman for listening and saying "Go for it" back in the days when this book was just an idea; and to Ronna Eley-Kelso for her editing expertise and Henry Ward for his legal advice and counsel.

To Kevin O'Brien, thank you for bringing Stephanie and me together and for knowing how to laugh and work at the same time.

To Stephanie's wonderful mother-in-law, Joanne Triplett, thank you for the babysitting you did of both Stephanie's and my children (and our husbands) during the many occasions we locked ourselves in a room together to work on this book.

To my beautiful children, Anna and Cade, thank you for continually showing me the joy of simply being alive to appreciate this wonderful world. You are both my sunshine.

And I'm immensely grateful to Stephanie Triplett for being my abiding friend and the funniest damn girl I know.

— **Sara Ellington**

Recommended Reading

The Baby Book
William Sears, M.D., and Martha Sears, R.N. (Little, Brown, revised edition, 2003)

Birthing from Within
Pam England, CNM, MA, and Rob Horwitz, Ph.D. (Partera Press, 1998)

Dispatches from a Not-So-Perfect Life
Faulkner Fox (Harmony Books, 2003)

Games Babies Play from Birth to Twelve Months
Vicki Lansky (Book Peddlers, 2nd edition, 2001)

The Girlfriend's Guide to Pregnancy
Vicki Iovine (Pocket Books, 1995)

The Girlfriend's Guide to Surviving the First Year of Motherhood
Vicki Iovine (Perigee Trade, 1997)

Mother Shock
Andrea J. Buchanan (Seal Press, 2003)

The Pregnancy Journal
A. Christine Harris, Ph.D. (Chronicle Books, 1996)

What to Expect the First Year
Arlene Eisenberg, Heidi Murkoff, Sandee Hathaway, BSN (Workman Publishing, 2nd revised edition, 2003)

What to Expect When You're Expecting
Heidi Murkoff, Arlene Eisenberg, and Sandee Hathaway, BSN (Workman Publishing, revised edition, 2002)

A Note to New Mothers from Sara Ellington

Each year thousands of women experience depression after giving birth just as I did. Unlike the baby blues, which are typically a couple of days to weeks of weepiness, postpartum depression (PPD) lasts longer and is characterized by a pervasive sense of feeling down, a loss of interest in normal activities, changes in sleep and eating patterns, lack of interest in the baby, a feeling of impending doom, and even thoughts of death or suicide.

The experience varies for each woman who goes through PPD. If you feel that you may be depressed during your pregnancy or even afterward, *do not hesitate to talk to your doctor.* He or she can help. Please don't feel ashamed to ask for help—getting help was one of the best things I've ever done for myself and my family.

PPD Resources

BabyCenter
www.babycenter.com

Depression After Delivery, Inc.
800-944-4PPD (4773)
www.depressionafterdelivery.com

iVillage
www.ivillage.com

The National Women's Health Information Center
800-994-9662
www.4women.gov

Postpartum Support International (PSI)
805-967-7636
www.postpartum.net

About the Authors

Stephanie Triplett (left) lives with her husband, Tim, and two children in Atlanta, Georgia, and currently owns Writer's Block, a marketing and copywriting company. A graduate of East Carolina University and a former advertising executive, her past projects include the marketing and promotion of everything from sunblock and dog vaccines to cable networks and gas pumps.

Sara Ellington is a freelance writer whose advertising work has appeared in *The Charlotte Observer* and *Southern Living*. She holds a B.A. in marketing from Lynchburg College in Lynchburg, Virginia, as well as a B.A. in English from the University of North Carolina at Charlotte. She lives in Charlotte, North Carolina, with her husband, David, and their two children.

Please visit: **www.themommychroniclesbook.com**

Mommy's Notes

Mommy's Notes

We hope you enjoyed this Hay House book.
If you'd like to receive a free catalog featuring additional
Hay House books and products, or if you'd like information
about the Hay Foundation, please contact:

Hay House, Inc.
P.O. Box 5100
Carlsbad, CA 92018-5100

(760) 431-7695 or (800) 654-5126
(760) 431-6948 (fax) or (800) 650-5115 (fax)
www.hayhouse.com

———

Published and distributed in Australia by:
Hay House Australia Pty. Ltd. • 18/36 Ralph St. • Alexandria NSW
2015 • *Phone:* 612-9669-4299 • *Fax:* 612-9669-4144 •
www.hayhouse.com.au

Published and distributed in the United Kingdom by:
Hay House UK, Ltd. • Unit 62, Canalot Studios •
222 Kensal Rd., London W10 5BN • *Phone:* 44-20-8962-1230 •
Fax: 44-20-8962-1239 • www.hayhouse.co.uk

Published and distributed in the Republic of South Africa by:
Hay House SA (Pty), Ltd., P.O. Box 990, Witkoppen 2068 • *Phone/*
Fax: 2711-7012233 • orders@psdprom.co.za

Distributed in Canada by:
Raincoast • 9050 Shaughnessy St., Vancouver, B.C. V6P 6E5 •
Phone: (604) 323-7100 • *Fax:* (604) 323-2600

———

Sign up via the Hay House USA Website to receive the Hay House
online newsletter and stay informed about what's
going on with your favorite authors. You'll receive bimonthly
announcements about: Discounts and Offers, Special Events,
Product Highlights, Free Excerpts, Giveaways, and more!
www.hayhouse.com